A Memoir of Holstein:
An Engineer Traces His Origin

By Gary G. Ruhser

Copyright 2013 Gary G. Ruhser

For Jean, Gayle, Janis, Jayne –
An approximation of the me that was before I came to love each of you

Contents

Preface
Roy Rogers and the L.A.G. Club
Family
School and Young Love
Big Brother
Special Gifts
Acquiring Infinity
The World of Holstein
The Why of Holstein
My Home
Measuring Worth
Young Friends
Life as an Only Child
Jesse
Kinfolk
Brian
Sunday with Axel
Man in the Sky
Mike
Tractors and Wind Tunnels
The Holstein I Knew Then
Sex Education
Paradise Valley
Leaving the Boy Behind

The Cottonwood Rocket Club

On the Hunt

Self-Propelled

The End, The Beginning

Epilogue

Sources

Preface

I did not picture myself as an author, a scribe, an essayist, or a writer until I came under the tutelage of Mrs. Christie in high school. She demonstrated her conviction I was not to be excluded from the world of writers merely because I was a young man, or a high school sports athlete, or a farm kid, or good at math and science. Mrs. Christie, our English instructor, subtly implied that I, and many of my peers, could also be writers, if we so chose. She did this through instructing us to keep a personal journal. She provided guidelines of subject material or content category, she reviewed our work and provided comments for improvement, but she did not grade our journals, and best of all, we students could write whatever we wanted within her broad boundaries. The experience was quite liberating compared to the narrow confines of most of our high school subject assignments.

During college my voluntary creative writing primarily occurred in the form of near daily love letters written to Jean, my future wife, who was remotely ensconced in her own college of choice, some 150 miles from mine. It was not until I had more free time of my own after completing college that I began to engage in some writing and concluded I would like to write more someday, something significant, something thoughtful, and because of the way my brain worked en route to becoming an engineer, something non-fiction.

Over the years I have dabbled in personal essays, some humorous, some sober, and often related to my enjoyment of the outdoors and nature. In addition there were numerous letters to friends and relatives. It was not until I was almost ready to retire from my vocational pursuits, in some introspective moment, I at last recognized I had already been a writer for many years as an engineer. Many of my engineering assignments, at some point, required the organization and expression of multiple thoughts and facts in a clear concise manner written to others: letters, short memos, meeting minutes, engineering reports, preparation for various group presentations. Being a writer, then, was not the issue. What was now at hand, given my retirement from the world of earning a living, was finally having the time to write whatever I wanted. And what would that be?

A few years ago, Jean, my wife and life partner, and I wrote a joint memoir about our dating years for our daughters. That effort was 24 pages long and proved to each of us we could write together as well as individually about things we wished to share with others. It also showed each of us what was still missing from the story of our lives. We have future goals to tackle and write something about the parental years, about the period we call the "Peregrine Years", and about our retirement years. Having each pursued our genealogical history and having developed huge questions about persons long gone, questions which will always remain unanswered, about the particular lives of these ancestors of ours, I think we feel compelled to leave a documented story of our own lives. Within a story context lives become real and memorable. Without the story only dry data remains, and not much of that. What is one's life, but a story?

My marriage family, those I now hold dearest, know the least about my life from birth to age 18. After age 18 I have a certain amount of backup redundancy inasmuch as Jean could tell part of my story. But who can tell my story up to that point? Only me. If I want my readers to know about me in the tenuous years of the beginning of my path through this life, I'm going to have to do the story-telling. The advantage this offers for me, of course, is I can be prejudiced and only share what I choose. But I wanted this effort to be more than just a boring litany of things I had engaged in. What could broaden its appeal to my family readers, or to any reader for that matter?

After some years pondering how to make my personal story more interesting, how to develop a story line in what I now knew would be a multi-page effort, and after writing numerous notes into a spreadsheet, I recognized a lot of my old memories encompassed a culture and other people and physical surroundings all of which are passing into history. I began to see myself not necessarily as only an individual, but as a product of the community into which I was born. I couldn't tell my story without also sharing the context of the world into which I was born. John Donne said "No man is an island, entire of itself; every man is a piece of the continent." To which I might add, partly based on my awareness of each of our genealogical histories: There is always an earlier starting point which one could choose for their own story. Although my story could start with the origin of humans in Africa, or the grand sweep of time and history as mankind found its way around the eastern Mediterranean, or at any point where my ancestors entered northern Europe, my story starts in Germany in the mid 1800's and quickly the loci or focus point of my observation of my own history comes to Holstein, Iowa.

The community in and around Holstein nurtured me, as all good communities can do, in my journey from infancy to adulthood. But as I grew older and learned more about my own community I gradually learned that Holstein is, indeed, special. Some of its current occupants may not be aware of how its origin and growth molded its character and the lives of past Holstein citizens. And so, I have elected to share what I perceive as special about Holstein with the reader of this memoir and wrap Holstein around my own story, and thereby hopefully add a level of interest. In the absence of Holstein and the surrounding area, my life story would be dramatically different. And because of its impact upon me, Holstein also impacts those to whom I dedicate this effort.

With the exception of private personal journals or diaries, written largely for the author to more fully understand or express himself, many writers likely hope their effort will be read and somehow perhaps even be appreciated by readers other than the author. Scientists, researchers, psychologists, philosophers have speculated about a fundamental need for meaningful communication in the human species to which authors, performers, actors, even preachers may be responding. But trying to write or perform for a broad audience can be an intimidating stultifying experience as well. The end result for many who try is to give up or not even make the effort to share their story, their idea, their acts. I understand and had this fear as well when I thought about writing and attempting to garner a large audience. I became free of the fear when I decided to write this memoir on the assumption only my family and closest of friends would read it. Like Mrs. Christie's ungraded journal, I found this to be a liberating concept for writing the story of my young years and at last was able to proceed. Having completed the writing of this autobiography, if anyone else beyond my closest ring of acquaintances should choose to engage in the reading of what follows and, furthermore, if anyone responds with empathy, understanding, or appreciation for what I have written, that is an unanticipated bonus.

Roy Rogers and the L.A.G. Club

Four brief vignettes begin to illustrate my amazement and appreciation for what once existed in and around the community where I was born, which, during those first two decades of my life, I characterized as Home.

I first met the woman to whom I have been married for nearly five decades while she and I were classmates and young friends in first grade. She then transferred to an adjoining school district and we attended separate schools for the remainder of our elementary and high school years. I first expressed my affection for her when she returned to visit my class (her former classmates) for two days in third grade. As young adults in our first years of college, we met again on the street corner of the main intersection of Holstein. By the time I left her at her home that night she and I had talked to one another non-stop for over 3 hours. Exactly two years later we were married.

When I was 61 years old I met a man who was 8 years my senior whom I had not seen since my High School days. He and I began to share a few memories of the common home town area he and I had both grown up in. In so doing he related his memories of a High School football game I had played in during my Junior year. He remembered the long pass I caught, which set us up for a narrow one point win over our rival. He remembered the name of the school we were playing and the precise score of the game. And this 45 years after the fact. The only thing I remembered was catching the pass and how it made me feel.

In the last two years of her life, my mother shared her room in the community nursing home with the mother of the girlfriend I had dated throughout my Junior High and High School years, 24 years earlier, and with whom I had broken up a year prior to dating my future wife.

My parents and the parents of my wife are all, or will be, buried in the same cemetery, each within 10 yards of the other. From the hilltop setting of the Galva Township cemetery one can see the lands where three-fourths of those parents were born and raised, while the lands of the fourth are but eight miles west.

Stories like these are possible only within the unique characteristics of the rural community and time where I spent the first 18 years of my life until I moved away to attend college.

How now to tell the larger story, the story of one's life, which can encapsulate how the four vignettes came to be, and why they can be representative of the world enveloping and protecting me during those early years?

I am naturally tempted to start with my birth. That is the beginning, is it not? Well, yes, the beginning of me as an individual being but biologically we all now know my being came to be started nine months earlier. Many children have a natural reticence to think of their parents doing "it", engaging in the most natural act of procreation. My life partner, Jean, is fond of recollecting how, upon first learning of the sexual act between humans, she began to count the number of children of couples she knew and could thereby safely deduce each couple had engaged in "doing it" at least the same number of times as there existed children by that couple, a revelation most of us probably came upon also in our early sex education. Being now myself a grandparent, I can confidently report I have become immured to the concept of my parents co-mingling and can now look upon their act of conceiving me with quiet contemplation and reverence.

With my parents silently enveloped now in that lovely cemetery on the hill, I can but imagine a scenario of that time so long ago, when farm life was propelled by seasons and weather, and when special conditions I can still remember might have resulted in my conception. It must have been a night in June, when the three older children, my siblings, were already asleep, June, when the weather was warm on a summer night and my father had cut hay behind the horses as he rode the wheel driven mower around and around the field of alfalfa, brome, young timothy, early clover. Tired and sweat laden he had cleaned his body on the porch where the wash basin lay in the dry sink, fresh water pumped from the cistern in the bucket near by, warm water heated on an electric hot plate. After a late supper, the children now in bed, Mother had finished some hand mending of torn clothes, and retired, pulling on a long loose night shirt before reclining in the bed with fresh sweet smelling sheets from the day's washing. Some moments later, Father padded into the room, pulled on a similar garment, and stood briefly in the dark room lit only by starlight and moon glow, in front of the open window, noting the fresh cut smell of new hay, and listening to the night insects buzzing and creaking, a Screech Owl singing a few notes in the Pine grove north of the house, a quarter moon suspended over the ash trees to the west of the window which my Grandfather had planted over 3 decades earlier. Their characteristic good night hug and kiss, which I never saw, only heard as a young child some years later, was executed perfunctorily, but yet, yet on this night it led to a second hug, and then eventually my conception. I can imagine this because I can still see in my mind those upstairs rooms of the house where I lived, sense the same night air, aromas, sounds which my parents sensed. I have responded to those same warm touches of a partner's embrace. And been surprised by what results from a mix of emotions and sensual experiences when in fact I thought both I and my partner were quite sleepy upon initially going to bed.

Nine months later I was born in a room on the second story of the Cushing, Iowa hospital, becoming the only child of my parents who was not born in the house I grew up in. My father drove my mother the six miles to the delivery site in a high sprung, narrow-tired old Ford, the first 4 miles being muddy from the spring rains and thawing activity, no doubt causing some nervousness on his part. Just down the hall of the small rural hospital, a little boy born the previous day, Bryan, would become my best friend in high school and my college roommate. What was once a small hospital for a private practice eventually became someone's home and still stands there providing shelter for a family, its occupants very likely unaware of the lives and stories which began in the home they now inhabit. My coming into the same birth proximity as Bryan on my first day of living is but the earliest start of many marvels of those younger years of my life which stun me with the magic of their being.

With rare exception, most people as adults, me included, don't really remember life events which occurred to them from birth to age 4. I used to think in my 30's and 40's that one of my first remembrances was myself as a little lad, age about 3, playing with kernels of corn on the sidewalk east of our farm home. But then I discovered an old family album which had been misplaced for a few decades which showed this exact image as a photo. In retrospect, the photo had become the image I remembered, and I had transferred it to my own impressions. Many of the stories of our youngest lives, prior to school, most likely come from family stories, the memories of others, and old photos.

One of those stories, shared by my mother, and reinforced recently by a 55 year old note I found, begins to yield the first inklings of my self-described, self-accepted, introverted personality. That is – I was a shy child. As indicated by my mother and confirmed by neighbor women her same age, I would literally hide behind my mother's skirt when confronted by strangers trying to get to know me. When pressed by these adults, bending over and around my mother's imposing presence, presenting their too-large faces to me from a distance of a few feet, and confronting me with their question of what my name was, my response was total silence. When pressed, I would occasionally answer, "Roy Rogers". That was usually enough to get them to back off.

As a younger woman, my mother was invited to join a local women's club, consisting variably of 10-12 women, officially chartered as the "Let's All Go" Club, and she remained a member for decades after, literally until death. Formed in 1934, one of the founding members was Lillian Blenner, the first cousin, once removed of my father. Three quarters of a century later it was my privilege to be bequeathed the final documentation of the end of this remarkable club. The group's structural cohesiveness was built on genuine love, the deep sense of neighborhood at the time, friendship, and an unspoken need for reinforcement of the qualities binding the women together. Today we would call this a support group. Those things that drew this group of women together, that kept them as friends for their lifetimes, in my opinion simply cannot be repeated in today's society. We have good replacements for what they had, but what I learned of the totality of their group would be difficult to replace. Oh, yes, they had some petty differences, some minor complaints about someone in the group, voiced in the privacy of one's own home to their own family, but their need for one another and their overall acceptance of one another is remarkable. As a child, as an adult, as an older adult, I could sense pieces of their story as a group, as a club, but it was not until 2010 when I read the Club minutes regarding "shutting down" of the LAG Club. This final entry was written in 1993 by the last able member, a few others yet surviving but in failing health and unable to attend meetings; I read these words with tears in my eyes years after the last club members had all died. And so after nearly eight decades, the story now lies before me, not all the details, but the wholesome rich unity of their bonding.

Organized and chartered on October 11, 1934, the LAG Club was, to my way of thinking, surprisingly formal, likely indicative of the time of its origin. Minutes were issued for each meeting, funds collected for group-approved purposes, officers elected, a schedule laid out for hosting meetings. But, perhaps some of this formality helped enable it to survive so long. At this time, farm neighbors still knew one another for miles around. Farmers still needed the help of other neighbors to accomplish some of those big farm jobs: threshing oats, harvesting hay, building fence, constructing buildings, butchering farm animals. Average farm size needed to support a family then was about 160 acres, some having more, some less. This then yielded a population density of 3 to 4 families per square mile section of land. Transportation was largely by Ford Model T type automobiles, but horse transportation by buggy also still existed, particularly for younger children going to country schools. It was a younger society then, many farm families had children, and the number of children per family was higher than it is now. If you were a farm wife of age 20 – 40 it was not difficult to find peers of your same age and lifestyle, near enough to your home that one could get to another's home in less than an hour, regardless of transportation mode chosen, horse or self-propelled vehicle. Convenient traveling range then would put somewhat more than a dozen friends and neighbors as available club members. But meetings were held in member's homes, whose size was limited to that of holding a single family. Thus, an upper limit of club members occupying a member's home for the get-together could number no more than a dozen. And so, the group membership was held at a variable upper level of 10-12 women. Over time some would move, or drop out for their own reason, and the group would invite in an agreed-upon replacement.

    LAG members had ever so much more in common than today's once a month neighborhood meal clubs or many of modern social clubs. All had the same occupation: farm wife. None of them had paid jobs outside their homes. All lived in the same type of house, a single family farm house. Some homes were more expensive, some were larger but all served as a farm home. All members' husbands were engaged in the same occupation, farming. All members had a household income common to the others. No family earned any where near 10 times the lowest earning family such as can exist in today's society. All members were only one or two generations removed from their forebears' immigration to America. All members had the same ethnic background of northern Europe, mostly German heritage, and a number of them could trace their roots back to a common localized portion of Germany. So local, in fact, that several members were related. Many members could and did speak a second language,

Low German, because of their heritage. All members had children and could relate to children.

The primary value and goal of their meetings was to be together and to visit, keeping up on neighborhood stories, each other's family, but to justify the event other actions were also under way. Numerous quilts were jointly made – a process I found most amazing as a child. Quilting boards were always stored in our back closet and readily available. Card games were sometimes held. Once a year a club picnic would be organized at a local park and the husbands and children would attend as well, the husbands gathered in one group discussing farming, the women in another group chattering about one another's children and organizing the food.

There was a time, back when I was hiding behind my mother's dress, when at one of these functions I was purported to have said, "I doon like doz ol' jadies." Fortunately, the ladies gathered forgave me for my youthful indiscretion, and found it to be one of those "cute" comments they would remember for some years later. They found the term "jadies" to be delightfully unique, and I was periodically reminded of it by one or more of the club members as I matured into a responsible adult. In September, 1984, on the occasion of their 50th anniversary of their founding, Lurene Stamp, a Club member, wrote in the collected memoir sheets of the Club, which came into my possession in 2008, "Gary hid behind his Mom's skirt because he didn't like 'the old ladies'". She had several memories noted of other children of the Club members as well. At that time of her writing that I was 40 years old and lived 300 miles from Lurene and my mother. Their continuing faith in, and support of, the members' children was a welcome feature of their personalities. Those ladies, gathered in a member's home once a month, were undoubtedly the first social group I ever was a member of, well before church or Sunday school, well before Cub Scouts or regular school. Those "old ladies" were my first outside-the-home teachers, and good teachers they were, in more ways than one.

Month by month, year by year, decade by decade, through the Depression, through World War II, the Korean War, the Vietnam War, through personal loss, through the weddings of their children, through the births of their grandchildren, through holidays of joy, turmoil of suffering, through laughter and tears these women kept coming to one another.

On the occasion of their 25th anniversary, my Mother submitted a poem to the group, several lines of which illustrates their bonds:

"For few things seem more precious
In days of strife and stress
Than the kindness freely given
Through pure neighborliness."

Their annual dues were still 25 cents each in 1959, the same as it was in 1934, but additional funds and efforts had been contributed over the years to the Red Cross for Tuberculosis and Polio, Legion Auxiliary, the Holstein Advance newspaper Soldier Subscription Fund, Buddy Box, and they were always sending boxes of cookies and goodies to their sons and relatives in the service of their country. By 1959, the Club had held 21 bridal showers and weddings for the children of Club members, and that was before my sister, Gloria, and I and several other Club children had been so honored.

On the occasion of the Club's 50th anniversary held on October 18, 1984 the club was down to seven active members who gathered for a sumptuous meal at Maxine Arny's catering establishment. Along with acknowledgement of fond memories and the "real fun time" the Club has been, Lillian Blenner, Club President noted in the meeting minutes: "Our dear member Sophie and Husband Henry (my parents) are confined to the Good Samaritan Home in Holstein after suffering from a stroke that left them confined to wheelchairs."

On December 27, 1993, fifty-nine years after the founding of the LAG Club, then President and also a founding member of the Club, Lillian Blenner, made the last entry into the club memory booklet and minutes of the Let's All Go Club:

"Our good club is having troubles. With: Marie Bumann has been in the nursing home 5 years now. Pauline is in hospital past 6 weeks. Light strokes and very poor heart? Henry and Caroline are at home both very poorly right now. After both have had light strokes able to get around in home. Lurene has taken Lilly in to live with her. Both very poorly with many ailments. Bearly able to be at home with Russells help. Laverna has been confined to her home because of alishimer and her son lives with her their on the farm. I am doing pretty good yet. 1993."

On October 15, 2001 Lillian sent the LAG memory and minutes booklet to my sister Delores as a gift for Delores's 50th wedding anniversary. On March 7, 2002 Lill Blenner passed away, both her son and daughter having predeceased her.

But, with myself as an infant in 1944, the end of the Let's All Go Club was five decades into the future, and my overall awareness of the role it was to play in my knowledge of my birth neighborhood was also five decades into the future. In the meantime, story after story was unfolding for me, and for everyone else in the greater community recognized as Holstein, Iowa. Many stories I cannot know, many stories I can only infer, my own stories of how I grew into the community, and what the community gave of itself to me are the only ones I can tell adequately.

Family

Crawling around as a baby underneath the card tables and quilting frames of the LAG Club may have been my role within the first non-family social group I was brought into. But family always came first – in birth, in sickness, in joy, in death, and in rearing. My siblings, sister Delores, brother Duane, sister Gloria were all older than me. The youngest of the three, Gloria, was eight years my senior. So, yes, I was an unintended surprise to the family, but welcomed. That's what those German families did. Took care of their own, made adjustments. I mean, from their way of thinking what other options were there? None at all. The baby crib was taken out of storage from the Summer Kitchen, and set up beside my parents' bed in the upstairs bedroom of our home.

The Summer Kitchen was a single room outbuilding of the farm, constructed to the same standards as that of the house: cedar shingle roof, cement and stone foundation, overlapping cedar horizontal siding, stout 2 by 4's, brick chimney at the north end. It was located about 25 feet east of the house and its interior dimensions were 12 feet by 16 feet. The name defines its original intended use, that of being the kitchen in the summer when the use of a wood burning cook stove in the house would make the whole house uncomfortably warm. Sometimes we called it the Wash House because by the time I came along the primary use was as the laundry room and it contained the reliable Maytag wringer-washer and a galvanized rinse tub, and the former cook stove had been replaced by a wood burning pot-bellied stove that pleasantly warmed the interior on cold winter days.

Sister Delores became an alternate mother to me. She was 14 when I was born and thus of a perfect age to learn mothering and play a big role in my care. My mother had already cared for the rearing of three infants, knew the work and time involved, and was no doubt somewhat pleased to have the help of Delores, by then a young woman who could be trusted with some major decisions always needed in the safe care of a small baby. A very few pictures of my infancy, one of myself and my siblings taken on the lawn between the house and the Summer Kitchen, show this child-rearing role of Delores. In that photo I sit between her knees and Delores holds me upright, her hands positioned in comfortable cradling of my body. After Delores had her own children, after she had raised them to adulthood, I had finally come to realize similarities in her children and myself which could best be explained by the simple fact that the same person had participated significantly in the rearing of both them and me. The mere fact that we may engage in common experiences does not negate the fact that it may take many years to come to a comprehensive understanding of what the experience did to us.

Outside the immediate family of siblings and parents, the closest extended family members whom I would have seen most were my Grandmother, Evalina Ruhser and my father's brother, Clarence Ruhser who lived with Evalina, and my Uncle Fritz and Aunt Anna Schroeder. My first outing as an infant was to visit my

Grandmother Ruhser in Meriden, Iowa one month and two days after I was born. While I remember my Grandfather Ruhser, I do not remember him well, as he died when I was but nine years old. His was the first funeral I remember attending. Funerals and death were a great mystery to me as I am sure they are to any child, and because we remember how we felt as youths, this probably explains the care and concern most of us can give to children being called upon to participate in this most mysterious of human conditions. I respect what I remember of Grandfather Richard Ruhser. He was soft-spoken, kind, but had that rigid disciplinarian look emanating from his eyes, perhaps aided in my young impression by a rather thick mustache draped under his nose, the hairs of the mustache requiring some maintenance and wiping when engaged in the drinking of coffee or consumption of soup, straining the very top surface of such liquids. In his hands he usually held a cane to assist his mobility at that age. And I can remember him using it as a reaching tool and as a way to make a point in the conversation, tapping it upon the floor. Forced then to look upon him in the coffin, I could not grasp why and how he could be alive one day, and so immobilized by what people called "dead" the next. What couldn't I see? But that was a small boy's view. Had I had the cognizance then, or even for that matter, to have asked my Dad of his impressions of his Dad, what a world of a different answer I would have gotten. And that is one of the other facets of stories—it matters ever so much what your viewpoint is. My dad's memory of his father included visions of strength, decision-making, action, teaching. My own memory of his father included none of those things, and my view of what his father, my grandfather was, is thus incomplete. That is part of the answer to the question of why stories are needed, to fill our visions and thereby make our view more complete, more real, more lasting.

I am glad I could come to know my paternal grandparents. I was unable to know my maternal grandparents, their deaths occurring before I was even born. Each of us has to deal with some level and form of tragedy in our life. It is the inescapable reality of life, the other side of what life is capable of giving us. It gives us great joy, love, friends, but because you have, for a moment in time, life, the other aspect of this circle of reality you will inevitably have in life is grief, loss, death. With life you will face sadness. Without life you cannot have joy. Could any of us give up willingly the profound joys we have had from living in exchange for not knowing them at all and thereby avoiding the negative aspects of living?

I am convinced the greatest tragedy in my mother's life occurred, just as she was becoming a woman at the age of 13, when her own mother died. How do I know this? Because until my mother's dying day, those of us that knew her well, remember the story of "the death rattle." And my mother, right up to the last years of her life, could refer to the death rattle she heard her mother sigh, and it could evoke tears from my mother's eyes at whatever age she was upon sharing this story. When Mom was herself an old lady of 81, lying helpless as a child in the nursing home, sharing again the story of hearing her mother's last death rattle while she sat waiting at my Grandmother Schroeder's bedside located in the same home in which I was raised, seeing Mom tear up, one could not but see the 13 year old girl there in front of you, still saddened by the loss of her own Mom.

My mother's mother, who would have been my grandmother, died at the age of 33. Died on December 18, 1918 of the horrible Influenza, which was then marching through the entire world like one of the Four Horsemen of the Apocalypse, sweeping its scythe with broad strokes through 50-100 million people on Earth, of which 550,000-675,000 were Americans like my grandmother, who died 26 years before I was born.

There are tragedies deeply felt, like what my mother felt as regards her loss. There are other tragedies less personal, less felt, but which still can affect one's life. When growing up I knew vaguely of my Grandmother Dorothea Marie Sophie Wink Schroeder's death story, of its affect upon my mother, and then through more family stories, of its affect upon my Uncle Fritz, who I knew, and its affect upon my grandfather Carl Fredrick Schroeder, who I never knew. But I did not learn of its affect upon me until over 50 years after I was born. It was then, while working on my family genealogy that I was able to piece together the larger tragedy and its affect as a loss of relationship with others as applied to me. For, you see, it was not only my grandmother Schroeder that died in that terrible month of December, 1918. On December 6, 1918 my grandmother's mother, living one mile north of where my mother and grandmother were living, Catherine Marie Meyer Wink died of the same Influenza. And then on December 23, 1918, Catherine Elisabeth "Dora" Meyer Koetke, my great aunt, my grandmother's mother's sister living in Moville, Iowa, died of the same plague running through the winter-covered land and hills of Northwest Iowa. Within 17 days, three members of my mother's maternal lineage, the only three members of that lineage who came to America, were wiped out of corporeal existence, and thus effectively erased from any potential of coming into my active memory. And because during this age, perhaps any age, it was the women who best held family ties together, I was precluded from coming to know any of my Wink relatives in Moville, Iowa, one of whom I played against in High School sports without realizing he was related to me, I too partook in the tragedy of loss occurring in 1918, even though I was far from even being born then.

In 1918, even though Moville was 23 miles from the homes of my grandmother and great grandmother, the families of Carl Schroeder and Fred Wink would still have visited Catherine Marie Meyer (wife of Fred) Wink's sister there in Moville. Or Catherine Elisabeth Meyer Koetke would have come to visit her sister at Holstein several times a year. When all three of them died the maternal lineage linkage with those families was also severed, and for this reason and others perhaps of a more personal nature, I never came to know any of my Wink relatives in the Moville area, even though one was my same age. It was not until I was over 50 years old that I learned and confirmed I had a great grandfather buried in Moville. I had grown up and spent the greater part of my adult life under the impression that great grandfather Wink never came to America and was buried in Germany. Certainly the near simultaneous loss of those three pioneering women affected my life as well by interjecting some loss of kinship, thus tragedy, into my life also.

As a little child just beginning to move down the stream of life in 1944, it was as though I had entered the waters 26 miles/years downstream of the rocks upon which those three women died. Their lives were long over, gone in the past upstream somewhere. I was just starting my drift of discovery. During infancy our cognizance is not yet ready to absorb history, we can only live. But as children we can only survive and thrive well within some frame of family. My greater frame of family was somewhat typical: a good Grandma Ruhser who could come down from Meriden, Iowa for a day or several nights to care and nurture me in case Mom was ill or had to go somewhere, a good Uncle Fritz and kind Aunt Anna who would come to our house, or we to theirs for those family events worthy of recognition—birthdays, wedding anniversaries. I had siblings to pick on me or watch over me, neighbors and friends. For those days, from birth to pre-school, an individual's "memories" are best crafted from old photos, and any stories that came from those old photos during the sharing of them over the years.

One photo begins to reveal the role of siblings in my upbringing. The four of us, and our farm dog Pudgy, are gathered on the lawn east of the house near the Summer Kitchen, sprawling Elm trees forming a backdrop. Resting on his knees, my brother Duane, age 12, is holding Pudgy. Sister Gloria, age eight, is standing between Duane and my sister Delores. Delores, she in the role of alternate mother and caretaker at 14 years of age, is kneeling and holding me, a small child of six months propped upright next to her thighs. I find it to be a comforting picture, and one of the earliest to portray the growth of closeness and camaraderie which would wax and wane through the years until we too were old, or as old as we can get. A hazard of looking at old pictures is in retrospect we can now see the things that happened in life, and possibly be saddened by what came to be. My brother would not live to be an old man. It is thus important to look at old pictures for what they were intended, not to be a portent of the future, but a historical look at the moment that was. And I find this moment in this picture to be one of sibling bonding on a house and farm yard we would all call home, in the beginning sense of the word, the home in which you launch your lives, and with good fortune, get a good start on your lives in a secure and permanent setting. Such was my good fortune.

Another of the early photos beyond my helpless infancy is the picture of me when I was three, playing with shell corn on the sidewalk, dressed in a shirt handmade by my mother from feed sacks, my body attired in small overalls, shoulder straps over the shirt, hands full of corn looking straight away apparently bound and determined on a little boy goal. Then perhaps a year later, another photo shows me clothed against cooler weather, perhaps of fall or spring, snug in an overcoat and a small cap complete with ear flaps held tight with the strap passing under my chin, and petting two of the ever-present, ever-ubiquitous cats then on our farm and likewise present on all farms of the area.

Every year I lived on my parents' farm and for all the years when my parents were retired on the farm, cats were present. I can still see my father, dressed against the cool of that day, when in his mid-70s I watched him from the house as he trudged to the barn carrying a small bucket of cat food he had prepared on the porch. Dad had to walk a bit carefully, wary of the cats quick legs, a few of whom were leading the way to the barn and capable of potentially tangling in his legs. A small sea of upright tails mounted on cats' backs following him, appearing rather as a pack of wobbly periscopes appraised on the bucket in his hand and the beckoning open barn door ahead. Seeing him on this evening devotional mission, his charges following his every step, I was forced to contrast my teen-age years' vision of him as a stern, well-meaning German farmer, with what was before me, a kind old man taking care of his cats, and enjoying the obligation. Even now I can still see him bend over and grasp a favorite cat in his huge thick hands and give a few quick strokes to soft hair beneath, the cat struggling to get back to the food, and a small grin of contentment on his normally silent mouth. His handling of the cat or kitty was not what one could classify as gentle, but it was nonetheless caring.

Nearly all the cats on the farm were outdoor cats relegated to the barn and the farmyard. Most knew and cared where their daily rations came from and some always lingered near the door of our porch, some becoming clever enough with their timing they could slip into the slow-closing door. A few, even more clever, could hook their claws in the very corner of the door and open it themselves if it had not latched properly. It was a rare picture of our house that did not show several cats sitting, lying, or crouching on the front stoop of the house. My sister Gloria had affection for cats and selected a few pretty and precious cats for extra taming and petting. These special status cats were granted occasional permitted entry to the house. But their entry was for the humans' satisfaction, not for the cats, and they could not be called house cats in today's sense of the term. No one in my home knew anything about a litter box, and the concept was unknown where the whole farm was available for litter box duty without the need for anybody to clean it later. Favorite cats tended to be white and mostly white cats were not at all rare on our farm or in the neighborhood. Gloria's favorite cat was Snowball. One of my early pets was Tom, yes, a cat.

My mother records that at the age of three, when I was asked my name, I would often respond "Roy Rogers". In my three year old mind that certainly made a lot more sense than Gary. I heard about, watched movies of, looked at books about Roy, and knew all a little boy could about Roy Rogers. It was not till I went to Kindergarten school and discovered there were two other little boys named Gary that I met and knew anybody named Gary. Sixty years later I am still friends with Gary L and the third Gary, and Gary L and I communicate yearly. So a picture of me wearing a large brimmed cowboy hat at age 4, looking dead on with determination into the camera, my right hand on the pistol strapped around my hips, the left thumb hooked into the gun belt, was most assuredly, and family lore sealed the identity, that of Roy Rogers. Anyone else looking at this picture might note the two large knee patches sewn onto the bib overalls of the small lad and conclude this is actually little Gary. But try to imagine confronting this little tyke in his attire and asking what his name was. My mother told me he would not have answered, "Gary".

Having had to commit our own little daughter, Gayle, to surgery at a tender age, I can imagine the trepidation my parents might have felt committing me as a child aged five to surgery in 1949. Only a few days after starting Kindergarten school in Holstein I had to have an inguinal hernia repaired in the recently constructed Sioux Valley Hospital in Cherokee, Iowa, where I was kept two nights. I am sure my mother would have been called upon to read to me from my favorite book called Patchy the Pony. Patchy was one of the fuzzy wuzzy books and whenever Patchy appeared on a page his body was flocked with a fabric coating. On each page I would reach out and feel his soft fur. My full-time small companions for the hospital stay were Ted, my stuffed teddy bear, and Bun, my stuffed rabbit. Ted and Bun were always reliable friends and well-matched company for me wearing small shirts my mother had hand-sewn for each of them. After coming home I was granted the small privilege of being able to lie and recuperate on the downstairs bed, in the same bedroom where the grandmother unknown to me had died of the 1918 Influenza 31 years earlier. A mother's concern for a little boy recovering from surgery is no doubt colored not only by what she sees before her but by memories of older events within the same setting. My recovery was quick and typical of healthy children.

    Recovery, given modern psychological discoveries, was likely aided by what is known today as a "support group." In the downstairs bedroom, permitted only limited physical activity for some days, I could lie on the bed and receive frequent attention or comments from my brother and sister, from my mother and father. In the fall of 1949, my oldest sister, my sub-mother, Delores, had moved down to Omaha to attend a secretarial school following her graduation from high School in Holstein. Friends of my parents, neighbors, and relatives stopped in briefly to see "little Gary", all of them so concerned in those days to have such a young person need to go through surgery, it being far less common and routinely procedural than today. Get well cards for the little boy were received nearly daily, delivered to the mailbox at the end of our lane by the rural mail deliver, George Will, and then brought to me on the bed by my smiling mother; pleased herself to know others cared about her boy. Many of the cards came from families of the Let's All Go social group.

How is it I can possibly know about those cards and visits 60 years ago? Delores, in Omaha, unable to be in attendance during my operation and recovery, had mailed to me a spiral bound 9" X 12" scrap book, along with a starter selection of magazine pictures of dogs, horses, fish, farm animals, birds--anything a boy might find of interest. This was to be a project: I could select and assemble a scrapbook by gluing onto the pages spread before me while resting in bed. After the get-well cards arrived they too were positioned by me and my mother into the scrapbook and this scrapbook lies before me as I write. I am thankful my mother did not throw this away years ago. But given that it yet exists and I am getting older I do have to ask what should or will become of it. With each passing generation and year it has less and less importance to those remaining cognizant of its origin.

As I open it now, old voices, old memories, come back to me, brought back by such a simple act as the turning of a yellowed page, glue beginning to release, dried beyond adherence, scotch tape pieces yellowed and cracked and falling loose from their role of holding an old get-well card in position. The Johnnie Wiese family, my young playmates David and Diane Lohff, LaVerna and Clarence Ludvigson family, Lafrentz no further identity required because everyone in the neighborhood knew who the Lafrentz family was, Mr and Mrs Wm Kalhl, Ronda, Loretta, and James who were cousins of my cousins and Ronda was my classmate. Rosa, Rozella, Carl, and Myrtle, with Myrtle being the sister of the husband of my father's cousin. Ervin and Marie Bumann family, with Ervin being the cousin of my father. The Hammers. Mrs Sinky, the lady whom I shared the room with in the hospital. Rosdail family, with Mrs. Rosdail, Minnie, being the cousin of my mother. Lorna, my cousin. Olga and Harry, neighbors. Uncle Fritz and Aunt Anna, Delane, Marlene. The Jensens, closest neighbors to the north. Carol Dittmer, cousin of my father. My grandmother Evalina. Reverend Geske of our church and 4 other couples visited my mother and me in the hospital before I was even home. Mrs Fahan, best Kindergarten teacher in the world, included a short note in her card, "Dear Gary, Well, that was a big operation for such a little boy – but Mother said you were such a brave little soldier – We'll be glad when you're back with us." Do teachers have an impact on young people's lives? Yes, they do.

In retrospect, by the time I was all of five years old, I had already been shown the broad outline and many of the details of the family and community life that would sustain me for the rest of my life and which I have not adequately recognized until these 60 years later and can now put thought and words to all that happened to me and why.

School and Young Love

My school years, as they must in a German community, began with Kindergarten, its very name denoting its origin in Germany. My first class consisted of 55 children, the large size in a small community having been caused primarily by the baby boom of World War II. By large, being a relative term, I mean the largest that our community of Holstein had produced. A number of my classmates had fathers who served in World War II, Nina Ann, Gary L, Roger, among them. My own father, and the same also applied to other of my classmates, was in a subset of individuals too young to serve in World War I but too old to serve in World War II. Our kindergarten was organized to be a half day session with half of us attending in the morning. The other half would be attending Mrs Fahan's kindergarten class in the afternoon.

The school building was the largest building in our small town, constructed of dark reddish brown bricks in 1916, and towering a full three stories into the air. To rise to its top level, the third floor, meant you were the oldest children in the school and thus could tower over the small rank and stature of all the lesser children on the lower levels. But, for me, that was the future that beckoned, not the immediate reality of kindergarten. Our class met in the room in the southeast corner of the school building which in turn sat on the northeast corner of the city block it dominated. The original wooden framed town school was built in 1884. In 1895 a brick building constructed of lighter, tan bricks with a castellated roof and impressive bell tower, was added onto the front of the frame building and was on the west side of the same city block. The area between the two schools was covered in pea gravel and was our play ground during the precious recesses and noon hours. One can only assume the pea gravel was purposely selected by knowing adults wanting to avoid injury to the children playing there, but we, as eager children can do, still had numerous cuts and abrasions, as we ran, tripped, played games, scuffled, and were thrown in fights to its pebbly surface.

Our kindergarten classroom had separate cloak rooms for boys and for girls with hooks assigned to each child where they could reach up and hang their outer garments. Appropriate attire, set by social standards of the time, not rules, dictated girls wore dresses or skirts, boys wore pants or overalls. In the winter snow and severe cold conditions girls would wear warm pants under their dresses to stay warm and then would "disrobe" indoors in their cloak room for privacy from the curious boys, who at that age were not actually so much curious as just plain troublesome. A small playhouse was in the back of the room which enabled play indoors during adverse weather outside and which served the needs to pretend and play act for us children. Each of us had our own small rug which we would roll out on the floor for our assigned nap times, doubtless important to the needs of the children but surely an important time for our eminently kind and patient Mrs Fahan to regain her strength and will to carry on in our training.

Kindergarten was my first real opportunity to spend extended time with other children my same age. Classmates became playmates, playmates became friends, and friends I made as a five year old became life long friends in continuing relationships carried on these many decades later. Why is that? Does that sort of thing still happen in schools where entering classes number in the hundreds? What matters is it worked for me. In the Holstein community of the early years of the 1950's there were social and class differences but compared to today's magnitudes of differences, ours were perhaps in the order of a factor of two. That is, the "richest" parents of my classmates did not likely earn or spend much more than twice what the "poorest" parents did. There were nice houses, and less nice houses, but there were no homeless, no hovels, no mansions where I or my classmates lived. Many classmates were interrelated by virtue of their heritage and their families' origin within this community. Divorce was virtually unknown, if known, it was a singular rarity. Farming formed the basis of the economy. If one did not farm directly, one provided goods and services to those that farmed. Economically all citizens were tied together. Somewhat more than half of my classmates were born and raised on farms, those that weren't were still well acquainted with the farmers' world and rural living. Our parents, by and large, were not college graduates. Most had only a high school education, some of the older parents, mine among them, had only an 8th grade education. Thus we were a relatively "classless" set of children, with the possible exception of the religion of our families. We, as children, could tell who among our classmates did not come to our Sunday school or church, thus we concluded they went to one of the other two churches in town, and over the years could gradually ascertain who went to which. What set us apart or together was not our social class, not the income of our parents, not the houses we lived in, not the educational level of our parents, but our personalities

The conversations with friends in kindergarten have drifted from the river of time, but singular events, and memories of where one spent so much time still remain a half century later. What is of some interest to me now is not that I have those memories remaining, but the realization that my parents, my grandparents, all other individuals now like me entering old age also had memories from their upbringing of over a half century's worth of their own precious memories. They experienced what I am now experiencing. They lived young in their minds as I am living young in mine. And this ring of people's experiences and recollections of experiences lived goes on and on and on. What a vast vista everyone's mind holds. Can you even imagine a scene of all those memories combined and revealed? What a marvelous world and life vision that would be.

In my mind I can still walk up the sidewalk from the city park and approach that corner of the school building where my first school classes were held, where my first friendships were formed. I see the raised concrete pad surrounding the school on its south, east and north sides with its concrete buttressed corners on either side of the steps leading to the pad leveling the basic structure of the school. Children laughing, playing, yelling, climbing, chasing one another, or talking quietly with one another or in small groups as they wait for the school bell to summon them back inside for more training on the tenuous road to adulthood. In the early morning hour, a little before eight o'clock, I disembark from bus number 4 and hop to the pavement carrying my small brown lunch sack of a sandwich wrapped in wax paper and a cookie and with orange slices already peeled and separated by my mother. Setting my lunch sack, emblazoned with a bright crayon color with my name, "Gary R", on the south side of the school building up against those bricks in its usual spot to protect it from being trodden by small feet, I rush off to join my several young friends waving at me. As the bell rings I return in time to see Sue's large, but friendly, Golden Retriever dog named Rusty, with soft long fur the color of an autumn leaf, its eyes laughing playfully, running off across the street with my lunch sack suspended from its mouth, to Sue's and the dog's house, directly across from the school. With surely some degree of frantic in my voice I raise the alarm of what has happened and where my lunch has gone. Sue easily retrieves it. Another school day carries on, other details lost to memory, except for the vision of the moment. I might have been upset, angry, overly concerned, perhaps crying at the time. But now, now, I thank the dog and Sue for what I can still see, oh, so clearly. Given all that happened there, at that school building, it hardly seems possible the building is gone and all that physically remains of it for me is a single brick setting on the top shelf of the bookcase in our living room. The building's useful life to the community expired in 1998 and the building was torn down. Ethereal touch-less personal memories outlast and are stronger than the concrete and brick building.

    Miss Johnson was my first grade teacher, she of the long light hair and pleasant disposition, whom a number of the boys (NOT shy little me) kissed as they left school for the day, and which some classmate girls hold against Miss Johnson to this day. The students were purposely mixed up from the associations we had been placed in during kindergarten and so a tall brunette girl named Jean Beyer entered my young life. Fifteen years later she would become my life partner, my wife, and she already struck me then in first grade as someone special. Mrs. Jackes was my second grade teacher, an older woman with gray hair piled on her head, a disciplinarian who invoked appropriate fear into us children. By now we had advanced to the second story of that school, moving up in the world, the cast iron steam radiators tutoring us with their hissing crackling sounds emanating from the south wall of the building, the wall where we could look out upon the alley below and see the city park play area beckoning to us, the only obstacle being rules and a set of houses lining the street on the south edge of that city block. The cloak room was now on the west wall of our classroom, its open swinging doors reminiscent of the saloon doors portrayed in movies did not lead to the bar but to clothes on hooks, rubber galoshes in season placed on the floor under one's assigned hook, childish mayhem occurring there before and after each recess. Second grade was the last year the cute girl, Jean Beyer, and I attended school together. Although Jean's parents did not move, they were halfway between two school districts and decided to send their children to the closest district which offered bus service past their lane. Her parents did not seek my approval before implementing this plan and it was with some sadness I made note of her absence when I joined third grade under the tutelage of Miss Cain, a rather petite short brunette-haired teacher, another teacher that children could love and would remember for her kindness, rather than for her discipline. By now we had moved on from small tables and been assigned individual desks. Our room was in the far northwest corner of the school building but we were back on the first floor. I remember marveling at my elderly parents and their ability to remember the names of nearly all of their teachers when they went to school, that time period being now nearly a century ago, their country schools being all within a few miles of the school I now was attending as a wee third grader. And here I sit at my computer, a century removed from their teachers teaching them, and I too can remember all the names and faces of all my grade and high school teachers.

    One morning when I walked into Miss Cain's classroom, there before me stood Jean Beyer, looking fetchingly attractive as ever. How could this be? Jean did not have school at her Galva, Iowa school that day and so came to my class with her first cousin, Christine, to make a re-acquaintance of classmates she left behind when she transferred to Galva's school. Struck by a little boy's passion of instant love (easier to recognize when it has been taken away for a time) and knowing Jean would be with us one more day, I went home that late afternoon on the bus determined to find or create the perfect gift to announce my love for this charming girl. While my mother was outside gathering the day's eggs I went into her dresser drawer where her jewelry was kept and took a lovely, seldom-worn rhinestone necklace. Next I proceeded to weave an art object we had recently learned in school – an overlapping interwoven layering of purple and gold construction paper. It was a beautiful heart-felt creation. The next morning, back at the classroom and before lessons started, I boldly presented both the artwork and necklace to my young love, fully expecting, I am sure, Jean's instant adoration and devotion to me. But, …shock and pain numbed me to the core of my little boy expectations when, ….Jean refused my offer. What? Why? Although tempted by my gift, Jean remembered her mother's admonition not to accept gifts from strangers (What!!! But we're friends, you are my classmate!) and having been separated by our different school locations I now ranked as a possible stranger and she felt she would get into trouble if she brought my gifts home. Avoiding a total rejection I proceeded on that same day to instead give my gifts to Connie, another pretty girl, another cousin of Jean's. Connie accepted. Thirteen years later Jean and I discovered we each shared basically the same memories of that day in third grade, a most memorable day for each of us. Does Connie remember any of this story in the same detail? Doubtful. Jean and I wanted to ask her at the class 50th reunion, but Connie could not attend.

Big Brother

Being the son of a father who was 40 years my senior, I believe gives one a different, unique father-son relationship than being born the son of a father who is 25 to 30 years ones senior. In my case my father was also identifiably German in his treatment of the father-son relationship. It is not that he was not loving or concerned for my future, but rather that he was a patriarchal disciplinarian, reserved and aloof in any display of affection, and fulfilling the role of father as he had learned it from his own father, the first generation born on American soil, and from his grandfather, a man born in Germany as it then existed in 1845. Instead of the family oriented father-son relationship as characterized within the rearing patterns of the late 20th century and early 21st, I instead was blessed with time and circumstance of having an older brother who was 11 years older than I.

Duane was (I must say was because Duane left me far too early and far too abruptly) my Big Brother. Duane was the Big Brother a young boy could only wish for, if only he knew the best things to wish for. And he was mine. My best and fullest awareness of what Duane came to mean to me of course comes only with the advancement of years and with appropriate reflection. Within the time period we are currently visiting, I am a little kid just coming into a time of cognizance and being able to maneuver through life on my own without constantly holding onto an older person's hand. Duane was an older teen-ager just finishing his High School years and contemplating what his future roles as a new adult should be. My father was busy trying to provide support and direction for his family. My brother, on the other hand, had time available to devote to his kid brother, had family affection available to give, knowledge and wonder to share, and an artistic crafting ability which allowed him to create those items a little boy needs in his life: things like guns and horses and drawings from his mind which delighted my own.

The gift of a little boy's toy riding horse, a caricature of a horse's head mounted on the end of a stick which a child would straddle as though it was the horse's body and thus "ride", precedes any direct memory of its receipt but that does not diminish the great significance of this toy to me. In a house occupied by a 4 year old Roy Rogers and given my brother's creative and thoughtful talents, it seems quite obvious he would create my Trigger, my Roy Rogers' Horse for me to ride about the house and out to the open range of our lawn and farmstead. Duane first drew a pattern for the head upon a piece of light drawing paper and then made pencil correction to the proportions deemed appropriate for realism. The pattern was then traced to a broad one inch board, cut out with a hand coping saw capable of following the contours, and the rough edges relieved and given final contour by deft strokes of Duane's folding pocket knife. Next he colored with a brown crayon the horse's mane, eyes, mouth, on each side of the head, and then he crafted a leather bridle, reins, and the horse's ears from old leather scraps left over from old boots and other farm projects, leather then being a much more readily accessible farmstead item than now. These leather components were tacked onto the head with tack head nails, the completed head assembled to the riding stick and the complete toy was presented to an undoubtedly surprised and delighted little boy. Given my penchant for pretending to be Roy, the horse automatically and instantly became Trigger, which was the name the famous cowboy of the 1940's and 1950's had assigned to his own Palomino horse. Trigger is the only name I have recognized for this wonderful, special, yet simple toy, never such demeaning titles as my horse, or the toy horse. Sixty-one years after first seeing Trigger, his now somewhat stained and aged head, leather parts stiff with age, still hangs above my workbench in the basement, and I still can admire the effort put into his creation by a 15 year old Big Brother.

What will happen to Trigger when I die and am gone? What will happen to other objects of affection, other physical manifestations of Duane, wooden planes, tanks, a wooden miniature Battleship Missouri, old drawings, artworks that he created that still mean something to me, that evoke memories no one can relate to? For that matter, what will happen to anything physical that I own which means something to me, but which comes from days of yore? These things we call precious keepsakes bring back marvelous memories, some memories you think you've lost, until in gazing upon them after the item's resurrection from an ancient storage box or remote shelf or cupboard in attic or basement, suddenly memories, visions, conversations, pictures come flooding back: things no one else but you can see or feel, near sacred scenes, but invisible and undetectable by anyone else. What will happen? Ashes to ashes, dust to dust, nothing lasts forever. What is so important to you or I now at this moment in time will be less and less important to anyone with the passage of more and more time. But that's okay. That's how the world works. That's how life works. So, if what I have left behind when I am gone means something to someone and they want to keep it a while, that's okay. But if it loses its meaning, or has none for the new possessor, or if it becomes a burden and a bother to keep around, then properly it should be disposed of. All physical objects within the sphere of what we know exists always get recycled. That's all that is going on. Fire can speed up the process. And a ritualistic fire of dissolution could create a spiritual cleansing for the individual involved in the recycling of physical possessions. It is not the physical that was ever fundamentally important anyway, it was what the object evoked.

It is natural enough to view one's personal history through one's own perspective. It can be a bit more challenging but much more revelatory to view one's history and personal relationships if you but take a moment to note things from another's perspective. The 15 year old Big Brother in 1949 was but 4 years removed from being an impressionable 11 year old at the end of World War II. From such a perspective of age and time then, and knowing the thoughts and emotions I could grasp as an 11 year old child, I can now see why the tools of the military and war could play a large role in his imagination. Thus I can have a view and explanation for Duane's art capabilities being expressed in hand-crafted toy guns, toy turret-carrying tanks, toy airplanes, pencil drawings and crayon or water color paintings portraying these same objects. He could draw, he could create, he could carve. And why not would any artist draw, create, and carve those things that interested him?

While Duane kept many of his artistic works and hobby expressions for his own enjoyment, as a younger brother I was the recipient of a number of his creations. During church services on Sunday mornings, when my mother tired of the gentle, much beloved by myself, back rubbing she utilized to calm her little boy during those long and boring (to a six year old at least) sermons, Duane would sometimes fill in to distract my squirming by drawing a quick sketch of an airplane, a boat, a farmstead or wild animal. I was a mesmerized by the act of drawing and the results just as little children of today may be mesmerized by cartoons on television. His sketches came out of nowhere and appeared unspooling upon the page of paper in front of me. Initially I wouldn't know what he was creating. It was a mystery appearing complete before my eyes. Then I recognized what it was going to be. A few minutes, a few strokes later, there it was: an airplane diving out of a partly cloudy sky, guns blazing, bullets arcing out of the wing cannons toward the ground below, the pilot's helmeted head in the cockpit. Duane smiled down at me, I smiled in appreciation up toward him, and I had that emotion for what had just happened – the best Sunday Sermon so far this year!

The M1 .30 caliber carbine developed for use in World War II was a light weight, short barreled, military weapon carried by our troops, especially valued as a back-up rifle for armored columns. I know it was an important weapon, important to me because by the time I was seven I had my very own. Made of wood, made by Duane. The stock was cut and carved from a 2 X 6, the barrel was a slimmed down piece of a broom handle tapered down toward the muzzle which had a carved wooden front sight mounted on it, the cartridge magazine was a squared off piece of wood cut from the end of a wooden peach crate, the trigger guard was a shaped piece of tin cut from a gallon can, and the sling was a select piece of leather from the afore mentioned leather collection available on farms of the era, the entire gun painted in brown and black to replicate the original.

For a young man in his mid-teenage years Duane was a natural and skilled artist, very creative in his materials, very adept at bringing his imagination to reality. The bulk of his projects for me were created both shortly before and shortly after he served his draftee time in the US military, a time that coincided nicely with my greatest childhood needs for such "toys" as he was able to craft. I was the fortunate little brother who could be the recipient of a number of his works:

1) The miniature military tanks were scale replicas of World War II and Korean War tanks, both German and American. The American tanks were patterned by Duane after the M46 Patton, the M26 Pershing, and the M41 Walker Bulldog tanks. Their greatest

utility for me were being able to pull them with a piece of twine around the farm in winter when there was snow on the ground. They were made out of 2 inch thick lumber, sometimes sandwiched to a greater thickness, all of them sharing the characteristic tank treads which glided through the snow and made parallel tracks. Pulling two at a time or sharing in the activity with a friend one could imagine the deathly military maneuvers which these impressive machines engaged in the rough forbidding terrain of our farm, especially out there in the pasture where, exposed and in the open, they were subject to bombing runs of enemy aircraft overhead.

2) The wooden airplanes did not come into my direct possession until after Duane's death, but as a child I would touch and envy their construction as they were stored and displayed on shelves on the east wall of our Summer Kitchen, in amongst the stuffed Great Horned Owl, coon skins, mounted deer head, animal skull collection, mounted Ring-necked Pheasant and other projects of his taxidermy hobby. Writing this now, with the perspective of five decades and facing the paucity of outdoor activities available to today's children, I can see I was one lucky little kid. The thing about the airplanes: a B-17 bomber, a German Stuka dive bomber, the British Spitfire, the F-51 Mustang fighter, that amaze me as an adult is their exceptionally good proportionality. These were crafted before the days of plastic model airplanes and at a time when any dimensional statistics would have been hard to come by. I presume he collected the overall length and wing span possibly

from some magazine or newspaper article, but wing location on the airframe, engine location on the wing, gun turret location on the plane – all these he created very accurately just by his sense of proportionality as compared to pictures he was using as the origin of what he would build.

3) He built a complete collection of miniature farm buildings from the wood of peach boxes then extant in stores and homes: a barn, machine shed, hog house, corn crib, all to the size which a young boy could carry from dry storage and have organized into a farmstead in the cool shade of the elm grove north of the house in a jiffy. And, what is a farmstead without animals? So, he carved miniature animals, cows, horses, pigs, to the correct proportions to go inside the buildings. On those infrequent Saturday or Sunday afternoons when a young friend could come for a visit, oh, the joy we would have for undisturbed hours pretending at farming, positioning the animals in their new yards, harvesting grass from the lawn to feed them at chore time, bedding them down for the night with dry tree leaves, crafting a dried tumbleweed, sticking it in the dirt, and pretending a mighty oak was shading the barnyard. Toy tractors and machinery completed the scene and provided additional explorations in pretending.

Special Gifts

Duane did not make all the gifts he gave me. But the purchased gifts were selected with a view toward quality, being able to last the handling of a young boy, and toys which reflected his own interests. In 1951 he gave me a realistically scaled model operating construction crane for Christmas. Little cranks on the side of the cab would raise and lower the boom and raise and lower the dirt bucket which would automatically latch closed on its next lift. Pulling on the trip string would release the dirt bucket to open and drop its load of dirt after small hands had pivoted the main crane body and extended boom into position over the target drop zone. Naturally at that point I was in my young life I knew the crane had been magically delivered to our Christmas tree by Santa. As the years passed I gradually figured out I had been hoodwinked by a loving family.

In those times, the times of the late 1940's and early 1950's our family Christmas traditions included erecting and decorating an artificial tree that folded and was stored in the attic upstairs. There were the traditional glass balls, small crocheted and starched doilies and angels made by my mother, and numerous other hanging decorations that were pulled down from their storage on the shelf above my bed upstairs. Several strings of 7-watt electric multi-colored bulbs provided the lights. Upon replacing one failed bulb one day, as stupid children are wont to do, I discovered the empty base for the bulb was just the right size to contain the end of my finger. Unfortunately I quickly discovered the light string was obviously plugged in and while 120 volts delivered to the contact points is just right to illuminate a light bulb, it far exceeds what a young boy expected. Thankfully, the poor contact I likely made and the rapid involuntary reflex of a child was quick enough to save my parents the embarrassment of having such a careless child fall dead under the Christmas tree, or at least that is what I conjured after the event. Fortunately for my embarrassment factor no one else was in the room at the time and I could learn from the mistake unimpeded by older sibling or parental admonishments. There are times when it seems to me we are all very lucky to be able to grow to old age given the numerous opportunities for failure to do so, which youth and inexperience provide along our trek through this world. (Like the time of my first trip to a big city, Omaha, to visit Big Sister Delores there. Somebody failed to hang on to my hand and I stepped boldly into the street to cross it, dozens of cars racing by, until someone quickly pulled me back. In another darker Universe there would have been a flattened and crushed little boy lying in that street. But see, the thing is, in my small town of Holstein, Iowa, there was very little traffic to watch for, what traffic there was would be driving slowly, and any car would have stopped for me. But I am rambling. Very difficult to keep all these memories under control and to tease out a logical progression through a life lived 5-6 decades ago within a communal setting which no longer exists.)

In my mind I can see a montage of past Christmases. Christmas for a farm family of German heritage in Holstein, whose parents were members of the community Lutheran Church, meant I would be practicing on the preceding Saturdays in December with my Sunday School classmates and getting ready for the annual Christmas Eve service. All the children had some role to play in what was an organized pageant. Who organized the ones I was in? I am not sure but whoever it was had a backbone of steel to deal with the mob we must have been. Except for the girls, of course. The girls were all angels. Most figuratively. Others literally as performers within the play. The most impressive part for us boys to play was to be Joseph. The same factor for the girls was to be Mary. You had to reach a certain age to play such a significant part. I suspect many of my pals wrestled with the same quandary I did. One never quite knew whether the fame of being Joseph and getting all dressed up in that wonderful robe and headdress was enough to counteract the very real risk and embarrassment of forgetting your lines at a critical juncture and having who you thought were your friends instead make great fun of you. One never knew whether to hope and pray (we were in a church, after all) for the relative anonymity and safety of being selected for the choir or to hope for the academy award opportunity and be the Big Man Joseph. And when, during most of those years when I was not selected to be Joseph, or, at a bare minimum, one of the Wise Men, I always breathed a sigh of relief and was happy to be in the choir.

Two large and impressive decorated Christmas trees were erected at the front two corners on either side of the altar. The green needles of the pines were accented by the multitude of electric lights wrapped endlessly around the entire tree. With the main overhead lights of the church off it seemed as though you were on a dark planet where two multi-colored suns were rising side by side into the dawning sky. Within the context of my life at that time I knew of no other Christmas trees so large and so beautifully lit. Unknown to me at the time those two trees very much bespoke and represented the rich German traditions and German origin of my community.

At the end of the annual Christmas Eve church service, just before exiting the church for your ride or walk home, a huge collection of brown paper sacks appeared near the door, attended by some of the caring adults who had lovingly assembled the sacks and the contents. In my younger years I and my playmates gazed with some small amazement at these sacks and were thrilled to be given one, one sack to each and every child. As we aged the mystery diminished and we came to expect we would be given these small parcels and had become ourselves, traditionalists, confident of their receipt each year. Inside each bag were always an orange and a handful of peanuts in the shell, some small candies – treats which any child would enjoy, a gifting ceremony by the church community to ensure no child would be without some type of a gift each Christmas.

With the stress of the pageant now behind me, my brown bag of treats in hand, I would walk with my parents and siblings to the family automobile, the first I remember was a black 1951 Chevrolet, later a 1954 blue Ford Fairlane. The six mile ride home in the dark was always greatly anticipatory for me. I knew this night I would be staying up late, as long as my eyes would carry me, and I could imagine going into the house and finding presents underneath our tree, presents which weren't there before we left for the church service, but which had magically been delivered by Santa Claus while we were at church. For a young boy, my Christmas Miracle fully entailed wondering how to explain such a fortuitous appearance of presents with such fortuitous timing. During the years of my "belief" I fully expected and knew Santa would deliver, never doubted his intentions. With the development of my analytical inquires I did indeed wonder how Santa could accomplish such complex tasks all over the neighborhood, let alone the world, but I didn't want to work too hard at cracking the mystery. At that stage of my life, belief was more important than resolution. And besides all my close friends had the same miracle going on at their houses, for some of them on Christmas Eve like me, for others on Christmas morning (however did they wait so long!?), verification enough to prove what was going on, and given the substantiation provided by every loving adult whom I came in contact with during the exciting Christmas season.

What I remember most clearly though about those rides home on Christmas Eve was not necessarily the anticipation but the snow. In particular the snow shape appearing in the headlights, most often over the left front fender, and always directed in a quartering fashion directly to me as the viewer regardless of which direction we were going. I am sure now this vision, in fact, probably only rarely occurred exactly on Christmas eve, and was likely reinforced on my consciousness by many other rides home in the snow in the dark, but it seems correlated most strongly to the family-filled, present-filled ride of the night before Christmas. During the ride, when it was snowing, as we sped down the road, the faster the speed, the more dominant the vision, what appeared was a bright white whorl of thousands of wind-driven particles of snow, driven from a central cone directly toward myself in the car, driven out of the middle of an all-encompassing blackness of the night. Fascinating. Beautiful. Mysterious.

During those years the Quaker Oats Cereal company, in its production of the products called Quaker Puffed Rice and Quaker Puffed Wheat, advertised the products as the breakfast "cereal shot from guns." The illustrations for the advertising included a cannon, with generous quantities of individual grains of the cereal being propelled out of the end of the barrel, again toward the viewer. The vision of the snowflakes in the headlights of a speeding car then appeared remarkably similar to the advertisement, with the exception of the "cannon barrel" being invisible. But the endless discharge of snowflakes from the barrel of nature appearing right there over the fender was very much the same. The glare of the headlights illuminated each flake as it came from the center of the cone of discharge until the flakes fell out of the light as they passed closer to the windshield. When my father slowed the car for corners or parked on the farmyard to discharge the family, the falling snow resumed its "normal" appearance drifting prettily downward. And so I knew I had witnessed an artificial image, caused by speed and light reflection, but nonetheless I very much admired the images seen, both as "shot" and as slowly falling, both real images.

Just as I had the draft conscription process of the Vietnam War to deal with as a young adult, Big Brother Duane had the draft to deal with for the Korean War. He and his friends did not need a lot of time or research to consider college or post High School training given the North Korean invasion of South Korea occurred only one month after his graduation from Holstein High School. As the ebb and flow of this major international conflict occupied newspaper headlines, any young man of military age did not need to be much of a prognosticator to know his immediate future would very likely involve some kind of military service. Duane worked for my Dad and neighboring farmers until he was inducted into the United States Army on March 10, 1952, drafted by the locally operated county Draft Board. My parents and he were fortunate inasmuch as he was not assigned to the fighting corps but instead his main accomplishment was to help build airports near the northern border of South Korea by driving a D-8 caterpillar tractor. One of these airports is still in use by our Air Force, the outline of its runways and revetments, as constructed by Duane, still visible from outer space.

Because my birthday was in mid-March, prior to his leaving the family farm, Duane bought a special present and presented it to me as an early birthday gift. A Daisy Red Ryder, lever action B-B gun, one of the most coveted gifts for any young boy in that carefree era before civil action lawsuits made any significant dent in the public's thinking about what constitutes danger. Every farm home had one or more guns tucked somewhere into the accessible family possessions. We were just at the end of the time period where guns were still a necessary tool, for dispatching the wayward, possibly rabid, skunk or for collecting wild game as supplementary table fare. Roast pheasant, fried rabbit, and squirrel stew were occasional meals at our table, collected by my brother or myself, cooked by my mother, enjoyed by all. The small gun collection of my family, then used mostly by Duane, but my father and mother were capable shooters as well, rested on the butts of the guns in a corner of the kitchen formed by the south kitchen wall and the projecting edifice of the brick chimney, the ends of the barrels leaning into the 90 degree corner thus formed. There was a .22 slide action repeater Remington model 121, an older .22 single shot bolt action Remington model 12, and an old 12 gauge break action shotgun which Duane would trade off after the war for a 12 gauge Remington 870. The cartridges, then called bullets, were on an open triangular shelf on the opposite corner of this space behind the access door to the kitchen, the shelf being high enough so the door could swing under it in the summer. There were no locks employed, everyone could see the guns there, could observe the bullets, sometimes the bullets were just left on the window sill, but everyone in the family knew the potential dangers of the weapons and nobody played with them or touched them unless they were about to be used. The guns were highly respected but were stored no differently than the broom on the adjoining porch.

And now I was the proud possessor of a new gun which would be stored there in the corner with the others and it would be mine to use as I saw fit. Big Brother showed me how it worked, taught me how to use it, taught me how to aim by setting up some distant empty tin cans to shoot at, taught me how to carry it safely, taught me how to load it, how the action worked, how to maintain it. But cocking the weapon so Little Brother could shoot it by himself? Now that was a problem. Duane just cocked the lever from his hands and arms and presto, the B-B gun was ready to fire. Trying to duplicate my brother's motions I could not even manage to budge the huge resistance which that air powered weapon provided to a little boy of 7, going on 8, years old. Working together, under Duane's tutelage, he and I finally worked out a method where little brother could cock his own B-B gun after Big Brother was no longer available to do it for him. Standing with my feet spread far enough apart to contain the butt stock of the gun held perpendicular to the axis of my two feet, I held the upper end of the barrel slightly away from my body with my left hand. Then I bent over and with my right hand grabbed hold of the lever and, with all my small might, pulled it upward until my Daisy Red Ryder was cocked and ready to shoot. Success! The feat could easily rank as one my first tasks which resulted in a genuine sense of self-accomplishment. Does mastering one of those video games of today upon reaching the age of 8 give the same sense of self-accomplishment? Hard for me to believe.

Duane was a good son. While he was in the military, while he was in Korea, he would write home about once a week, our mother would write him about once a week. Periodically in those letters, those letters now over 60 years old and kept in a box in my basement, Duane would ask how Gary was doing with the B-B gun and give me encouragement to keep practicing. Any old letter is a bit like a time machine. Reading an old letter enables one to transport themselves back through time, back to the time when the letter was written, and to look around and see things as they were then. As an 8 year old when the letters were written I had youthful, short-term priorities: eating, sleeping, playing with the dog, going to school, getting on the bus. Now, as an older man, I can step into my parents' and my brother's world as it existed then and look upon them as fellow adults. They were courteous, informative, expressing their love and devotion without saying so explicitly. As a young boy I could not see the concern my mother undoubtedly had for her older son in the military. Now I can read her comments, her questions and imagine her feelings. As a young boy, I could not see Duane missing home, wondering about his brother, teasing his sister via written comments to his mother. Now I can read he was trying to reassure them, give my parents a sense of comfort through letting his parents know he was OK, enjoying his comrades, sharing stories of his days. So when Duane asked about Gary in one letter, Mother would respond in the next, sharing a small story, telling Duane Gary had taken the flashlight last night and his B-B gun into the hog house and shot a couple sparrows. Stories told, stories written, stories shared with family and friends – all the stories are important. Stories are one of the few things that can outlast ourselves.

Acquiring Infinity

One of my first friends was David Lohff. David was one year older than me and the closest neighbor whose age was near my own. Many of the neighborhood children were more in the age group of my older siblings and were enjoyed by and friends of my siblings but not of me. David lived one mile north of my house and would walk the one mile road on an occasional Saturday morning so we could play together. David's parents, Willard and Ann, were renters of the house and land where they lived, renting being a concept I would not understand until I was older. To me, his parents, his siblings, and David were neighbors, and David was a nice kid I could play with.

David was being raised and lived, until the Lohffs moved to a farm outside our school district, in the house in which my great grandmother had died in December 1918 of the terrible flu ravaging the country at that time. The farm where David lived was once owned by Fred Wink, my great grandfather. Fifty years before David and I played in his house and my house, his house was the family home of Fred, his wife, Catherine Marie, and their seven children, one of whom, Dorothea Marie, became my grandmother. David and I didn't know it at the time but the world in which we existed was historical and enveloping.

One Saturday morning in winter, the temperature slightly below freezing, the winds were calm enough to allow David to walk to my house, comfortably bundled in his winter coat, with a long ruff collar pulled around his neck. David did not intend his dog, a collie type of mixed unplanned lineage, to accompany him but I am sure David enjoyed his companionship as the dog padded along the road near him. Young boys, unless the dog was exceptionally trained, lacked any wherewithal to send a dog home, preferring to be with a companion that was so much a daily friend in their lives. And farm dogs of the period were not "trained", they were just farm dogs, their chief virtue being that of an alarm which erupted in barking when a car entered the farmyard, barking loud enough to be heard inside the house by its occupants. Awaiting David's appearance from the west window of our living room I spied David walking down the hill on the road west of our house and preparing to turn the corner into our lane. I then rushed to bundle myself for the outdoors and went to join him.

There was only a small amount of snow on the ground. Many bare patches awaiting the full arrival of Spring, lay scattered about covered in brown grass, provided easy transit for two boys bent on discovery and mutual entertainment. I saw David's dog lagging somewhat behind him but the dog was deferential to strangers and merely tagged quietly along following us wherever we went. David and I grabbed my toy wooden gun, the M1 carbine crafted by Duane, and some other suitable armament so we could attack and deal with the imaginary Indians or Chinese or Koreans hiding in our grove of trees in back of the chicken house. Eventually we called off the war and padded our way down to the alleyway of our corn crib where my Dad was getting ready to grind some oats and shell corn for our chickens, hogs, and cows, always a weekly chore for him.

Inside the corn crib alleyway, accompanying my father, was Pudgy, our farm dog, and he was busy keeping a sharp eye out for any mice or rats which might attempt an escape as Dad prepared to grind. Pudgy was a short haired, black and white spotted farm dog with bobbed tail, possibly a terrier, but again of mixed ancestry, who had come to our farm yard before I was born, recognized a good thing when he found it, and never left. Pudgy was a loyal family member, and although he was the first dog I came to know and love, he was primarily Duane's and my Father's dog. Pudgy was busy enough with my dad, he was unaware there was another dog on his turf. David's dog was busy enough with David and I that he was unaware of where Pudgy was. Dogs being dogs I am sure David's dog knew by this time of Pudgy's existence somewhere on this farm.

As David and I walked into the corn crib each dog suddenly saw the other and each went into alert mode. Approaching one another for the circling and sniffing tests, there suddenly wasn't any more time available for circling and sniffing and an all-out dogfight erupted much to the surprise of the humans in attendance to this major arena event. This was no minor barking growling snapping biting event. This was a full-fledged clamped on vicious dogfight, David and I backing out of the way to avoid the fracas, my Dad's voice suddenly screaming commands and curses at the dogs. But the dogs were locked on to each other and fully involved in a test of final supremacy. Carrying the only clubbing option in hand, and standing too near my dad, my father grabbed my beautiful M1 hand crafted carbine, swung it fast and hard, crashing it down on both dogs backs, stopping the fight, and leaving only half of my toy gun in his hands. The butt stock had snapped off at the trigger guard and lay there on the corn crib floor, fully severed. I'm sure my mind was temporarily blank, it had all happened so fast.

What next then? I don't know. I don't know how David's dog got home. I don't remember when David left that morning. I don't think my father apologized for what he had done to my gun, he had other priorities that morning, and although brutally striking the fighting animals, had probably saved the lives of two good farm dogs. Neither dog bore any lasting harm. I didn't blame my father for anything he had done, likely just feeling guilty myself and that I was somehow the one responsible for blame. All I know for sure is the gun was repaired by someone at some point in time with a few judiciously driven nails and some glue, and the gun was used again by little soldiers in future wars carried on in the willow saplings south of the house, in the rugged little gully east of the barn, in the more distant pasture grasses near the big Cottonwoods, and now hangs on the wooden 2 X 10 joist over my workbench in my basement in Wisconsin, an artifact that can bring David back, and Duane back, and my father back, and Pudgy back, and the corn crib back, just as valuable now for what it gives an old man, as for what it gave a young boy on a farm in Iowa, six miles northwest of the community of Holstein.

After Duane was discharged from the Army in December of 1953 he came back to the farm, to home, and worked for our father as a hired man for a short while until he was able to line up his military assistance through the G.I. Bill and went to Business School at Commercial Extension in Omaha, following in the footsteps of our sister, Delores. Having operated a large Caterpillar bulldozer during his time in Korea, and having now secured his own automobile, a 1954 Plymouth, Duane became very interested in a nearby construction project, the rebuilding and blacktopping of a new highway being built between Correctionville, Iowa (named for the surveyor's "correction" in township demarcation lines) and Washta, both small communities adjoining the Little Sioux River, with this new road being about eight miles west of our farm. Snatching some spare time from the farm he would drive over and watch the project underway. Once he took little brother with him, and based on his own experience, was able to explain to a wide-eyed little boy what was taking place and why, what would occur next, the type of machine he had driven, and how this construction related to what he had done during the war. The following Christmas, Duane bought me a long beautiful red toy Tournascraper, a dirt hauling machine that scrapes soil in one location, can haul it away to another location, and then deposit it in a layer wherever the construction boss and driver decide it is needed. Mine was nearly 3 feet long , built to a 1/16 scale, its engine perfect for a boy to lay a hand upon and drive that machine down roadways being built in the grove north of the lawn, its size perfect to crawl on hands and knees alongside directing its motion. By now Duane had taught me to peak the center of the roadbed in triangular cross-section, then doze it flat to secure the road bed. The Tournascraper was built totally of metal, as strong, secure, and usable today as it was in the early 1950's. Oh, except for the rubber "smokestack" exhaust pipe emanating from the engine compartment that broke off years ago.

To make financial ends meet on the small 80 acre farm my father had married into, in addition to running the farm, he had worked his way into a full time job as office manager of the county Agricultural Stabilization and Conservation Office, in Ida Grove, where he had a small staff of clerical assistants working under him. With Duane to help out, Dad would not need to rush home in the evening to do chores as Duane would have that function as his responsibility. Chores were also apportioned to me as a function of my size, strength, and maturity. I would feed the growing chickens in the brooder houses in the field east of the barn. Then I would walk out to the pasture and bring the cows home, trailing behind them in the well-worn cow paths of the bluegrass pasture shimmering in the late day heat, the lead cow knowing exactly where to go and why, for the evening milking. This was an easier task than it might sound to a city-born reader because the cows were tame, very much creatures of habit, could feel the urge to be milked, knew my coming was the sign, and would gather up and walk home single file, one behind the other, in the same common cow path (there's a good reason it is named that), swishing their long tails from one side to the other, and go gently to the barn. I would top off the cow yard water tank from the nearest hydrant, the discharged water flowing smoothly down the cast iron catch mouth under the hydrant then thru the eight foot long two inch diameter steel pipe projecting through the board fence until the water stream leaped into a graceful cool arc into the galvanized cattle tank beneath. If you were young and thirsty, that now well-cold, smooth flowing, stream of water could be irresistibly tempting to drink from, never mind the cow slobber at the end of the pipe. That would be washed away by the time you got to it. Same thing with the 50 pound white salt blocks kept somewhere in the pastures of every good cattle or dairy man in those farms of northwest Iowa. As a young boy lured to taste the taut sharp flavor of raw salt away from the table, you learned to just lick the clean edges of the salt block, not those cavernous concave depressions where the cattle had been licking with their rough tongues, their share of the block. That, or some judicious chipping at a fresh corner with your pocket knife could get you a little nibble to suck on as you headed on through the pasture, either doing your chores, or engaged in a youthful mission of exploration.

    Back at the barn, Duane would have put a small scoop of ground ear corn, cobs plus the kernels, into the small grain box of each cow's assigned stall in the milking area. In the winter, sections of hay bales would also be put into the adjoining manger.

The barn doors, as all good barn doors were constructed, were in top and bottom halves, capable of being opened independently of the other half. Frequently used doors, except in winter, had the top half permanently fixed open to allow fresh breezes to enter the barn. Upon the bottom half door opening into the barn yard, Duane would find the milking cows gathered in a small group outside the door, which they then immediately commenced to enter, each cow going to its own specific stall. No need to argue or watch over who went to which stall. Every cow knew its position in the hierarchy. As they thrust their massive furry heads, ears always twitching one way or the other, into their grain box, Duane, or myself when I got older, would walk up the head and neck of each cow, reach around the neck to gather the other end of the chain, and latch the two ends of the loose fitting manger chain together to bind them to their stall area. In the summer, when flies were bad, we would grab a hand pumped sprayer filled with liquid pesticide/repellant, and spray the cows' head, neck, back, wherever the flies seemed the worse.

Clean milk buckets would already have been brought from the Summer Kitchen near the house down to the barn and be lined up in ready reach. Over time, and as each of we three men of the family co-mingled with chore responsibilities together or separately, we would next reach up to a high shelf in back of the cows, along the east wall, next to where one of the many Barn Swallows always had a mud daubed nest, and pull down our favorite milk stool, a broad single leg like a 4 X 4 or an appropriate tree branch piece, mounted to a flat board on the top of the leg, and one of us as the milker would sit on the top of the board, and balance and pivot as necessary, our two legs forming the rest of the 3 point support, with our forehead nestled softly into the flank of the cow. Each milker had his own favorite stool. We didn't share.

With a pail under the cow our hand milking commenced. The farm cats, handy critters to have around for keeping mice under control but always in danger of overpopulating themselves, would be lined up in back of the cow along the wall. They knew better than to get in the way of a well-placed kick, either from the farmer's foot or the cow's sharp hooves. Some cats were beg-meowing gently, others licking their fur pretending their expected treat wasn't all that important to them. All were waiting for the small dish of milk that was poured for them at the end of the milking session. The bowl surface was covered with small furry heads, the surface punctuated rapidly by lapping kitty tongues, their tails thrust upright in a larger circumference of feline spikes. But sometimes at the start of the milking of each cow, or merely for one's personal entertainment and delight, one of us would aim a stream of milk and arc it over the 5 foot intervening distance where an alert cat would sit back on its haunches, thrust its mouth into the stream, and lap the milk as quickly as it came, smiling a cat smile as soon as the stream ceased, the milker smiling at the cat

Being too young to yet be an assigned milker while my big brother was the hired man, with the conclusion of my chores I would climb up on the 5 barred pipe fence outside the south barn door and perch with my rear on the top railing while my heels were tucked onto the railing at midpoint of the fence, and sit there to keep Duane company while he finished up the cows near this door. It was on one warm sunny late afternoon, there on my perch, that Duane introduced me to Infinity. Television had barely made an entrance into our neighborhood. Although going to a public library was not something my family engaged in, we did keep a World Book Encyclopedia upstairs on a shelf on the north side of the stairs, along with a small collection of books, both novels and non-fiction. The daily newspaper and magazines were the chief method of staying literarily engaged in the world. Copies of Good Housekeeping, Life, Successful Farming, Farm Journal, Outdoor Life, Field and Stream, Capper's Weekly, lay in profusion about the house, older issues piled up in the Summer Kitchen. Whether it was from a recent magazine article or his high school or military training, Duane had learned about Infinity and introduced it to me there from his Philosopher's Bench beside the cow while I listened and questioned from the top rung of the Student's Rail. The issue arose during an astronomy discussion involving the distances to the moon, to the sun, to the planets, to the stars. And beyond. Beyond, you say? Infinity, you say? You mean forever and ever? Out there in Space? Never ending? Never ever? Why, the thought had never occurred to me. It was kind of magical and put into view a new way of looking at our physical universe. Instead of falling off the edge of the world or the universe, I tried to wrap my mind around the fact that you could just keep going. It was a big concept for a young boy and a great way to receive it. The moon coming up over the neighbors ripening field of corn or the 3 stars on Orion's belt went from being simple objects of beauty to being wondrous increments of a fascinating Entirety, the literal World without End.

The World of Holstein

As a youngster, one very gradually attains an increasing awareness of the world around them. As the awareness increases so too does the size of the world. As an infant my world was my mother's arms and embrace, and then it enlarged to my bed and the room surrounding it, then the living room and kitchen. As I learned to walk better and more, then the farm yard was added to my world, then the inside of a car, and while I was yet too young to comprehend it, then my greater community, our neighbors, and town, the town being Holstein. At that time nearly everyone's world was yet small enough that you did not have to say you were going to Holstein. If my dad or my brother, or Jesse, our closest farmer neighbor to the north stopped in and said, "I'm going to town, need anything from the store?" one did not have to respond, "Which town?" the town would be Holstein. Coming then to the age of awareness in which I became aware of my community town, it did not initially carry the name Holstein, but was instead "town". No doubt my analytical comprehension of town and of the town being Holstein quickly increased as it became the destination in which I would spend increasing amounts of time as I became a student within the Holstein school system and as I began to attend Sunday School at the local Lutheran church. The emotional comprehension of Holstein as being a community initially began to develop at the same time as this age 5-7 time of increasing awareness, but continues to develop as I study Holstein's meaning to my life from a time 6-7 decades beyond being introduced to it.

The safety of the community and my comfort at being within "town" and outside the bounds of my house and farmstead are perhaps illustrated by a story which I don't even remember but was told to me by my mother and later recorded in one of her notes written in my baby book. For some reason or failure of adult arranged logistics, as a first-grader, I had failed to get on the school bus for my ride home to our farm. Instead of crying or wailing helplessly until some adult would notice, I resolutely walked 2 blocks north to the parsonage of our preacher, presented myself at their door, and somehow explained my situation. Mrs. Striepe assessed the situation and called upon her oldest son, Bill, the older brother of my friend, Paul, and Bill drove me out to the country and delivered me home. End of story. Satisfactory conclusion. But in these times we are only too awfully familiar with the dangers such a short walk can bring in today's communities for such a young child, and the trepidations which the average caring parent might have to contend with.

Gradually my sense of town, of Holstein, increased. I learned where stores, homes, friends, the school buildings, the city park, the football field were located. Some Saturday mornings I would ride with Dad as he drove to town and delivered the eggs to the Vohs and Johnson produce store. Near the store, English Sparrows would appear in abundance, chirping and peeping, and feeding on spilled grain remnants. While he took care of some town business I might walk to Kerslake's drug store for a ten cent Butter Brickle (always Butter Brickle) ice cream cone. Or I might walk with Dad into Casey's meat market, where friendly Casey Brechwald, wearing a white apron, would be standing behind the white counter and refrigerated display cases where his hand cut and hand selected meat products would be displayed. Dad would pick out a beef shoulder roast which Mother would pot roast with carrots and potatoes and a few bay leaves for our Sunday noon meal. Some Saturday nights we might go a movie where my ticket for admission would be ten cents, a good Roy Rogers or Gene Autry Western being favorite fare, or perhaps Ma and Pa Kettle for a little levity. We had several good grocery stores to choose from, Keitges Grocery or the Council Oak store run by Norman Weiland. Later Tom's Super Valu. Being poorer than I realized we did not eat out very much but the Green Lantern Café on Second Street carries its unforgettable name and location in my memory.

When I grasp now for dominant images in my mind of the Holstein I knew then, there are of course some easy selections as best candidates for illustrating my Holstein of the 1950's. There was the centrally located tower mounted town water tank in back of the movie theater, an impressively tall structure to a growing boy. It might have excited some of my earliest inclinations toward my later engineering career as I pondered how it could be erected and how much strength was needed in those 4 legs to hold up enough water to supply an entire town. From my farm chores I knew how much a 3 gallon water bucket weighed at the end of my arm and 5 gallons was almost too much for a little boy to lift, unless he was showing off to a friend. Up there, high in the air over the movie quonset building, there were just an awful lot of 5 gallon buckets of water. The tall set of Felco grain elevators at the north end of town, near the railroad tracks are a potential selection for a memory dominating image. The white elevator buildings were and are easily visible from miles outside of the town. It's gone now but the old German Turnhalle, representative of the German founders of Holstein, lingers in my memory. Some of these founders organized the Turnverien Society in 1884, based on German exercise and fitness groups of that time in Germany. In 1889 they built the Turnhalle, a large indoor facility to host their events and as a place for routine exercise.

By the time I came along the Turnverien Society was extinct but the Turnhalle remained for use as a dance floor, various social events of local organizations, occasional group banquets, but, being entirely constructed of wood, its age was starting to show. Chiefly I remember it as being intricately constructed and one of the very few buildings in the area hosting a balcony with a thrilling railing keeping occupants from crashing dead to the floor below, or, at least that's what I thought. Stout thick climbing and exercise ropes attached to the ceiling high overhead, formerly used by Turnverein participants, added to the historical aura of the building. Oh, and another candidate for a boy's recollection of a memorable image – the old cannon in the park. What was a boy's time in Holstein worth if he had not climbed onto that cannon and lobbed a few artillery shells into the advancing ranks of the enemy as they approached from the Northeast? But the two images I remember best, as characterizing the old Holstein I see in my mind, was the several block section of Main Street in the "downtown" area, perhaps because I had seen and driven through it so very often, and the lengthy entirety of Kiel Street, appearing in the summer as a massive tunnel of green.

After one crossed the old railroad tracks and the immediate cross street of First Street, the next two blocks as one drove south on the wide avenue also carrying the traffic of US Highway 59, constituted approximately one-half of the downtown businesses. The other half of the businesses were largely located one block east or one block west of the main intersection of Main and second Streets, thus forming a plus shape (+) with each leg of the plus being one block long. If you parked anywhere in the four street lengths, then being all diagonal parking, each one block long, and stepped from your car all the businesses or professional services one could ordinarily need were all within a very modest walking distance. And, with rare exceptions, the Chamber of Commerce Christmas Drawing being one, you could always find a parking spot in these 4 blocks. Main Street was a broad avenue and there was no stop sign or traffic light until you came to US Highway 20, one mile south of the main square. The building store fronts, many of them dating to the early 1900's, were stoutly constructed of brick, in some cases of wood, some modernized, some retaining the classical appearance of their history. All welcomed your entry, several had a type of covered veranda where one could stop and choose when to rush out in the rain or to pull up your collar against the winter snow. Within these 4 blocks one could step into the offices or stores of: several groceries, 2 drug stores, the movie theater, 2 hardware stores, two clothing and shoe stores, the local newspaper, heating and plumbing shop, 2 barbers, the doctor's office, 2 dentists, the 'Dime" or variety store, farm implement dealer, the post office, several diners or food parlors, the State liquor store, about 4 or 5 bars, a billiards facility (then referred to as Pool), a bowling alley, the local Legion Hall for dancing and parties, a meat market, attorneys, insurance offices – in other words, a unique assemblage of essential goods and service unequaled within the same distance or square footage of any of today's malls or shopping areas. Things were handy and you needn't walk far.

    Kiel Street was located one block east of Main Street and runs from the north side of town all the way to the south side of town. From the Methodist Church south it is lined with big houses and small, ornate houses and plain, many with porches some without, but all were neatly cared for. The dominant thing about Kiel Street was the large mature stately elm trees towering from each side, meeting in intersecting boughs over the center of the street, in the summer forming an immense tunnel of green and shade. Planted there with much aforethought by earlier citizens, we, as the current occupants of what was their community, were the recipients of their efforts and plans. From the church south Kiel Street has a gradual slope downward, not necessarily noticed in casual walking, but when Roger and I kicked off on his bicycle you could coast almost all the way down to the swimming pool. Gone now from the Dutch Elm disease of the 1960s, I can still see those old tall trees, the huge tube of leaves, the pastoral shade beneath. One doesn't always have a camera, particularly a camera through a time machine, sometimes the best pictures are the ones you can only capture in your mind.

The Why of Holstein

A street named Kiel. That could be a clue to history. When you add to Kiel the names of the other north-south streets in Holstein: Hanover, Lena, Hamburg, Altona, Lubeck, it goes beyond clue and becomes origin and history. Holstein's origin lies in the German settlers who founded it. Davenport Street, one block beyond Lubeck, continues the origin story by giving homage to the path of immigration through Davenport, Iowa, at one time the major gateway to the newly accessible lands of Iowa.

On April 12, 1847, the sailing ship Harriet, classified as a bark, and commanded by Captain Hunker, left Hamburg, carrying 150 passengers bound for New Orleans. The ship arrived in New Orleans on June 8 where a number of the passengers were offered a bounty to enlist in the Mexican War. Those that continued up the great river arrived at St. Louis on June 19 and only several days later the remaining passengers disembarked at what was then the small village of Davenport, Iowa. The passengers largely came from the area of Germany known as Holstein, many of them from a smaller area within Holstein and comprising an area covering 51 square miles known as the Probstei. Of the 150 passengers, 90, or 60 %, have surnames which appear in my extended genealogical family tree, names such as Stoltenberg, Lage, Hagedorn, Wiese, Klindt, Ladehof, Ewoldt, Meyer, and, yes, even one Ruser (Ruser being the original spelling of my surname). However, nothing further is known of this particular Hans Ruser, after his arrival in Davenport.

When the 1847 immigrants arrived in Davenport, at least eight families from the Probstei had already made their homes in Davenport, one family dating their arrival to 1836. The German or Prussian or, indeed, the European situation during the mid 19th century offered numerous incentives for what must surely still have been an extremely challenging decision to immigrate to America. Those families or individuals that did finally commit to immigrating to the relatively little known lands in the center of North America, must surely have focused on a destination point as suggested by others who had gone before. Given any individual's fear or unsettling concern for the unknown, it seems logical that immigrants would gravitate to destinations where they already had relatives or people speaking the same language and from the same homeland village area. I am sure that was the case for these latest arrivals from the Probstei. And it did not end there. As more letters and more word gradually filtered back to people still in the "old country" more dreams were plotted, more voyages were made, more people from the Probstei or other locations in Germany speaking their same language came to join others already here in these United States of America.

From its start as a village, Davenport grew to a town, then to a small city, then to a destination. Early travelers had come to a steamboat port but with the invention and expansion of railway service, Davenport was selected by the Rock Island Railroad as the site of the first railroad bridge across the Mississippi River constructed in 1856. Now immigrants and travelers and their freight were provided a choice of how to get to the fertile farmlands and expansion area of Iowa. Instead of coming up the Mississippi from New Orleans they could come to Chicago, thence to Rock Island, Illinois, and finally to Davenport. Steamboat companies viewed the expanding railway systems as a threat to their livelihood. So incensed was one captain of the Steamboat, Effie Afton, that he deliberately crashed his riverboat into the new bridge on May 6, 1856, only a few weeks after the bridge was finished. John Hurd was the owner of the Effie Afton and he filed a lawsuit against the Rock Island Railroad Company. The railroad company hired Abraham Lincoln as the lead defense lawyer to protect their right to utilize their major investment. The United States Supreme Court upheld the right to bridge navigable streams and the bridge was allowed to remain. Numerous ancestors of the citizens of Holstein, Iowa were then able to travel to New York, then Chicago, and to cross into Iowa on the Rock Island bridge to meet fellow Germans who had preceded them.

By the 1860's, thanks to the railway companies and the new bridge, Davenport was becoming a regional hub and entry point for many immigrants, not only to Iowa, but to the upper Midwest region. At this time the need for accommodations was growing and what was last known as the Standard Hotel was constructed. This same building is now owned and occupied by the German American Heritage Center and Museum at 712 Second Street. Any resident of the Holstein, Iowa area who has a family lineage in Holstein, Germany extending to the last half of the 1800's can stand in this building, as I have done, and postulate with a fair likelihood of assurance, that at least one of their ancestors once spent one or more nights in this building when it was a new hotel or in other hotels once located in the same area of Davenport. It may be brief, but given the right degree of thoughtfulness, it is a remarkable experience to intersect earlier pathways your family once trod. My great grandfather slept here? Yes. If he came to Iowa in these historical times, he probably did.

Many of these early immigrants were farmers. It was land and opportunity that they wanted. Land and opportunity is what Iowa offered. For those farmers who had come early enough and worked hard, life had improved. By the 1870's some Davenport area residents perhaps were feeling a little crowded, or wanted more affordable land, or were ready to gamble a bit on new opportunity. August and Ludvig Schmidt of Davenport journeyed to northwest Iowa in 1875 to the location where Holstein would be built as part of a small hunting party, eager for some wild game the area then offered. Excited by what they had seen of the prairie and the soil supporting it, they returned to Davenport and encouraged a few of their peers to join with them and acquire some of this land for their own use and investment.

These recently transplanted Germans, after all, were not unfamiliar with the concept of opening up and tilling new lands. In 1762 Catherine II, known in history as Catherine the Great, who was a German native, took the vacant Russian imperial throne. One of her early major actions was to invite Germans to immigrate to vacant Russian lands along the Volga River to colonize and bring the land under cultivation. In the years 1760-1765 King Frederich the V of Denmark invited the colonization of the sparsely settled, thinly populated moor regions of Schleswig's Geest and Jutland. This area of what was then Denmark contained large "burst heath" and moorland habitat which proved quite difficult to bring into fruitful production. My wife, Jean, had several ancestors involved in the moorland project who moved there from southwest Germany along with 1000 other families. Now, within the freedom which America offered, these enterprising Iowa Germans could organize their own colonization instead of operating at the behest of some remote King or Queen.

Opening negotiations with the Blairtown Lot and Land Company, a subsidiary of the Chicago and Northwestern Railway, a combined 14 citizens of Davenport succeeded in purchasing 11,647 acres of land for $5.75 an acre, totaling nearly $67,000, a considerable sum at that time. The final agreement with railroad officers secured a promise from the railroad they would build a rail line to the area purchased. The new land owners promised to break at least 40 acres in each section. Of the 14 individuals who purchased land around what is now Holstein, 10 individuals have the same surname as the surnames which appear in my extended genealogical family tree.

I do not mean to imply through my analysis of the surnames of the early Davenport settlers or the early Holstein land investors that I can prove I am a direct descendent of each or any of those individuals, although given the commonality of surnames of my ancestry with theirs and given where many of these individuals emanated from in Germany it is certainly likely that some of us share in a family lineage. Just as a goodly number of others in Holstein have a share of some of the same lineages. What I have learned though is that my roots to Holstein, Iowa are multiple and deep, much deeper and of more historical charm than merely being born at a particular location called one's birthplace. All this came to me as a slowly developing revelation in collusion with an appreciation of my forebears' perseverance and cohesiveness.

In the spring of 1876 the new landowners sent out a group of young men to break the prairie soil and carry out the landowners' part of the bargain. It took a few years longer for the railroad to comply with their portion of the contract but in the autumn of 1882 the first train came rolling down the tracks near the site then known as the German Settlement, which was actually one mile north and one mile east of the present city center. Knowing firmly at last where the railway was located the city originators platted out land for a town site, laid in First Street parallel to the railroad tracks, and began to sell initial lots at auction. Joachim Thode was an early 1876 settler in the area, having come from New Holstein, Wisconsin, and was elected as the first mayor. Because Holstein in Germany was the name of the province where so many of the new town's settlers had come from, Joachim proposed Holstein as the new town's name and it was quickly adopted. Within a short period of time Holstein had houses, two lumber yards, general stores, two hotels, hardware stores, physicians, meat market, bank, shoe shops, several all-important saloons with their ethnically vital beer and the voluble transmission of the latest news of interest, and a population of 400 persons. Holstein was recognized within Ida County as having been very methodically settled and more than any other town within the county, as being dominated by foreign born people, largely of German descent. My hometown was born in 1882, six years after earliest conception in the minds of some Germans in Davenport. By 1883 it was a community of common concerns and goals.

In 1864 the first Ruser that I can trace within my specific family, my great granduncle Claus Ruser came from Stakendorf, Germany to New York, where, to secure his first money-paying "job", he volunteered to fight in the American Civil War. During those years it was legal to avoid being drafted by paying someone to be an official "substitute" to fight in your place. Claus became the substitute for George L. Maxmell of 250 West 23rd Street in the 16th ward of the 6th district of New York City. Claus served in the Civil War in the siege of Petersburg, Virginia where, as a member of the 10th regiment of the New York Infantry, he was shot in the right shoulder. After the war he returned to New York where he became a painter and he lived there until September 2, 1868. Likely hearing news of opportunity and of fellow Germans from the area of his youth, Claus moved to Davenport, where he lived until April 10, 1883 when he moved to Holstein. There Claus lived with his wife, Margreta, until his death on October 28, 1909. My father introduced me to this relative when we visited Claus's grave site and I was a teen-ager, now finally old enough to appreciate some old family stories. It was on a Memorial Day and my dad was proud to point out Claus as one of the very few individuals in the Holstein Cemetery to be recognized with an emblem on his grave as having served in the Civil War. The dates on Claus's grave, and the little metal emblem were the basic extent of what my dad knew about Claus. But it was enough to carry his tone of pride for Claus's uniqueness on this hallowed hilltop. How I wish that I could have shared all I have since come to know about Claus, about all the Ruhsers and Rusers, both in America and those still living in Germany. My Dad would be SO AMAZED and appreciative.

Claus lies in the ground next to his brother who is my great grandfather, Heinrich Ruser, the first direct ancestor that came to America in my personal Ruser lineage. Claus and Heinrich were each born in the same small farmhouse in the village of Stakendorf in the Probstei of Germany. These two brothers, Heinrich was the younger, now share in the common earthen home of a community named after their German Province, and located 4460 miles from their common birthplace. How did this come to be? Family members sometimes follow in the paths of other family members. This was the case for Claus and Heinrich. My great grandfather,

Heinrich, came to New York in 1867 and lived in the same city as his brother, Claus, until 1868, when each moved to Davenport. Each lived in the Davenport area until Claus moved to Holstein in 1883. Seven years later, in 1890, my great grandfather moved to Holstein to once again join his brother. Brother had followed brother through four communities and thousands of miles.

By the time Claus came to Holstein, he too had been following earlier paths blazed by friends, acquaintances, fellow Probsteirs, and relatives. In its founding days, and continuing through to my youth, early or continuing residents of Holstein had an abundance of near and distant relatives within the Holstein area. Not that the relatives were always recognized as such. There are numerous examples of immigrants arriving who did not know or chose not to seek out relatives who had immigrated to America before them. Some were separated by several generations, but the commonality of family surnames as one goes back in time is profuse among Holstein residents for the time period of 1882 to, let us say, 1982, to select an arbitrary point of now diminishing relationship. Many early residents of Holstein shared a common heritage, a common German origin, even down to what we would define as counties, and a few common genes.

Partly the relationships possible within a community or within a greater community were formed by the population dynamics of the time. It was not unusual to find families containing 4 to 8 living siblings (infant death being more frequent in the 16th, 17th, and 18th centuries). It is not that difficult to find familes containing more than ten siblings or step siblings (Remarriage and combining families then being the socially-accepted means of family survival, for example in cases where one spouse has died.). As one moves backward or forward in time studying birth records, such a profusion of children and the lack of transportation, makes for many opportunities for genetic relationships and relationships through marriage. To present a small example within current context to illustrate the background of Holstein compared to today's society: My wife had 40 first cousins, of which 36 were within several hours travel time as she was growing up. I had 15 first cousins. Our daughters have four first cousins; our granddaughter has none. A similar progression is taking place throughout American society today when compared to the society of Holstein, Iowa in 1900. The times, they are a changing.

I have chosen my Ruser surname to illustrate a pathway of migration and a basis for common origin. That is not to diminish the roles each of my other 7 great grandparents play in who I am and what my historical heritage is all about. Indeed, I am of the firm conviction that many individuals put far too much emphasis on their given surname and patriarchal lineage when in fact they owe their genetics equally to all ancestors on a generation by generation perspective. And in fact, matrilineal lineage should receive a greater emphasis, because as my wife is fond of stating, one always knows for sure who the mother is. But, before today's genetic testing, one did not know if the father might not have been the postman or traveling salesman, or, in harsher times, the invading soldier. All eight of my great grandparents came from the northern ¼ of Germany, half of them even had lived within a day's walking distance of one another. The community bonds were tight and many-stranded at the origin in Germany. Due to like finding or following like, those bonds continued down to the Holstein of my youth. The people around me not only shared in my heritage, a goodly number shared a few of my genes or were married to someone in the community who did. Not all of us knew or understood that at the time, but the older the citizen the more they were aware of it.

Vestiges of Holstein's German heritage were still common in the community as I was growing up. My mother and father still spoke some German at the dinner table and my older brother and sisters learned the language in their youth, but, due to the impact of the Second World War and my age, I was much less exposed to this second language and did not learn it. Older members of the community often exchanged some sentences in the old "Low" German of their youth, the older they were the more likely they shared some conversation in their native tongue, some still carried the pronounced accent into their English speech. May Day on May 1st is still celebrated in Europe and in Schoenberg, Germany, where some distant cousins currently live, and was still a tradition within the Holstein community of my early grade school years. May baskets of flowers and treats were exchanged or left on a doorstep, and a dance was held that involved weaving hanging garlands around a centrally erected May Pole. Kinderfest, or

Children's Day, is an old German tradition in Holstein of honoring the children and giving them a special day, celebrated by the community each year from before 1900 on up to the present day. My Aunt Edna (Ruhser-Coale), as a 90 year old vividly remembered attending the annual Holstein Children's Day each year in the mid 1920's. Her "Papa" would leave the horse and buggy at her Grandparent's house on North Altona Street in town and she would attend the festivities in a new dress hand-sewn by her mother (my Grandmother).

My Home

At age eight, I was still eleven years away from meeting my wife to be on the main square of Holstein on a momentous future Children's Day yet to be revealed to me. At age eight, I was still pondering why it was that the young girl on whose doorstep a May Basket might be left was supposed to rush out and kiss you if she could. At age eight, I was still surrounded by the protective care of my immediate family and neighbors and whatever I was engaged in was within their domain of granting or denying permission. But that puts it too strongly. It wasn't so much demands and orders that dictated my life; it was expectations, both those of others as well as myself. And not necessarily meeting expectations, as is too often defined in today's vernacular. No. Just expectations.

The most reliable and dominant expectation was that there would be three meals each day and we would all gather round the table for each of these meals. Further, the time for each meal was approximately the same each day. Sister Delores would leave our home and go to secretarial school in Omaha when I was only four. Duane left home when the military drafted him when I was age eight, but he returned home for a year or two after the war. Sister Gloria would leave home and attend the same business school as Delores had done when I was ten years old, so the mix around the table was in flux depending on how old I was. Dad sat at the head of the table and was the voice of authority although it was rarely used, it didn't need to be. The small 80-acre farm we lived on was actually my mother's inheritance. Because of that and because of losing her mother when she was only 13 years old, she had become a skilled politician in working with the men in her life, and so was not without power in the family. Again, it was rarely visibly exercised. Again, it didn't need to be. There were, after all, expectations.

I don't recall ever being sent to bed at a particular hour, or, as a teen-ager, being told when to be home. Given the expectations of the home, it wasn't necessary for any of us children to be given a specific bedtime or a time to be home. Chores were not mandated so much as they were assigned as what needed doing. Once assigned a task, we did it. If it needed to be done every day, such as some evening chore duty, at about the same time each day, we did it.

When at the dinner table, that being a term of today's use, not ours, we called it the kitchen table, I sat on the west side of the table. Breakfast was breakfast. The noon meal was either lunch or dinner, the terms used interchangeably. Dinner was never the evening meal. The evening meal was always supper. When I went off to college and then later joined the business world I had a tough time grasping what the word dinner meant to others and learned quickly to confirm the time of any "dinner" meal I might be invited to. Over Dad's head at our kitchen table was a tall shelf, reachable by the adults, which held the official clock, a somewhat ornate hand-wound clock, black numerals on a white face inside of a black wooden curved top body, which chimed on the quarter hour.

Dad was the official winder and often did the task as part of his early morning tasks. The clock was one of those family heirlooms which was generally treasured and appreciated by the whole family for its traditional appearance and now resides in the home of Gloria in Omaha. As a teen-ager, coming home late at night, it became a minor nemesis of mine because, depending on her wakefulness, my mother could tell when I came home, and if a bit later than she might regard as acceptable behavior, I would be teased the following morning. Did this clock contribute to my analytical time-consciousness? Or was I pre-disposed to be that way? Certainly the shelf clock was a highly utilized common reference to determine when to leave the house for the bus, or for church services, or for some evening event.

The other common reference point of the kitchen was the large wall calendar that came each year from the local elevator grain company. It seemed to be at least 18 inches wide and 24 inches long and had large numerals on each day, Sundays appearing in red numerals, numerals so large anyone could see them all the way across the kitchen. Inside each daily box was written the total number of eggs gathered that day, eggs being an important commodity gathered each day and sold weekly, providing one slight steady stream of income so important to the small farmer.

As a preschooler I vaguely remember the large cast iron wood burning cook stove along the south wall. It was positioned directly in front of the centrally located brick chimney and between the two windows opening to the south. These windows, because of their solar orientation, held my mother's collection of house plants and always posed a striking wall of green and variations of red tones consisting largely of the coleus and African violets, as one tried to peer out. When the cook stove had been recently fired up and the oven door left open, standing in front of that radiating warmth on a cold winter morning after you just came from the chilled bedroom area upstairs was often one's first stop of the day. Soak up the warmth, rub out the goose bumps. The wood and coal burner was replaced with an oil burning stove made for both heating and modest food preparation. It was designed with a cast iron hot plate on top and in the winter a round silver tea kettle would be left there, always containing hot water, whether for your morning tea or your noon coffee, or for washing and rinsing the mealtime dishes and utensils. In the summer an electric hot plate was used to heat the water and the stove instead supported just a few more of Mom's house plants.

The source of the kitchen, drinking, and washing water was an in-ground cement cistern just north of the house. The ground was not high enough to support gravity feed into the house so a hand pump was mounted over the center of the cistern. The water was supplied through underground pipe from the hand dug, shallow well in the pasture located down near what we called the little creek ("crick" in Iowa Speak). The electric pump over the well was selectively turned on by my father with a switch in the barn when he noticed the water level in the cistern being low. Several hours of pumping would rectify the low water level and he would judiciously, based on years of experience, turn the switch off and stop the further filling of the cistern, there now being enough water in the cistern to supply several days-worth of household needs and of livestock needs which were supplied by gravity from the cistern to two hydrants located near the barn and hog house.

One would grab the white enameled bucket with red rim from the kitchen or porch as needed each day and go to the cistern, pump the handle, and return to the house with fresh ground-cooled water. In the winter this bucket sat in the pantry adjacent to the eventual electric stove and on the countertop of what we called the pantry. In the summer the bucket, with a dipper in it, sat adjacent to the wash basin in the dry sink on the porch. If water was needed for washing or kitchen use, it was dipped out of the bucket with the long handled, enameled dipper. Not infrequently, as needed to quench one's thirst, you dipped in and drank directly from the dipper – no use getting a clean glass dirty or risk tracking dirt to the glasses storage cabinet. The soap dish was next to the wash basin. You washed up, took the towel from the rack on the east wall of the porch and dried off. If you had made the water too dirty for another use, you grabbed the basin, opened the porch door next to the dry sink cupboard and flung the basin water out on the lawn before the door closed again, the water scattering over the lawn and seeping away. That oval spot on the lawn, approximately 10 – 15 feet long, maybe 10 feet wide, as the days warmed up and summer progressed always grew grass and dandelions several inches taller than the adjoining lawn. Then one would step left of the door where a mirror was hung on the wall. I kept my personal comb on the horizontal 2 X 4 mounted over the mirror: I could grab it, comb my hair, and be good to go. When I was a teenager sporting my new butch flattop haircut my jar of sticky, pinkish Gary's Butch Wax (its real name, how could I resist using that brand?) perched adjacent to my comb.

Dishes were washed in a brown enameled rectangular wash pan set on the table after the meal was done. Later an electric hot water heater of 15 – 30 gallon capacity with huge thick insulated walls was positioned in the pantry. By means of this water heater, my family had advanced to having hot water available 24 hours a day at the turn of a handle instead of specifically heating it on a stove, hot plate or oil burner. We filled the heater with several buckets of water from the cistern poured in through a six-inch top opening, which had a rubber insulated lid. Hot water was dispensed by opening a faucet spigot at the bottom of the tank and catching the released water in a container of choice. Efficient use or expectations of hot water still had to be monitored to assure: a) the water did not run completely out and thereby burn out the heating coil, and b) fresh cool water had been added far enough in advance for the water to be the temperature you expected.

Running water inside the home was not delivered until in my middle grade school years when Dad took out a second mortgage and secured funds to do some repair work on the well facility and ran a new buried water line directly into the pantry where a new kitchen sink and cupboard system had been built. The drain line was a simple tile line in the ground extending south of the lane and emptying near the willow trees and waterway south of the house. There was still not enough money or family income to build an indoor bathroom facility complete with shower, sink, and stool. That wish still laid ahead out there in the future somewhere. In the meantime, not having had one, it was not exactly missed. Not having a full-fledged bathroom was just something the family lived with and we were all used to it.

Cleanliness and bathing of the body proper was accomplished in one of three ways. The most common technique utilized was the sponge bath; in this method the body was cleaned using a small hand basin of water, a small wash cloth and soap, followed by a fresh basin of rinse water. The water in the basin for washing and rinsing was freshened as often as needed. The second approach, not often used and only in the cool months was to put warm water into a large galvanized oblong tub brought up from the cellar, set it up on the unheated porch, or, if very cold, in the kitchen, and sit in it. The third approach, only used in warm months, was to mount a gravity feed shower bucket and spigot with attached 4 foot long small hose onto the side of the Summer Kitchen (or what was sometimes called the Wash House, named for the laundry facilities, not for the showers of which we speak) and to bathe with it. Mother had sewn a large cotton cloth curtain for privacy around the bucket and my father had mounted the curtain around the concrete platform and entry door to the building. One could disrobe in the building, step out to the shower area, bathe and then towel off and dress back inside the building without others potentially viewing the process. The cloth enclosure was visible from the entry lane to the farmstead though. Although anyone that drove onto the farm yard could not see you, such an unexpected and rare arrival did have a tendency to shorten the length of the shower as one bolted for the full privacy of the building.

The stoutly constructed outhouse built on a concrete perimeter foundation was located at the end of a small narrow concrete sidewalk running past the Summer Kitchen and about 60 feet northeast of the house, beyond the tool shed, under the tall elm trees and just south of the pine grove, and was utilized day in day out, whether it was 100 degrees in the shade and calm, or 30 degrees below zero and a blizzard raging. Outhouses on farms were not a rarity as I was growing up, but they soon came to be. The few remaining that I was familiar with were most often vestiges of the way things used to be on a particular farm and were utilized most often by the adult males of the family to avoid taking muddy boots off to access the indoor plumbing. For my family and for just a very few of my classmates, the outhouse was the only option. Again, we accepted it. We were used to it. I'm sure it would be much more difficult to accept for those who had gotten used to indoor plumbing and then had to go back to outdoor facilities, whether temporarily or semi-permanently, such as in the case of being a farm renter and then having to move from one farm wherein the landlord had indoor plumbing available for his tenant farmers to that of a landlord that did not provide indoor plumbing to his tenants.

Indoor plumbing finally came to my farm home, sometime around 1970, after I had gone away to college, married and become a parent. Dad had secured enough surplus funds that he could afford to build his own bathroom addition onto the side of our kitchen and pantry and then he hired the plumber to complete the project. I'm sure Mom appreciated it immensely. When I was young enough as a grade schooler I was not embarrassed about the absence of a bathroom, which is not an item of great concern to a little boy. As I became more aware of society though and got into Junior High School and High School, it did embarrass me. But the older I got the less likely it was that particular social settings within the family home would occur. By then I and my close friends were spending time in town, at the movies, at the school, or at friends' homes that were "modern". And my oldest friends and closest relatives already knew the bathroom situation at my house.

Looking back at my early life without a home indoor bath what impresses me most is that it was basically a non-event. I had the embarrassment factor occasionally, sure, but, so what? It didn't give me any lasting harm. These things all revolve around physical functions that need performing, regardless of accommodations. My good friends were still, and stayed, my good friends. Mom and Dad's friends and relatives all accepted them for what my parents were internally, not for what they possessed externally. The Let's All Go Club, my mother's neighborhood social organization of women friends, didn't stay away when it was Mom's turn to host the monthly meeting. They might have planned accordingly, but they didn't stay away. My parents' community and my parents' associates accepted my family for what it did, not for what it should do. The social settings of my family members were inclusive, not exclusive.

Adjacent to my father's spot at the kitchen table was the doorway leading into the living room. Once immediately inside the living room a door to the right led into a small bedroom, normally unused when I was young. As a five year old and new kindergartner in Holstein I had lain upon a bed in that room and finished recovering from my hernia surgery in the Cherokee, Iowa hospital, cards from my classmates and relatives and from my teacher, Mrs Fahan piling around me. My mother's mother, who would have been my grandmother, died in that room of the 1918 flu, 26 years before I was born. My siblings were all born in that room. As my parents marched into old age and got tired of climbing the steps upstairs to their bed, they moved down to this bedroom, now so very handy and close to the new bathroom. This small unpretentious quiet little room held it all: new lives coming into the world, a ravaged life leaving it, a little boy's recovery and napping, my parents' calm contented retirement and evening rests. For a small space this room held a lot of stories.

Back in the living room, an oil burning heater, the wood burner having been removed years before, was centrally located along the east wall between the doorways leading into the downstairs bedroom and the door leading to the stairs going up to the second floor. The far north wall contained a door, the door's upper half being window to admit more natural light with the door opening to the outside. This door was never used in winter but provided a quick supplementary exit in the warm months. Twenty feet from the door, a large, ornate white bridal wreath bush, 6-8 feet in diameter and height, redolent in blossoms, was a real eye-catcher in the springtime. Left of this door a large round mirror was hung, magnifying a bit the relatively small confines of the room. The dominant feature on the west wall was what my mother called the "glaashop", a holdover term from her German youth, describing literally a glass case. The top third was a shelved unit which held the special occasion dishes, antique heirlooms and modern glass or pottery display items, and some gold rimmed wine glasses, rarely used. The middle third was a desk unit with ornate carvings on the front door which dropped down to expose the contents and provide a writing surface. This was used more as a storage unit than as a desk, what fascinated me was the intricate little wooden drawers inside. In the bottom third were several slide-out drawers, which held old photo albums and piles of more recent pictures, most of them taken on Mom's old Brownie camera.

    The south wall of the living room, which separated the living room from the kitchen, had, as its chief feature two large wooden cupboard doors, decoratively grooved vertically in narrow strips as wainscoting might be, each mated door of the pair being approximately 30 inches wide and 60 inches tall. Therefore a large portion of the wall was consumed in a dark wood varnish tone. What was interesting about this cupboard or storage unit was the north wall of the kitchen also held the same size and style of doors except painted white to match the décor of the kitchen. When all 4 doors were opened, which they hardly ever were because some living room furniture was invariably placed against the doors, one could see straight through the wall. On the bottom shelves within this storage area were the rags and old discarded clothes. The next shelf up held an array of crayons, writing paper, and books and stories which had been favorites of mine as a small child. The top shelf held Dad's old shaving soap mug and straight razors, frighteningly sharp and wicked looking, now relegated to a place of relative inaccessibility. It seemed the old cupboard held an endless menagerie of obscure items with no other better place to store them. Among the collection was an old rubber enema bulb, which the men folk had liberated from its designed use to be applied instead as a clean method to add distilled water to the tractor and car batteries.

 Between the door to the upstairs and the door leading to the bridal wreath bush was the door that led to what we always called the closet because that is how my family used this tiny room, half of which was tucked under the sloping stairwell going up. At the time of construction, late in the 1890's, this room was utilized as a second downstairs bedroom. During my time a high rod six feet long supported all the dress coats of the family and all the formal or "going out" clothes of the whole family. Card tables and spare wooden folding chairs were stored in the room ever ready for the neighborhood gathering or birthday celebration guests. The room's treasure for me and my young friends though was the large collection of colorful and exciting comic books, 10 cents each when purchased new at the drug store, and stored in two piles, one on each side of the two-compartment wooden box, just big enough to contain the comics as they lay piled one on top of another in this box. Those were impressive and heady times when the piles of comics exceeded the height of the storage box and the lid no longer could be closed. The vast selection included Archie and Veronica, Roy Rogers (of course), Gene Autry, Donald Duck and his nephews, the beautiful physical form of Rulah Jungle Goddess, the older I got the more Goddess she became, Buck Rogers, and dozens of others.

The stairway door was always closed except on the coldest nights in winter when it might be left open to allow a little more heat to flow upstairs. That decision was Dad's and it was not taken lightly due to the cost of the fuel. The heat from heavy bedcovers was free. Fuel oil was not. The upstairs rooms were unheated except for the floor register in the main room upstairs. The register had an intricate system of vanes which could be open or closed with a hearty push of the flat lever on one side of this foot square opening in the floor covered with a grille. This register had 2 main advantages for me. One, it was a swell place to stand over on a cold morning to catch the first rays of heat as one was dressing in a cold room. Secondly, if the register was open it made a great place to look through and down onto anyone in the living room without their necessarily being aware of being spied upon. This spy game necessitated two caveats, however. One, don't let the floor squeak on your way over to lying down and spying through the grille. Two, don't try to open that register if it's closed. Either mistake will get you caught.

The upstairs only had two rooms with walls and surfaces made of plaster board and lathes, the same as the interior walls of the remainder of the house. However, through the use of cloth curtains suspended from cord rope the number of rooms upstairs was doubled, albeit the total small square footage remained the same. As one came up the relatively steep stairs from the living room, one automatically rose into the midst of the first room. Each room upstairs had a vertical sash window in the respective end of the house which that room occupied. The size of the house and the rise of the stairs meant there was only a landing about 18 inches wide at the top of the stairs. You had better be prepared to turn instantly because there was barely room to secure your standing on the small landing between the top step and the outside wall of the house. In both of the rooms, the ceiling slanted at a 45 degree angle, the same angle as the gable roof of the house, starting about three feet up each side wall, until it met the flat part of the ceiling at eight feet above the floor. What this meant in practical terms for each room was you could stand straight up in the center one-third of the room, but as you approached the north or south wall in either room, the more you had to bend over to avoid hitting your head. Few heads were actually hit in practice because when you lied down on a 2-foot tall bed next to the short wall, you were nicely tucked under the ceiling although if you reached straight up you could touch it. When you rolled out and sat up in bed with your feet on the floor, the ceiling increased in height as you did, because now you were four feet away from the wall. As you stood up from your bed, mine in this particular example, your head advanced to five feet away from the short wall, and again your head was safe from contact with the ceiling. Like the bathroom facilities, we were all used to it, and it seemed no imposition.

As one rose up from out of the stair well, you quickly turned right 180 degrees, and if you were going to the west room, walked along a 3 foot wide landing through the door into that room. On the north or left side of the stair well was a slanted roof miscellaneous storage area about 4 feet wide where my mother's treadle sewing machine sat unused after the new electric sewing machine came into use sometime around when I was born. Book shelves occupied the short north wall holding assorted novels, old school books from my parents' time in country school, and, best of all, a set of World Book Encyclopedias. The encyclopedias were somewhat dated but still a fascinating world of knowledge as I got older and read more. Being a little more impulsive than realistic I, at one point set out to read the entire collection, but only got part way through the "A" volume. I did considerably better on my next vow, which was to read all the articles pertaining to astronomy. One of the first books

I ever read cover-to-cover was a youth science fiction book about the boy Tom Swift and his rocket ship. As I read more of the astronomy section in the World Book, I got more and more interested in the subject.

In the Popular Science magazine of that time, I found an advertisement in the back pages for a collapsible telescope with change-out lenses to adjust the power and available for a mere $3.95. I purchased a money order at the post office and in a short period of time was in possession of a cardboard tube telescope with an impressive amount of power. It was at least 20 power, perhaps as high as 60, but certainly at its upper magnification I could no longer manually hold it still enough to acquire a clear view. So I went to our wood shop in the tool shed and built a wooden trough device to hold the body of the telescope and then mounted this fixture in a pivoting and rotatable stand on top of an old wooden fence post I had set up in the yard down by the clothesline with a clear view of the overhead sky. Once I had sighted in on the moon or some planet and adjusted the focus, I could release my hands and the scope would remain still and offer a clear view. Well, clear enough for a young boy with a $3.95 telescope. But the views it gave me were really quite amazing and lent the incentive to continue reading more astronomy articles in the World Book. The view through the scope also gave me my first concrete illustration of the relative speed of planetary motion as I noted how quickly Venus or Jupiter would move out of the image window of the telescope, almost sweeping across the small field of view.

As I aged I acquired the ability to build a small desk, which I labeled my very own. I constructed it from vertically-orientated, used fruit boxes, positioned a board on top and painted the whole assembly white. I have always been in possession of, and used, my own desk since I was ten years old. On the back end of the stairwell, over your head as you rose up the stairs was a board lying on the floor on each side but bridging the intervening gap over the stairs. On this board lay a very old, but very massive, brown-gold cloth covered Merriam-Webster dictionary, 6-8 inches thick. Too heavy for me to lift as a youngster, it became a valuable adjunct to my self-taught sex education classes as I got into those precarious, curiosity-filled teen age years.

The south half of this first room (the east upstairs room) was walled off by a cloth curtain hung from a stout cord between the door jamb of the next (west) room and the edge of the window on the tall east wall. The curtain provided a privacy barrier and entry to what was initially my brother's "bedroom" and what later became my room after he moved to Omaha. All six members of my family slept upstairs and the other five would all pad quietly past this curtain and enter the second room through a doorway that was never closed. This second room, the west room, was also subdivided with a hanging cloth curtain like the east room was. Behind the curtain, south of the door frame, again under a slanted ceiling overhead, was the "bedroom" of my two older sisters, who shared in common a double bed. In the corner of their room opposite from the bed, between their large set of dresser drawers and the short wall, was the quilt box, a large open wooden box which held a heaping collection of sheets, quilts, blankets, and pillows.

My parents slept in a double bed in the main portion of this west room. Dad accessed his right side of the bed down an aisle which also held an old small writing desk, which he utilized as a dresser. Mother accessed her left side of the bed down a small aisle. Across this aisle within her reach was initially a crib where I first slept. Later, the crib was removed and a single "rollaway" bed was provided for me. So with aid of a curtain, five people slept in this room. One person, my brother Duane, slept in the other upstairs (east) room through which all had to transit. Lighting was available through one bare electric light bulb in the center of each room's ceiling, plus each person had their own flashlight nearby to access as needed. The light in the west room where most of the family slept was controlled by a chain pull built into the lighting fixture. A one quarter inch wide soft cloth strip 5 feet long dangled from the chain to allow ready access to control of the light. The east room light control was the same until my brother-in-law, Earl, installed "modern" electric wall switches at top and bottom of the stairs to facilitate safety and convenience for all concerned.

Measuring Worth

By now the unfamiliar reader, one not acquainted with the rural setting and community of my youth, may begin to conclude my family was "poor". Technically, that reader would probably be correct within the context of average Iowa income for the 1950's, and based on the percentage of Iowa homes which had indoor plumbing, or the average amount of square feet of living space per individual household member during that time period. But in financial terms, I always felt my family was "average" or normal within our community. I was basically content and happy with the world around me. I had no feelings of remorse, anger, or plans for vengeance against those better off than me. I thought those around me, basically all of them, were about in the same situation and mode of living as I. It was not until I got to college that I finally deduced, "Hey! I grew up poor. Well, how about that!?" I was actually surprised by my late discovery of this fundamental fact of my existence. Naturally, a lot of the credit for my growing up contented and "average" goes to my family. But the rest of the credit goes to that small tight-knit, genetically interwoven, related by marriage, and if not that, bonded by custom, tradition, and cultural heritage, community that I called home. I felt accepted by both family and community, and did not feel as though I carried the burden of any social labeling. And, if in fact, I did carry any label assigned by anyone else, I was blissfully unaware of it.

By the time I got to college, I was thrust into a much wider network of peers from a much broader origin. My and Bryan's college roommate, Alex, was of Russian ethnic origin, born and raised in Chicago, who had performed scholastically very well in a school system that had 6 times as many students as Holstein had residents. After I got to college, while my parents searched for funds to sustain me there and I was advised it was time to get my own loan, I learned Dad and Mom were carrying two mortgages on the farm. In college I met a lot of good new people, and because it was Iowa State a goodly number of them had come from backgrounds very similar to mine. But I also had my first acquaintance with snobs, "rich" people's kids, who had expensive cars, expensive clothes; I also encountered a thing called "social status". Gradually, as young adults must, I pieced together the broader picture of how I fit into the enveloping new world into which I was growing.

Back in Holstein, in 1954, my world was smaller, simpler, and more uniform. In 1954 the average new car cost $1700. My Dad bought a new 1954 Ford having traded in our 1951 Chevrolet, so ones state of "poorness" is related to a broad spectrum of measuring indices. Holstein had two automobile dealerships then, Tharp's Ford on the south end of town opposite the swimming pool, Vollmer Motors selling GMC brands one block west of the main square. Oh, how we high school Juniors and Seniors, then entering driving age, loved to walk down to the dealerships upon release of the year's new styles. With a broad variety of brands to choose from, both for the well-to-do and for the not-so-well-to-do, still the most expensive cars one could procure were only around two to three times as expensive as the lowest priced car. Contrast this to today's most expensive cars being upwards of 15 times as expensive as the cheapest new transportation. For those cars normally readily procurable today in the central United States one could drop that ratio to four times as expensive as the average low cost family sedan. That is still a broader range than was experienced in 1954.

In the Holstein of the 1950's there were old homes, and a very few new homes. There were big houses and small houses. There were nice homes and some not so nice. But taken as a whole, the nicer, newer, bigger homes, were still only perhaps 2 – 3 times as expensive as the average of the smaller, older homes which families lived in. Like the automobiles in the preceding paragraph the range from average low to average high was not that broad. Contrast that situation to today's home prices. Today, many perfectly nice, livable homes are available for $100,000 to $200,000, which is a fraction of the cost of the many million dollar homes we have all been exposed to today whether through seeing the mansions on television or driving past the exquisite stately one-of-a-kind home on the hill with a view. Most of the families in Holstein at mid-20th century lived in a manner and style not that different from the rest of the families. Our lives and our happiness were not derived from an artificial construct of economic well-being.

These same valuation ranges can likewise be applied to family incomes during the time of my youth. Whether looking at the income of the vocation they maintained or how they lived in their home, Jim the baker, Lloyd the barber, Jesse the lawyer, Bill the gas station owner, Bill and Robert the clothiers, Jim the auctioneer, William the pastor, Norman the grocer, or my Dad and his near neighbors, none of them lived all that much differently from the others. The range of how we lived in that community, compared to the America of the 21st century, was relatively narrow. I think the small range of economic disparities and corresponding narrow range of lifestyle choices gave all of us a sense of commonality and comfort more difficult to attain now.

Within the farming community that was Holstein, perhaps the commonest measure of accumulated wealth was land – how much you owned, how much you farmed. And, usually, as is the way with small communities, we all had an idea of who owned how much. But one cannot wear land on your shirt sleeve and thereby demonstrate wealth, nor, in the personality types upon which Holstein was founded, was there necessarily the desire to be that demonstrative. Then too, land can carry hidden burdens, like operating debt and mortgages, and not actually be the asset one might assume. In the mid-20th century many local citizens were only 2-3 generations removed from being new immigrants. New immigrants usually arrived in America with essentially nothing. That's why they came to America – to better themselves. Due to the laws of partible inheritance in much of Germany, the property rights accorded to any individual kept being subdivided constantly smaller until the land one managed was insufficient to provide a living.

Starting with nothing upon arrival in the United States, many hard working German immigrants, those immigrants who founded Holstein, learned that with effort expended they could quickly better themselves compared to the lifestyle which would have been theirs in their old homeland. I have a letter written around 1890 by my great grandaunt, Catherine Elizabeth Meyer Koetke, to her mother in Germany. In the letter Catherine proudly writes of the 120 acres of land they are leasing, of the 5 horses they own, of the sewing machine they purchased, the new barn being built, all representing significant wealth to anyone struggling to make a decent living in Germany. One can read this letter and see the pride shining through. Sixty years later, the farmers around me still carried the quiet pride of Catherine Elizabeth for controlling the lands they lived on and for having bettered themselves compared to what their great grandparents left behind in the old country.

Although family income and family lifestyle choices provided a sense of union within the overall community, there existed a widespread sense of literal relationship in the Holstein area of the 1950's, along with a network of friendships both within and without ones extended family. I would even propose the sense of extended family relationships helped foster pure friendships which were without a genetic or marriage linking. I did not come to a genealogical understanding of the Holstein of my youth until I reached my senior years, but from a genealogical perspective let us now consider some details of the world of my youth -

As a child my hair was cut in the barbershop of my father's Uncle Bill. We bought our baby chicks for the farm from, and sold the eggs from those chickens to, Dad's cousin Sid. Sid and his wife, Pauline, sang in our church choir. The wife of Dad's farmer cousin, Walter, was Viola, our church organist. Dad and Mom bought clothes from Dad's cousin, Bill. Both Elsie and Lill were my mother's good friends and members of the Let's All Go neighborhood social group. They were also my Dad's cousins. My mother's cousin, Minnie, and her family would come to visit us periodically on our farm. We would go to theirs at nearby Schaller, Iowa. Mom's cousin, Hugo, farmed one mile south of us, and was often an exchange member of the neighborhood farm work crews then beginning to go out of existence. As a child, I could not know nor understand that certain older adults with whom my family came into contact with were my relatives, just as others in my age group could not know or adequately define their relationships with adults they saw. But these older adults, the aunts, the uncles, the cousins of my parents, or of my classmates' parents, nonetheless knew that I as a child, or my peers who were children then, these adults knew and recognized the relationship and very likely treated each of us children slightly differently, better in fact, than a stranger's child, and thus we were blessed in a modest way without knowing it at the time. More distant relatives were scattered about through the Holstein area. Some relatives were so distant, the current individuals had lost track of the fact they were actually genetically related and had originated from the same small area of Germany.

Of the 46 graduating members of my Holstein High School Class of 1962, eight are genetically related to me: three 2nd cousins, two 4th cousins, and three 6th cousins. An additional fifteen members of the class are connected to me through marriage(s) which joins their extended family tree to mine. I was certainly not unique in this respect. Many of my peers and many older members of the community have their own set of relationships, friendships, stories, and a woven web of existence easily equivalent to my own. Many other members of my class and many members of the greater community had a broad and complex interlinking similar to my own but with a different set of individuals, some of whom had links to my own network previously described. Not everyone who lived in Holstein had this type of traceable bonding. Some families came later to Holstein; some moved in while I was growing up, some were directed here through knowing someone who knew someone. Because the community had a small population base, newcomers could not stay strangers for long. Because the community was used to dealing with a narrow set of diversity and was accustomed to knowing those around them, I think this may actually have helped them to welcome strangers into the community. Newcomers became friends of long-term residents and through time and circumstance became long-term residents themselves or moved on, driven by needs applicable to that family. The Holstein community during the 18-year window of my youth appeared to be culturally stable with little change. With the broader perspective of more than six decades, and technological and economic development, I can see the Holstein of my youth has slipped into the past, just as the Holstein of my great grandfather's youth slipped into the past as I was coming into the world to look at and admire what he had left behind.

Young Friends

In my youth, my comprehension of Holstein's culture and heritage was yet to be learned. My understanding of it awaited me in the future. In the meantime, drifting in the sea of maturation, I was being supported by other community members who had preceded me, and were willing to lend support to me in my voyage. As a child my safe harbor was my home. I remember those occasional sick days or when one of winter's fevers would strike and I would curl up in the rocking chair beside the living room heater, the side heat vent doors open with the radiant warmth emanating about me, rocking slowly to and fro in idleness of thought. Hot tomato soup or sweetened green tea would be a potential remedy for a not-all-that-hungry child. Recovering after a day or two, I could get back to some missed schoolwork or the latest comic book or some dawdling drawings I created of hilltops, and airplanes, and ships. The soft plush easy chair under the mirror had massive flat arms on either side that readily supported the "Board", which, when retrieved from the closet and positioned over the arms served as a very fine writing and reading desk.

With the attainment of early social interaction which caring parents foster in their children, I began to have occasional visits from my friends to my home and I also visited their homes, although the ones I remember were more often at my home. Perhaps the lure of the farm and the unfettered outdoors slanted the ration of visits in favor of the farm for my town friends. Bruce and

Danny would be delivered on a Saturday afternoon by one of their relatives and the three of us would race off for several hours until one of their dads picked them up or my dad would deliver them back to their homes. We would climb the bale piles in the loft of the barn and play "King of the Mountain", the defender on top gladly pushing the offensive yelling climbers back down the incline of bales, until through some temporary cooperative venture, the defender himself was sent tumbling downward and rolling in the chaff and leaves and hay stems of alfalfa and clover. Tiring at last we would seek a new activity, one, as witnessed by the camera, was collecting several turreted tank toys and dragging them about the farm, staging mock battles.

Sadly, our friend and classmate, Bruce, would be gone from our lives before another decade had passed. Time was frozen in place for Bruce while Dan and I marched through an additional six decades of slowly turning into old men. Do we seek to know the end of the book before we open the cover and engage in its chapters? Are there not millions of books around us being lived page by page? Don't many of the stories in many of those books overlap our own life story? And therefore have an impact? And doesn't impact give meaning? These are questions old men ask when pondering loss and time.

When the new preacher came to town he arrived with one of his sons, Paul, being the exact same age as I and in the same grade at school. We quickly became friends when early in the Pastor's stay at our church, my parents invited the new family out for a meet and greet hospitality visit. Lacking the refined organizational complexities of a Newcomers Club many parishioners would periodically extend a luncheon invitation early in a preacher's stay to bond the congregation's tie to the new sermonizer. Paul and I no doubt dallied in some reserved shyness before being kicked outdoors after the meal was done to fend for ourselves. As kids do, we got along and became good friends. The Lutheran parsonage north of the church was Paul's home and sometimes it would be my turn to visit him there. This familiarity was fortuitous for me when one afternoon he and I were invited to a movie theater birthday party of one of our classmates. After the movie let out, my understanding was my father would pick me up there after the movie. Unfortunately, I was in the wrong, or my father was in the wrong because nobody came. Nobody came for a long time. Eventually, as a little tyke, I tried to steel myself up to asking to use the phone on the wall behind the popcorn machine. Even at my tender age I knew such a thing was possible - a person could ask to borrow the phone, the theater manager would let you, and presto, you could speak to someone. But, phone-a-phobia struck hard. I was not used to using a phone. These fancy city phones didn't look like, nor did they operate the same, as that wall hanger we had out on the farm. So I was never able to make the call. Instead, long after the party had dispersed, I walked the three blocks to the parsonage, pity was taken, and my problem was resolved.

Much to my mother's embarrassment and chagrin, I later came to bragging up the delicious taste of the hamburgers Paul's mom made for us. They looked the same size and shape of those I was used to at home, but they tasted really GOOD. It was not until I came to an older age of maturity and understanding that I discovered my mother routinely made her burgers with oatmeal and an egg added to the mixture before forming, an egg because we had them in abundance, oatmeal because it was cheap and stretched out the expensive meat supply – tactics of a frugal German mother. Mrs. Striepe's burgers were 100 % pure fresh ground beef. We farmers made the meat, but we didn't always eat it straight up.

One of Paul's most common means of visiting me was to ride home with us after the church service given by his father. Paul would eat the noon meal with us at our kitchen table, often some delicious pot stew which mother had left on the stove while we attended the service, and then Paul and I would have all afternoon to play until his parents would come from one of their visits to another parishioner and pick Paul up. One of our favorite games was simply called "War", as in "Let's play War!", a game which came to haunt me with intermittent and unnecessary guilt over the years since those innocent times so long ago. Paul and I loved the game and our farm offered all the right accouterments for the activity. How I would love to talk to him now about his memories of what we did and the fun we had at such a pleasant time of care-free youth. But that is impossible.

After dessert, perhaps a dish of cold ice cream from the new freezer, or a warm cherry pie from my mother's oven, Paul and I would first go to the Summer Kitchen. In that outbuilding 25 feet from the house, hanging on a hook on the wall near my brother's taxidermy collection was a helmet liner with strap, left over from some forgotten World War II surplus acquisition. It was not the steel dome itself but was the hard plastic inner shell, and shaped the same as a military helmet. It fit Paul's head better than mine and he looked quite the handsome boy soldier with it on. My toy M-1 carbine gun and several other pretend weapons of choice were gathered along with a small American flag and hand staff which my mother would hang out and display on Memorial Day and the 4th of July. Appropriately outfitted and assisted in our perilous mission by several imaginary private first class soldiers our small platoon would set out to the dangerous reaches of enemy territory down in the willows south of the clothesline. These willow trees lined the intermittent waterway, which meandered toward the creek on the other side of the single car garage building.

    The willows were near the orchard of apple and cherry trees and because of the orchard no farm animals grazed there. Consequently, due to the large intervening willow trees, except for some random grass and brush cutting seldom done under the fruit trees except at harvest time, the bulk of the area under the willows was overgrown in 6-foot tall hemp and ragweed. It was a veritable jungle. Dashing into the stalks of these weeds quickly drowned out the shape and location of our small boy selves, and we each independently fought against one another, or in a quick change of the imaginary forces we were united on the same side, in ambushes, patrols, shooting, sniping, lobbing grenades, the shots and explosions coming as real as we could make them from our voices, as we traveled from one end of the weed patch to the other, occasionally arguing about who was hit or wounded and how badly, occasionally taking shelter and resting beside one another behind the massive trunks of the willow trees, laughing and chuckling and planning the next foray. It was all great, active fun and left two young boys very ready for a good night's sleep that evening before school the following Monday morning.

Would I, could I, change what Paul and I did in those times? I guess not, but it sure takes a lot of rationalizing and speculative discerning of life and its meaning to work one's way through it all.

Thanks to forestalled love, the arms of passion, the joy of being home again - the home of their Holstein youth, the boys of our community had come home as men, after the Big War, the real war, and with the close of World War II created a small population boom of children of my age classification. My own father had been too young for World War I, too old for World War II, like other fathers of some of my classmates. But there were enough returning soldiers from 1943 to 1945 that my school class in Holstein had to be split in two to accommodate the number of students in our cohort and provide an adequate teacher-student ratio to foster good learning. In August of 1953 I, along with 24 other classmates, found ourselves assigned to Miss Streed's 4th grade class. The other half of our class went to Miss Brinker. Miss Streed had, shall we say, the reputation of being a strong disciplinarian. The initial result of such a reputation, of course, was a number of us embracing fear as an adequate motivation for our behavior. Plus for me, I was counting on being recognized as a familiar entity within the classroom, on having my own reputation of coming from a good neighborhood family. Not that I knew for sure whether my brother and sisters had in fact been "good children" while under the authority of Miss Streed. For, you see, Miss Streed had also been the country school teacher of each of my siblings when they walked or rode in horse-drawn buggy to the little country schoolhouse one mile east of our farm. At any rate, I think Miss Streed treated me fairly. I did not take undue advantage of her previous relationships with my siblings. And she only called me "Duane" a few times.

Our 4th grade room was on the second floor of what we called the "old school". This building was in the northwest corner of the city block, sufficiently back from the corner to allow room for a small softball diamond with the tall steel flagstaff and suspended American flag located about where second base wound up. Between the old school and the school building where we had been housed during the previous grades lay a large expanse of pea gravel. As far as us kids were concerned the pea gravel had been maliciously put there by adults anxious to extract varying levels of pain from any of us as we tussled, tumbled, fought, and raced upon its surface and invariably fell down resulting in needless bleeding from some bodily appendage. South of the schoolhouse was a tall board fence separating school property from the large nice white 2-

story house with a beautiful wrap-around porch which we all walked past en route to the city park for permitted play periods. The metal swing sets and tall metal pole which we called a twirler were positioned between fence and school. It always scared me when some of my more vigorous and athletic male peers would hop on a swing seat and attempt to pump up the swinging and get the swing to go completely over the top bar. I don't guess that ever happened but it seemed to me then that it should. The twirler was a vertical pole with a rotating bearing set on top which had attached to it 8-12 long chains ending in a swiveling handle. Kids, for some reason mostly girls, would grab onto a handle, run in an endless circle and eventually through the combined centrifugal force of the other handle-hanging participants, one could rotate about the pole, twirling as one went, not touching the ground. Very cool invention. Much beloved by the children. And also (see pea gravel above) apparently erected by malicious adults, this time specializing in dentistry, based on the number of chipped teeth this thing created when children would get whacked in the head by the hanging handles.

The old school was built in 1895 of yellowish-brown brick and adjoined to the original first school building constructed in 1884. The floor of our 4th grade class and the steps taken to rise to it were all constructed of wonderful old squeaky wood, more warm and tactile and vocal in its response than modern tile and concrete. When recess or noon hour came there erupted a thunderous cacophony of footsteps and thumping of young feet on those floors and steps. Not to mention the increasing and echoing crescendo of little voices combining in undenied racket. One of the favorite activities for us boys was to race down to the city park and go to the expanse of mowed grass there where we could establish edge growing trees as perimeters, boundaries and safe zones for our game we called simply "Tackle". We didn't even have to choose up sides for this simple rough and tumble game. All we needed was one forced candidate or volunteer to start the process. The initial "tackler" stood in the middle of the defined field of play. Other participants lined up on one end or the other, didn't matter which. Then all the other kids would launch out and run from one end of the field to the opposite side, or goal, or safety zone in which no tackling was permitted. The object for the tackler was to catch someone and throw them to the ground, one way or the other, and then that caught person also became a tackler, and had to stay in mid field and catch others. The object for all the other participants was to run back and forth across the field from one end to the other without being caught and tackled, the premier object, of course, being to become the last man standing, at which time the entire rest of the players would be standing in mid-field anxious to throw you down. When the odds became stacked in this end of the game, there was no way to get past the last gauntlet. It seemed to us to be excellent pre-condition training for our rise to the high school football team, a mere 6-7 years in front of us, and I enjoyed playing "Tackle" immensely. The adults had been out to wound us on the school playground. At least here on the Tackle Field we were left to wound ourselves, usually just an occasional bloody nose or cut lip, but plenty of grass-stained blue jeans and shirts for our mothers to contend with.

One of my classmates was Don, who became a good friend when he and I discovered we shared an interest in astronomy. He visited my home one night when there was to be a meteor shower which we planned on witnessing. Unfortunately, it clouded over and rained that night. By this time I was well acquainted with my uncle and aunt, Fritz and Anna, whose last name was the same as Don's last name, Fritz being my mother's only sibling. Putting two and two together I asked my mother, "Is Don my relative?" "Oh, no.", came the quick reply, "We're not related, they just spell their last name the same as Uncle Fritz does."

The family of my Dad, his brother, Clarence, and their father all spelled our last name "Ruhser". When my Dad would visit his grandfather's grave and find the headstone spelled "Ruser", he always felt compelled to someday get that gravestone re-chiseled and correct the spelling of the last name to "Ruhser", the same as his. There were, at this time, several other families in the Holstein area with the last name "Ruser". One of the boys, close in age to that of my brother, also shared his given name, therefore there was a Duane Ruhser and a Duane Ruser. The classmates of each of these Duane's kept them separate by calling the first, "Big Roos", because my brother was a big man, and the second, "Little Roos", because of this Duane's younger age, slimmer stature, and shorter height. All of we children eventually came to ask our parents, "Are the other Ruser's in Holstein related to us?" "Oh, no." came the quick reply, "They are not related to us. They don't even spell their last name the same as we do."

It took my wife and I and Don's brother about five more decades before we could verify the facts, some several decades after my parents were already in their graves, but, sure enough, the same surnames have a bond of genetic relationship. It's just that the intervening years and lives lived and history passed gently drowned out old facts and relationships, rather like the wake of one's life in a ship crossing the sea, look far enough in back of the ship and you can no longer see the wake, even though the water is the same. Don is my 4th cousin through Hinrich Bauer and my half 6th cousin through Jochim Schroeder. Duane Ruser is the 4th cousin of my brother, Duane Ruhser through Peter Ruser. The reasons are lost to history and only speculation remains – all we can say for sure is my grandfather added the "H" to his last name.

Again, let me remind the reader, the complex and far reaching genetic relationships within my family are not unique. Because of how Holstein was settled and because of who the settlers were, similar relationships can be genealogically established for many current and past Holstein residents if they have family surnames in their history which are the same as the early Holstein settlers.

Life as an Only Child

Sister Gloria graduated from high school in 1953 and then went to business school in Omaha. After the Korean War, brother Duane soon followed in the path blazed by his sisters and attended the same business school they had. He also followed them in working and living in Omaha after finishing his schooling. For the next eight years, until I graduated from Holstein High School myself as my siblings had done, I was an "only child". Being a late and unexpected baby and with three older siblings, I suspect my parents might have by then gotten a little weary of the whole mandatory parental role, and it seems to me I was largely left to raise myself after my early years when my sister Delores had taken a role in my care. My dad by then was an office manager for the county agricultural services organization working off the farm five days a week, generally gone ten hours per day. At home it was just Mother and I throughout those years I can remember best of my youth. Mom did not, could not, drive a car and what I did each day, certainly each day of the summer, was largely of my own choosing.

On pleasant days, the sun shining brightly overhead or partly cloudy with clouds scudding by driven by the winds I heard emanating from the pine grove north of the house, I would be outside, playing in the creek east of the barn, down in the willows roaming through the tangled growth, in the haymow petting the kitties, or in the toolshed trying to craft something built of wood like my brother had done. On rainy days, thunder peeling over the neighbors corn field to the west, rain washing down the car tracks of the lane in twin rivulets, I would be curled in the overstuffed easy chair of the living room reading a selection of comics, or with plumbed water now available inside the house and the dry sink vacated of its water bucket and wash basin, I might climb into the dry sink on the porch, rig up a back rest and recline there surrounded by expansive windows reading the latest Outdoor Life magazine. Alternatively, I might be in the lean-to portion of the barn's haymow, roof slightly over my head being pelted in the comforting rhythm of raindrops on the cedar shingles, the short barn door there propped open, with me resting in the loose straw and straw bales just staring and daydreaming as I peered through the rain drops and viewed the distant green pasture and big creek area of the neighbors land.

By then I had grown old enough to adopt and use my brother's abandoned bicycle. I had access to sister Delores's bicycle too, of course. It had in fact, been easier to learn how to ride the "big bikes" by utilizing her bike, being as how it was a girl's bike without the top bar. As soon as my legs grew long enough to straddle the top bar of Duane's bike and I no longer risked that dangerous pressure point between my legs, I labeled our girl's bike as a sissy bike, gave Duane's bike a shiny new coat of red paint, mounted a large wire grid basket on the front handle bars, and the boy's bike was all mine, especially when I mounted the small replica license plate with the name "GARY" embossed into the surface onto the front of the basket.

Riding the bike gave me an easier access to a greater world. In that time, my bike and most others available were single speed bikes and the concept of long distance riding was rather rare. By long distance I mean rides of more than four miles, which meant that the six mile trip to town was beyond what I felt was my capacity for continuing to pump those pedals. Although I would have liked to ride to Gary L's house to play or even into Holstein to ride with my pal, Roger, it was just mentally too far. Too bad. But that's the way we saw it then. My pals farther than a mile or so from my house did not ride their bikes out to visit me either. So the greater world of my bike was limited to perhaps a rare ride around the section, the square mile of land, on the west side of which we lived, with gravel roads all around it. More commonly I roamed most often down to Jesse's pasture, or the bridge and creek one mile east of us, or the good little fishing hole one mile south of us, or just up to the neighbor's empty granary building on top of the hill southeast of our farm.

The stop sign south of our house at the closest road intersection marked the top of the nearest hill available for high speed bike coasting. As I biked down that hill, coasting as soon as speed permitted, I as a young biker could glide past the end of the lane and mailbox but then had to soon engage pedaling again to make it to the top of the hill adjacent to the west end of our pine grove. At that point a shorter, more gradual coast could ensue as I biked past the five dominant cottonwood trees in the waterway which formed a solid arch of green leaves visible from a mile to the east. Then it was pedal to the top again as I continued north. At the top was a field entry way to Mabel Sherman's section. Because Miss Sherman owned a whole section of land, rather unusual for the time, even more unusual that a single woman owned it, we neighbors all accorded her sufficient status and rank by giving the land a suitable moniker—Mabel Sherman's Section—and then everyone within a several township region would know where you meant. Whether or not I had the energy to keep pedaling northward or turn around and go home again, I still turned into the driveway with my bike, laid down the bike or kicked out its kick stand, and stopped to admire the view.

    The view was pleasantly calming. Well, at least it was to me at the time. As I sit here typing though I still find the view in my mind of that vista as comfortably pleasing. Normally it was all mine, unless my dog had accompanied me. Normally, with the occasional exception of Wendell Jensen driving up the road, or one of the other neighbors coming and going, it was quiet and free of neighborly traffic. This was the top of the hill that sheltered our farm from the north wind and from the view of many of the neighbors, given that our farmstead was on the side of a small vale. As I walked across the gravel from my bike and turned south I saw the wall of pine trees which my grandfather Schroeder, who died 14 years before I was born, had planted 50 years earlier to shelter the new farmstead. In front of the pines were two rows of honeysuckle shrubs, which my father had planted as an auxiliary windbreak to slow winter's winds driving the heat from our home.

Turning east my view slipped down toward the little creek east of the barn and the large, old willow trees between "The Big Hole" and our well. The willows had long limbs extending from their trunks and gradually arching upward from their origin at the base of the tree to only 10-12 feet overhead. The limbs were easily six inches in diameter and one could choose the mid-point of the limb, swing up, or walk up, and sit at that point and then bounce up and down in a gentle swaying rhythm. The Big Hole was a 10-15 foot diameter pool of water. After heavy rains caused a minor flood, the water would cascade down the small creek, usually only a foot wide trickle, and then plunge off an underlying layer of hard clay, eroding and scouring out the softer sands and silt underneath, and form a pool holding water 3-5 feet deep, always an attraction for a young boy. A hill rose up on the far side of the creek obscuring views of neighbors to the east. Coursing down the midpoint of this hill was a waterway often heavily weed-choked in the Fall and, when corn was planted on that hillside, the waterway always held a pheasant or two come hunting season.

As I turned toward the northeast, the large cottonweed trees of our pasture's east border hove into dominance. There was a tall, steep bank eroded into shape by years of passage of the little creek's water, gravel rocks exposed and ready to tumble below with one swift kick, or one small boy's hand-over-feet crawling up the incline. Another arm of erosion from early farmer's poor conservation practices held our "dump", placed there by my father in an attempt to slow down the water's passage. In that time period, every small town had its own dump for use by its residents to discard tin cans, old metal, other refuse, but farmers generally had their own disposal pit, this one being ours. It was a great place to take the .22 rifles and do some serious plinking and target practice, knocking over tin cans or blasting glass jars to bits. From my high point of the farm on my hill north of the grove, the little dump faded behind lush green grasses of the pasture, our cattle lying contented in the midst of the shade of the cottonwoods.

Behind and to the left of the cottonwoods of our own pasture, lay one of the biggest pastures in our neighborhood. It was a large expanse of mostly flat lands which bordered both sides of Ashton Creek, which we referred to as Big Creek, adequately differentiating it from our own Little Creek which joined the Big Creek in Florence Kastner's pasture. From this distance the pasture gave me the impression of what I thought the Texas plains might be like, large swaths of bluegrass clipped low by grazing herds, scattered clumps of Canadian and bull thistle popping up here and there taking the place of southern tumbleweed and cactus. This big pasture could easily graze ten times the number of cattle my father's pasture could accommodate. The Big Creek just clipped the far northeast corner of our small 80-acre farm and in that corner the natural growth was unhampered by any tillage, it being reserved as permanent pasture and also holding some willow trees and box elder trees clinging to the banks of the stream. In back of the creek and pastures lay a half mile of gradually upward-trending farm land alternately patterned in the vivid hues of the crops: bright green alfalfa hay, rowed lighter green of corn or soybeans, yellowing oat fields.

North of my vista point, over one half mile away, was the farmstead of Jesse and Malinda Jensen. North of them and on to the edge of my view nearly two miles away the land gradually rose and I could see the windbreaks, some of the houses, the dominant big barns of Ben and Dora Hammer, Bill and Lill Blenner, Louie and Lurene Stamp, Ervin and Marie Bumann. The lands surrounding these neighbors, the cropped fields, the pastures, the scattered small groves of trees, extended in a grand sweep down beneath my hilltop, across the flatter lands bordering the bottom of the valley's Ashton Creek, and then gradually climbing the broad hills to that distant northern horizon easily encompassed 1500 acres of Holstein, Iowa land supporting all of us. Between these horizon-positioned neighbors and the Jensens were the farms of Eldo and Dora Kahl, and the farm where David Lohff used to live. That house, where my great grandparents once lived with my mother's aunts and uncles was already then empty, a fate which would overtake more than half of the homes once in my neighborhood, once holding laughing, joyous, grieving, smiling, crying families living out their lives, the best they knew how, just like their forebears. Now it was Iowa farmland, for the forebears it was the German soils.

To the left of the hill, west, was Mabel Sherman's section, no farms on this eastern side of it. When I looked at it I felt the inviting call of discovery, of adventure. Because Mabel Sherman's residence was out of sight on the southwest corner, this section appeared to me uninhabited, untrammeled (save the seasonal tillage and harvest machines). It held swales and waterways and highpoints seldom reached and therefore all the more valuable to me when I hiked to them and turned around to see how far I had come from the hill north of our house. Mabel Sherman's section held what I called Paradise Valley. At the base of this valley, laying in a broad swath, was a tall luscious stand of Reed Canary grass, grass so tall I only had to kneel down to be hidden in it, grass which hid the old erosion of an earlier flood that had gouged trenches in the soft rich soil and with the grass arching over them I could sit down and be as though in a tunnel, above me only blades of grass and pieces of blue sky. I could lay there and listen to my dog trying to find me, the deep grass combing his coat of hair, as he snuffled his way toward me.

Turning to the southwest to complete the 360 degree circumference of my world extending to the horizon I saw the small house of Henry and Amanda LaFrentz, among our nearest neighbors, one-half mile south of where I stood, the house tucked into the shade and fruit trees of their farmstead. They were our oldest neighbors in age, Henry and Amanda might have been some of the more recent immigrants as their rich German accent still colored their English speech. Their speech flowed easier and smoother when they engaged my parents in the old low German language, then slowly going out of any common usage in the community founded by Germans, which nonetheless printed a German language newspaper as recently as 1886.

Climbing back onto my bicycle, I prepared to continue my ride, now headed down the road, down the big hill. My fishing pole was thrust through the back of the grilled bicycle rack, the rod tied to the front of the basket with a leather thong, appearing as a mounted spear on the front of the bike; looking rather like a jousting knight on his horse in the medieval times, I instead was on two wheels. When I turned the front wheel of the bike my fishing rod, my spear, extended forth and turned where I turned, always ready to meet the opposing knight. This was the steepest, longest hill in the territory of my youthful cycling, and I knew better than to engage it lightly without thought. One day a boy one year older than I pedaled past our house with his twin brother, launched himself down this same hill, and skidded to a tumbling, bloody, bruised halt partway down the hill, thrown by the loose gravel then common on all our gravel roads. Loose gravel was a particularly bad combination when mated with high speed and the narrow wheels of bikes. It was worse shortly after the periodic maintenance by the county grader which redistributed the gravel relatively equally across the road. A young biker might prefer to walk down the hill at such times or ride the brake all the way to the bottom. It was far better, if I wanted a swift smooth ride down this hill, to wait a week or two until the wide tires of passing automobiles and trucks had created twin tracks of hard and cleared transit paths for my own small tires. Picking one track or the other and riding it until I stopped opposite Jesse's pasture, I first came down an initial decline of the big hill, temporarily leveled out near the north end of our farm before the hill went into a final longer gentler decline, picking up speed all the way to the base, and coasting until I decided on a spot to park, whereupon I would position the bike well off the roadway and inclined against the side of the ditch between the road and Jesse's pasture fence.

 The Big Creek, whether in Jesse's, Florence Kastner's, or our own pasture, held relatively deep holes of water in its bed, especially at sharp bends of the stream or in places where high flood waters of the occasional heavy rainfall could tumble off a bank or tree obstruction and erode a deep hole, deep meaning three to six feet. At those holes the fishing was best and quite easy. No casting required, strip off some line, bait my hook with fresh worms dug up from the moist soil in back of the machine shed, toss it in and let it sink, no sinker required. Conservation practices like contour farming, terraces, and planning for erosion control were just then beginning to be adopted. As a result erosion of soils and erosive action in waterways and stream beds was much worse than what can be found around Holstein today. Now on my rare visits to the community the fishing streams of my youth which harbored big holes and long expanses of visible water are, by comparison, nearly trickles of running water, thanks to today's farming methods, today's farmers, and the various programs and conservation practices that are emphasized and incentivized by both government and private programs, such as Pheasants Forever.

When entering Jesse's pasture through his fence I always tried to approach at some point far distant from his herd of beef cattle. They seemed to a young boy to be a curious bunch and if they spotted me in their grazing perimeter they would often come to huff and puff about me, blowing out their nostrils from their rapid transit to join me and see this short stranger in their midst. In my beginning explorations they generally scared me and I avoided them. As I grew older I learned they were mostly inquisitive, not dangerous, and the worst thing you could do was to show fear or run from them. They were after all, domesticated and controllable, but it helped to have the experience to know how to deal with cattle which do not recognize you as an individual they know. It also helped to grow taller than they were.

My most common quarry was the then common chub. The fish of these prairie streams had scientific and common names related to types of minnows, shiners, redhorse, etc. but to my brother and I what we generally caught was called by us a "chub". Sometimes in the right creek hole you could catch bullheads, some even of edible size. When that happened it was like I had come across trophy fish. A bullhead was the trophy fish of the big creek. The chubs were everything else. On very rare times one might even catch a sunfish, but that was far rarer than bullheads and the omnipresent chubs. Big fish were six, maybe eight inches long. More commonly they were 3-4 inches. But I liked it. It was fun, and there was always the tempting mystery to solve. What might be swimming around beneath the surface, down there at the bottom of this hole?

Jesse

Once when I was fishing in Jesse's pasture his son-in-law, Joe Guinn, came out to visit me. He was very courteous and pleasant. Several times, depending on his farm obligations, Jesse came out to visit me to see how I was doing, what I was catching. Naturally, the best time I remember was when he invited me up to his kitchen for a bowl of ice cream. Even by that young age I knew Jesse well and there was no way I was planning on turning down such a fine tempting invitation.

I had known Jesse and his wife Malinda since my earliest self-awareness. They were our closest neighbors to the north, our two farms shared a common border, thus a common fence line that sometimes needed mutual mending. Malinda was a member with my mother in the local women's group. No doubt Jesse and Malinda were among the earliest visitors in our home when my mother and I came home from the hospital after my birth. Jesse and Dad helped each other out when farm jobs like baling hay or harvesting oats or shelling corn or castrating hogs demanded some extra hands on site.

One of my first nights away from home and away from Mom and Dad was spent in the spacious home of the Jensen's. My parents had a very rare instance where they needed to attend to some personal business or perhaps go to Omaha for one of my sibling's needs, and instead of my grandmother Ruhser coming all the way from Meriden, Iowa, I was delivered to Jesse and Malinda.

The choice of who should tend to my needs was not all that difficult. They knew I enjoyed the smiling countenance of these special neighbors and knew these good people would watch me like one of their own children. Jesse was one of the first in our neighborhood to purchase a television set. It was an impressive piece of cabinetry set in a prominent viewing position in their living room in the northeast corner of the house and Jesse turned the television on for me. Mesmerized by the black and white flickering images, but with few channels to choose from, I was introduced to professional wrestling, one of the few subjects then available to watch in the evenings. It was a world of strangeness to me, both the device and the subject material, and I am sure I sat quietly engaged.

Time marched on, I grew older, old enough to fish Jesse's creek on my own. I liked Malinda's infectious smile and felt comfortable in her warm short presence. She was not a tall woman and I did not have to look up so very high to see the caring farmwife devotion in her eyes. But it was Jesse I grew to admire and respect and think of as a friend. He had a zest for living his own life in his own way and I saw in him aspects of living that I had not previously witnessed. I can sit here now all these years later and still postulate a very likely paragraph which he could have said after Dad and I came to his farmyard preparatory to one of those shared farm jobs requiring our assistance:

"Goddammit, Hank, I'm glad you could make it. Jesus Christ, isn't this some shitty weather we're having? Sonofabitch, if this keeps up we won't get a damn thing in dry."

Some moralists might not think this is appropriate language to use in front of a young boy. But he wasn't speaking to me, he was speaking to my Dad. I just happened to be within hearing distance. Jesse never spoke that way to me. He treated me courteously and with circumspect and expected me to know the difference between two adults speaking to one another and an adult speaking to a child. Jesse's expectations taught me the difference.

My single biggest impression of Jesse was the language he used – the cussing. When I was growing up and into my early school years I didn't have much opportunity to hear the kind of words "decent folk" classified as "cussing", or "foul language", or "bad words". In particular, I never heard them in my own home. And the church my family attended taught me you could go straight to hell for using those types of words.

Wait a minute. Hold on, says I in my seven year-old line of logic when I could first grasp the meaning of some of the adult Jesse words I overheard. If you can go to hell for saying stuff like that, how come Jesse says stuff like that? Instant admiration. The only conclusion I could draw as a boy was, "Jesse's got guts. He's a mighty brave guy to stare hell in the eye and say 'Shit'." And somewhere along the line I picked up the implication he didn't go to church very often. Wow! The more I learned the more impressed I became . . . and Jesse turned into a hero for me.

Jesse's colorful language was at its best during his conversations with my Dad and the other farmers of the neighborhood. I'd be as nonchalant as possible but still try to be in earshot of those talkfests of the Dads of the neighborhood when they would get together for a day's common work effort or for an evening's social entertainment. Just to hear those words, the words I could never hear anywhere else. I heard them only because they were different not because they sounded bad or because I was offended. Jesse had a way of saying "Goddammit" so that it spurt out of his mouth in about a syllable and a half. He could weave more cussing into a sentence, and into more sentences, more skillfully than anybody I knew. It was music to my ears and I hung onto every note I could grab. Jesse had a way of talking with those words that was pure entertainment. The words he chose provided the emphasis he desired without giving the impression of a foul-mouthed individual. Jesse wasn't a gutter mouth, he was a farmer who cussed and used uncommon words in a common way. He couldn't change; it was his style, his method, his language, his means of communication with those who could relate to him. And if you couldn't relate to him and accept him as he was – well, he certainly accepted your choice and had no more time for you. He was what I call a Real Person, unpretentious in any way.

Jesse wasn't a big man. He was of medium height and was, well – wiry. He was slim and when he sat down and crossed his legs the crossed leg was close to and parallel to the adjoining leg it was touching, not jutting out at an angle the way it does in people whose thighs and knees have more on the bones than a high tension muscle and a tough thin layer of skin like Jesse. His back could curl up on top of a milk stool without his appearing to be oversized for sitting so close to the ground when he was milking his cows. His short, straight hair was black, appropriate for the rebel I saw in him. His eyes had a twinkle which came from the lines formed by his ready smile. He was friendly and always had a warm greeting.

Jesse's use of what to me was a unique language wasn't the only reason for my awe and admiration. I can be bought. For the right price. Like the bowl of ice cream he offered the day I was fishing. Jesse loved ice cream and he knew most kids must surely share his taste for the frozen miracle. "How about a bowl of ice cream?" he would say and my head started anxiously nodding up and down after I sat down in his kitchen. He laid into my bowl a super-sized scoop. And as my eyes grew bigger and my mouth started to water he'd lay in another scoop full. And with a quick glance to my face and a big grin he'd declare, "Not quite enough yet for a growing boy, is it? Better put one more in this bowl here." Hey, now I was starting to worry. I hadn't ever seen such a heap of ice cream served to me. Which he knew. Which is one of the reasons he did it. And then he'd fill a bowl for himself just as big. And he'd reach up in the cupboard and bring down the Log Cabin Syrup and show me what to do with it as topping. And together we would tie into that delectable dessert. I can't remember when he served me the first bowl. Probably it was one of those evenings when the neighbors would gather for a card party or someone's anniversary. But I do remember the size of the helpings. The ice cream was cool and refreshing but Jesse's home was lovingly warm and it was his burning spirit for life and living which kept it that way.

No doubt his spirit of living was partly due to the fact he had diabetes. As I grew older and joined the work crew of the neighborhood back in the days when neighbors helped one another I witnessed one of his occasional diabetic attacks. I was working alongside of Jesse when it appeared to me he was getting weak and then his speech slurred to the point where he sounded rather like a heavily inebriated person would. Fortunately, one of the other neighbors knew of the illness and also knew a corrective action response when I summoned his assistance. As I learned more about the strange disease and discovered Jesse was administering insulin shots to himself my admiration for our neighbor could only grow. I still look the other way when I have to receive an injection. Jesse couldn't look away from his problem. And he didn't.

Did you ever try rolling a cigarette? It's a skill. Guys good at it make it look easy. It isn't. I tried it several times after I reached adulthood – always utter failures. But Jesse did it. Did it routinely and used the old Bull Durham sack, opening and pulling it shut with his teeth while his fingers spread the tobacco, packed it, and rolled the paper. Just a tiny tip of his tongue quickly sealed the paper. He could then pull the reliable wooden kitchen match so quickly across his denim overalls that friction would provide ignition. As manufactured cigarettes gained in popularity after the Korean War they too gradually found their way into Jesse's house. But when we gathered on the lawn after one of those delicious farmer wife meals during a long hard day of baling for a short rest before returning to the hayracks, out would come Jesse's Bull Durham and tiny papers. A short smoke and we returned to the harvest.

Rolling cigarettes, injecting insulin, sharing ice cream, and cussing may seem quite a basis for hero worship, but these things were really only the outside, most obvious physical manifestations which I saw of the man. Within each hero lies a much more complex core, a core of love, and respect, and goals, and meaning of life. Jesse wasn't the kind to articulate these higher attributes. He could only demonstrate them by being what he was and responding to those around him in the only way he knew.

When he retired from farming and moved into Holstein to live in town I discovered from reading Jesse's obituary, that he was fondly remembered for greeting his friends and neighbors around town while riding his bicycle. The bicycle was a habit he developed for continuing to get some exercise which 60 years of farming had gotten him used to having. As a result of his late interest in bicycles, he was known to all the neighboring school children who would bring their bikes to him for repair and maintenance. I'm sure they were responding to the same twinkle and grin and inner core that I had 30 years earlier.

Yep, Jesse was worth knowing all right. Damn worth it. I regret not telling him so.

Kinfolk

In February, 1954, my father's parents, my Ruhser grandparents, Richard and Evalina Ruhser held their 50th wedding anniversary as an open house in their farm home in Meriden, Iowa. Richard had earlier secured possession of the farm his father owned southwest of Holstein, but when he tried to purchase a bigger farm to enable the security of his growing family, he lost everything to the tumultuous Depression of the 1930's. In 1948 he and Evalina moved in with their son Clarence on a farm Clarence purchased in 1948 northwest of the small community of Meriden, Iowa, 25 miles north of our home.

My father always maintained a close and good relationship with his parents and his younger brother, Clarence. In addition to the strong bonds of commonly revered family life, farming was the other glue that bound these men together. About once a month my father would put whatever members of his family were still left at home into the family car and we would drive up to visit Clarence, Richard, and Evalina. Somewhat less frequently the visiting might be reversed and Clarence would drive his parents down to our house. Usually Dad would take the paved Highway 59 through Cherokee, but my favorite trips to Grandma's House would be when we took the back roads through Quimby or along the Little Sioux River in whatever was Dad's path of choice to "see the country" and check on other farmer's crops to compare to his own.

These back- country drives were slower due to the gravel roads but were much more interesting and all of us spent a great deal of time gazing out the windows and commenting on whatever attracted our attention, as the dust cloud billowed out behind our car. One farm might have exceptionally tall corn, the tassels towering above the fence line. Or, someone would spot a Red-tailed Hawk sitting in the top of a cottonwood tree along the river. Rattling over the bridge that spanned the Little Sioux, we stared at the water hoping to see a fish jump or we might see the occasional fisherman, his car pulled to the edge of the road. Once, a little way south of Meriden, a White-tailed Deer bounded out of the ditch on the right side of the car, scaring us all, but we all exclaimed in amazement after it had bounded down into the left ditch and then effortlessly leaped over the barb wire fence easily eight feet above the base of the ditch. That picture has stayed in my mind for six decades because for me to see any deer at all in that time was very rare, their population in Iowa then being very scant, limited to treed river valleys, and still in recovery from the killing of the previous century and the altered landscape wrought by farm practices.

 A child's memories are hard to catalog and inventory. It must be harder yet for any parent to recognize what memories might last and cause a deeply held impression in their children. A half century after my grandparents 50th anniversary, we Ruhser cousins can still hark back to a single day in 1954 and feel a rather common emotion of closeness, joy, and a strong memory of that day. Partly I and they were newly impressionable, close to our pre-teen or teenage years. Partly, due the distances separating our various families, the families of the children of Richard and Evalina, sometimes years would slip away before we saw one another again. For these and other reasons it was a unique event, a Big Deal, and we saw it and remembered it that way. One could perhaps propose a line of logic that says, because we saw each other so rarely we might not want to accept each other as play or relationship partners, we might prefer to be with our school friends who were much better known to us, probably even better liked. But yet, yet, … there must exist a greater family bond, a sub-conscious genetic recognition that labels the young first cousin to whom I am being re-introduced to after an absence of some years, as being an undefinable part of myself. And so we ate of the bounteous food before us together, and visited together, and laughed together, and played together, and the day melted into evening, and the evening melted into slumber, and the memories were branded into our cores.

Life spans being what they were then, the rare 50th wedding anniversary was a noteworthy accomplishment and communities gave them due recognition. In Richard and Evalina's case, the children hosted an open house at the Meriden farm. Wilmer Lamont and other neighbors and friends in the Meriden area stopped in for cake, a visit, and extension of best wishes. Because the anniversary couple had spent four decades living in the Holstein area, old neighbors and friends from that long forged time drove up to Meriden and likewise participated in celebration.

Extended family relationships added to the participants coming and going that day. There were Ruhser relatives and Sorensen relatives, Dittmer relatives and others, a broad spectrum of uncles, aunts, and cousins passing through the home that day, people I didn't know but people who were likewise my relatives as well as of my parents and grandparents. Due to the family sizes and the shared heritage of Holstein immigrants I can now look back to that anniversary long ago and recognize the magnitude and uniqueness of the event and how fortunate I was to be a participant, albeit a young one. With time's perspective I can also recognize and be somewhat saddened that the vast majority of today's children will not be able to have the same emotionally-warm experience that I had. In general, family sizes are smaller, the number of relatives young people today have is smaller, friends and neighbors now move in and out instead of staying for a lifetime like our forebears, and the pattern of the establishment of Holstein, Iowa cannot be repeated. What my parents had, what I had in Holstein is gone. Time moves on. This change is not necessarily good. It's not necessarily bad. But things don't, won't, can't, stay the same. That takes some serious getting used to.

In September 1954 we hopped into Dad's new 1954 blue Ford Mainline car and drove down to Uncle Harold and Aunt Leona's farm near Burlington, Iowa. Leona was Richard and Evalina's oldest daughter and she and Harold were celebrating their 25th wedding anniversary. In spite of time away from our own farm and its never-ending obligations and Dad's job in town, he wanted to honor his sister by attending this event. I was certainly glad he did. This meant I would see those same cousins I had recently seen in Meriden, and the occasional trip to see relatives was the only family vacation I would be familiar with throughout my school years. We children spent as much time outdoors as we could. Cousin Stan had a small open-ended wooden box into which we rammed and packed dry grass. With two pieces of twine cut to length and draped into the box before packing we could make miniature hay bales. Not that there's a lot you can do with these small hay bales but we sure enjoyed the process. Very likely the conversations of our fathers were also about the shared enjoyment of their vocations. Their lives spent were not as much about the products created as it was the lives they led during the act.

In January 1955 my Grandfather Richard died. The first brick in my wall of family security fell silently away. One day he was there alive. I can remember a last visit to his house, Grandpa sitting upright in a straight wooden chair, both hands on his by then ever present wooden curled handle cane one hand on top of the other, his thick and long gray mustache hanging slightly over his top lip through which he would sip his coffee at the table, the slightest smile on his face as he listened to his sons talk of farming. The next day he was dead. I can remember seeing him as a silent stiff corpse with eyes shut lying in a coffin in our church. Grandpa Richard was my first memorable acquaintance with human death. I had been told about it, softened up, so to speak, but as a fourth grader released from school for his grandpa's funeral, I was still plenty worried about how to cope with the event, with seeing his old body not ever to move again, with what to say, how to react to the people that would be there. Like so many things in life, you do what you have to do. As a 10-year old, I did what I had to do, and I remember very little about that day, except that it happened. Now I can see it was another marker event into the rotational forces we call living.

Lives led, the circle of life, though, is continuous. Death is one component of the circle, a necessary component without which our lives might lose the recognition of joy. The start of lives led together, a marriage, was witnessed by my family in the same year as my grandparents marriage ended through the death of Richard. One stage of Robert Coale's life was about to begin. Richard and Evalina's youngest daughter was my favorite Aunt Edna. Edna's oldest child, Robert, my cousin, was marrying Jeanne Jeter. And what a wedding it was.

In July 1955 my family once again piled into the 1954 Ford and Dad drove us this time down to El Dorado Springs, Missouri to attend one of the most memorable events of my life. As I stop to reread that last sentence I feel I must ask myself a question to ascertain its reality. "Most memorable event". Really? Does it fit into a small classification quadrant which certainly would include my marriage to my childhood sweetheart on the exact second anniversary of our re-meeting as young adults? Or the night I spent with some fellow employees trapped in a Huntsville, Alabama hotel bar that night in 1974 when one of America's most violent outbreaks of tornados occurred and the twisting death dealers danced mere blocks from where we sheltered? Or standing in line for another Friley Hall noon lunch at Iowa State University when news of the Cuban Missile Crisis broke? So I check myself and still I answer, "Yes". Yes, it does.

In its own way, attending Bob and Jeanne's wedding was akin to points within the Hero's Journey, so aptly described by Joseph Campbell in his works on mythology. First, the struggle against adversity, for us it was the 400 mile drive down two-lane roads in a crowded car from Holstein to El Dorado Springs, Missouri. Then comes the sacrifice, we slept outdoors because there wasn't room or money enough within the family to provide alternate accommodations. Then the peak of joy comes with the beautiful wedding. But hey, what kind of allegory am I trying to draw here? For the impressionable youngster I was, it was all just plain exciting unusual dramatic fun, and there was a lot to absorb in a limited amount of time.

The Coale farm was in the gently rolling country of southwestern Missouri south of El Dorado Springs, large patches of woodlands dotting the countryside, fences for the cattle made of black locust trees. Their house was at the south end of a rugged gravel road which ended where their farm yard began. If you could see the dust of a car off to the northeast of the house you knew where that car would end up. An expanse of freshly mowed lawn lay north of the house sheltered by tall shade trees spaced far enough apart to keep the lawn underneath bright green and lush.

We arrived the day before the wedding. Family photos show our families bent over outdoors, our faces buried in the ripe red flesh of freshly harvested and cut watermelons pre-cooled in a tub of cold well water, seeds spurting from our mouths to the stone lane beyond. That night the girls of the assembled families and the older couples slept wherever there was a flat spot inside the house, some doubled up in bedrooms, some in the living room on the floor, some in the porch. But for a number of us menfolk—at age 11 I was proud to be part of the "menfolk"—our assigned sleeping quarters were under the trees just north of the house. Camp cots were borrowed and set up. In July no blankets were required in southern Missouri and we slept under sheets, noses buried in soft feather pillows to protect our heads from the intermittent wandering mosquito.

The next morning, after breakfast, the cots and sheets were folded and put away and we began to set up evenly-spaced, neat rows of folding chairs on the lawn just beyond where we had dozed. An outdoor wedding! I had never heard of such an event let alone attended one. And the whole thing took shape and unfolded right before my eyes, coming into existence and fruition much as a flower opening its blossoms in the day's light and then slowly closing down when the glory of the day has past. Bob was completing his military service as a holdover from enlisting in the Air Force during the Korean War and elected to marry in his uniform, very handsome, very dashing. His lovely bride, barely 18, was a svelte brunette adorned in a white flowing wedding dress.

They were a most exquisite and captivating couple, smiles on their faces as they passed up the center aisle, and with their backs to us, committing themselves to one another, there in the bold sun-filled outdoors, surrounded by friends and family gathered to witness this intimate event. Fifty years later, as they neared their own 50th anniversary, and with each of us waxing into our own older age like our grandparents before us, I was pleased and proud to share with Robert how impressionable his wedding had been to a young boy.

Brian

Friendships initially develop within our lives as a result of shared commonalities, shared interests, routine contact points, and some respect or fondness for one another. In order to continue and endure beyond the opportunity of contact, to this formulation must also be added the ingredient of commitment. In our youth and as we age to greater understanding of interpersonal relationships, and before we engage in our own self-propelled travel, our friendships are necessarily rather opportunistic. Brian Bruning and I, depending on how bus routes were organized, some years rode on the same bus to school. He also went to the same church as I. Although he was one grade ahead of me he was only a few months older than myself, but best of all, he only lived 1 ½ miles west of us, within walking or biking distance for each of us as young boys. We were each farm sons, each enjoyed the outdoors, each enjoyed creek fishing and hunting small game, and became great pals until he advanced to High School and got his own car. After he was able to drive himself to his own chosen events and after he was in High School while I was yet in Junior High, our interests diverged somewhat. He and I remained friendly but our close friendship had dimmed as we each experimented with what life had to offer. It is an altogether normal and expected transition. As old men I am sure we would have enjoyed swapping a few memories, embellishing a few tales, and puzzling our wives with the strange and crazy things we did when we were boys of the neighborhood. But trips to the hometown of Holstein became rarer, our time when in the community then became more precious, and I lingered and put off and did not give getting together with an old and good friend from the past sufficient priority before he slipped permanently and irrevocably into my history.

Brian lived in a large white wood frame square farm house with, when you counted the attic windows and space behind them, a full three stories of height, room enough that he and his three siblings and his parents each had their own bedrooms, a veritable wealth of living space compared to my own home. Not that Brian and I used that interior space of his home very often, we were usually outside or in the barn. Their farm lay essentially in the middle of a section and a half of land due to the surveyors' correction lines and the fact that instead of the road going past their house, the road ended at their house and was thus a long half mile lane. When I arrived at their property boundary, whether walking or riding my bike, I still had to go another half mile in order to see Brian.

Without Brian, I would have grown up without a horse in my childhood, save for those last two strong work horses of my father which rode out of our farm on the back end of a truck when I was barely old enough to remember seeing them go past the kitchen window and wonder what was going on. Brian's horse was named Bomber, which I thought was a wonderfully individualized name for a horse. Bomber was a brown mid-sized horse with dark mane and tail, and Brian and I rode him independently and simultaneously, both at his farmstead as well as ours when he rode over to my house.

Brian and I would get together on Saturday mornings or afternoons or Sunday afternoons, depending on what obligations or restrictions our parents might have given us. Sometimes we would walk over to the other's house, sometimes we would ride our bicycles, and sometimes Brian would come into our lane riding Bomber.

I had saved up and purchased my own canvas pup tent from one of the popular mail order catalogs of the time, Montgomery Ward or Sears and Roebuck. I was always fascinated by independent survival and camping and living on one's own with only whatever one could carry or drag on their own. This desire was partly fed by being a member of the local Cub Scout organization, meeting monthly in Mrs. Lloyd Luft's home as a member of Den Four. I also read my own subscription of Boy's Life magazine which fed right into my wish to rough it, providing such sage advice as using the multilayered paper livestock feed supplement sack, then springing into common usage and replacing the old cloth feed sacks, as a sleeping bag. Being then yet too young to want to engage in camping solitary and carrying a certain level of fear for what might lie in wait beyond the end of a flashlight beam in rural Iowa's moonless nights, Brian and I planned and devised overnight getaways into the secret recesses of Mabel Sherman's section, or the section of land north of hers, and whatever adventure we might find there. In my case I recall it was more of a matter of advising my parents when these overnight ventures would occur, and not that I had asked permission. With today's concern for child kidnapping and foolish decisions by children not in the company of adults, the other thing I find fascinating was our parents did not know where in that roadless (there was no maintained road on the north side of Sherman's section) two square miles of land we would be camped. Furthermore no one, neither Brian or I or either of our parents, concerned themselves with securing permission for two young boys to camp on someone else's private land. I appreciate the freedom and trust we were granted in growing up, and the wider realm of protection the neighbors provided for us through their knowledge of the families of the two boys involved.

One night, in what must have been in the early days of summer before the heat and humidity of July, Brian and I were camped on a grassy peninsula of land formed by the reverse twist of the Big Creek in Mabels' pastureland across from the end of Jesse's lane. The night was clear as Brian and I tucked into our sleeping accommodations and giggled and talked as darkness and sleep finally overtook each of us. Too clear apparently, because the temperature kept dropping beyond the available warmth of cover which we had carried in to our camp site. We awoke shivering and cold. It was a LONG night. Tossing, turning, shivering, complaining, dozing, curling into a ball to retain whatever heat we might generate on our own, wondering when morning would come and grace us with solar rays. We succeeded in toughing it out and making it to a new and warmer day, thankful for the heat coursing upon the canvas and restoring our wild habitat to a comfortable temperature. And after the campout when the parents asked us, "How was camping?" we naturally replied, "It was Great!"

Another night, once again headed out to the wilds of the Sherman Section, we had Roger join us. Having now to transport more goods, more food, more blankets, one of us had read about usage of a sledge to transport bundles of gear. I built a sledge of two long parallel runners of 1 X 6 boards on edge with short cross pieces of one-inch boards nailed onto the upper edge thus forming a sled of sorts but running upon the grass and gravel surfaces which we would transit first going up the road north of my house, then across the fields into the heartland of Mabel's farm. One or several of us could pull it with a tug rope I had tied to the front of the sledge. Damned heavy, though! To avoid carrying anything on our backs we had piled everything onto the sledge and we were too young to understand the difference between rolling resistance and sliding resistance. But we could feel it.

We set up camp close to a barb wire fence in a swale of bluegrass, milkweed, some goldenrod, and remnants of the old prairie grasses that had once lushly covered this area. Gazing northward over the broad big creek valley lying in the distance below our position on the side of a wide shallow hill we watched the scene gradually disappear into darkness as we discussed great things of importance to boys pretending to be men on a mission. After crawling into the confines of the tent, sleep eventually overtook our slowing conversation. The next morning, just as the sun was rising over the farm fields to the east the dawn chorus of birdsong wakened us from our slumber, local Dickcissels being the predominant voice of greeting from the top wire of the nearby fence. Unrecognized by me at the time, unrecognized for years thereafter, I am convinced it was that very charming morning when I imprinted on the sights and sound of Dickcissels and they have ever after been a favorite bird of mine. When I see or hear the rare Dickcissel all these years later the pup tent, Brian, Roger, and the vast view of my neighborhood cradling our camp still spring into my mind with a lustrous shine.

Sunday with Axel

Playing with my friends on a Sunday afternoon or planning a camping trip were not my normal Sunday activity. I am sure I remember them more like shiny gold nuggets in a broad stream bed of memories, visually stunning because of their rarity. Most Sundays, after the usual but not weekly church service, were spent engaged in my own solitary activities in my room, in the tool shed building a new project, or helping Dad keep up with the requirements of a small farm. Several times a year, instead of the monthly trip to see his mother and brother at Meriden, Dad would arrange to meet them at his sister Viola's house in Cherokee where she lived with her husband Axel. The small home of Uncle Axel and Aunt Viola was located on the curved street that wound up to the local Sioux Valley Hospital where Viola worked as an aid and helper after she and Axel quit farming at Quimby. Viola was a mild-mannered, pleasant woman with a soft gentle voice always filled with empathy for the person she was addressing. Axel was a rotund Swede with quick motions and fixed opinions, but very cordial. Their house always held one mystery for me which I did not unlock fully until just a few years back when I began to understand the power of research within the realm of computers.

Uncle Axel imbibed in a bit more liquor than my Uncle Clarence or my father did. Axel enjoyed just a single nip of brandy or wine, sometimes mixed together, with his peers at times like a Sunday afternoon visit in his home. Axel would walk in his heavy off-balance way and fetch his latest bottle out of the cabinet along with a single ornate shot glass dedicated to such purpose and he would pass bottle and glass amongst his male guests, taking the first pour for himself and thereby setting the example to follow. Both bottle and the common glass were passed on to the closest guest and the process repeated until they came back to Axel and he put the bottle away and the glass in the kitchen sink. Clarence and Dad never drank in their own homes alone, but were always polite guests and never refused Axel's well-meaning offer of cordiality. Witnessing it as I did, it portrayed to me a masculine ritual accompanied with their calm reflection on events transcended since their previous meeting. It struck me as a special sharing, both fitting and proper.

With their conversation slowed I had the opportunity to gaze around the room and spy, as I always did when there, a picture behind the glass door of a corner case cabinet, the picture portraying an impressively striking young man in full dress military uniform with a flat top, brimmed cap. There were other mementos or antiques on other layers of shelf but the picture dominated the center of the top shelf, was distinct and almost like an altar piece. I somehow had been made to understand I was not to ask questions about the picture, particularly of Axel and Viola, or maybe that is merely the impression I had. Rather narrow and limited answers were given to my poorly framed questions to my parents if I asked them, because I was too young at the time to understand the full story anyway. Time had passed, what healing was possible had been completed, and the vicissitudes of World War had somewhat corrupted the truth.

By the time I finally had the opportunity and ability to go back in history and resurrect my memories of that picture, and frame my questions more adequately, the chief question answerers were all gone. Axel, Viola, my mother and father, all were gone. It is a sad fact of reality and the circle of living that sometimes, by the time we ourselves are interested in and want to know the answer to a family question, the people that know the answers best of all are already gone from the scene and have become history themselves. Best not to wait too long to seek your answers.

Although Axel, as father of the man in the picture, had the best basis of knowing the truth I cannot now know what he was privy to nor what he might have passed on to his immediate family. It is also possible, due to the fog of war and the violent upheavals Europe faced after the D-Day invasion and the immediacy of the moment on the battlefield that the man's end fate remained unknown until some months or years later. And by then, grief had marched on and what could a simple farmer of the soil do then anyway? My oldest sister, Delores, knew the young man in military uniform in the picture in Axel's cabinet best amongst those to whom I could still direct a question. Family lore within my side of the family suggested, she said, that Floyd had been killed during the June 6, 1944 D-Day invasion and his body never found. And so my search to find answers to a young boy's questions commenced in March of 2007.

The military man in the photo, in the special glass display case in my Uncle Axel's home, was Axel's son by a previous marriage. His name was Floyd Johnson and he was born in 1924. He was killed in action during World War II in the same year I was born. Floyd was a member of the 110th Infantry Regiment, 28th Infantry Division. This Division trained in England until July 22, 1944 when it landed at Omaha Beach of Normandy. By the end of July, the Division was heavily engaged in the so-called hedgerow fighting. Numerous towns and cities were captured as the Division pushed eastward along the highways of France. On August 29 the Division paraded through very recently liberated Paris, France en route to Belgium. A famous photo of the war shows the 28th Division marching down the Champs Elysees, the Arc de Triomphe in the background. I find it fascinating to note Floyd may be one of the many soldiers shown. His 110th Regiment liberated the northern parts of Luxembourg and on September 11 the Division was the first American unit to enter Germany. Floyd died on September 19, 1944, most likely in the Monschau Forest of Germany just east of Belgium. He lies buried in the beautiful Henri-Chapelle American Cemetery of Henri-Chapelle, Belgium where meaningful honor is yearly accorded him and his fallen brethren.

Floyd grew up in the rural setting of Quimby, Iowa, a small farming community located 16 miles northwest of Holstein. Like Holstein, Quimby too has for years sent young men off to war. Had Floyd lived a half dozen miles closer to Holstein his name would have been added to the list compiled by the Holstein American Legion for publication in the Holstein Centennial Book listing community participants who served our country in World War II. At 395 names that list is appallingly long already. I read through that list and then shudder at the insignificance of the bulk of our social problems today when I contemplate the Holstein area sending 395 young men and women off to war. There could not have been a family untouched by what was taking place around them in the first half of the 1940's. There could not have been an individual around Holstein unable to point to a friend or relative and worry about the danger that person faced.

There is one more puzzle, one more enigma to face, for those who knew an American soldier facing opposition in the European theater. For this mystery, instead of pondering Holstein, Iowa's historical origin within Germany, we must instead be thankful for rapid assimilation of immigrants into the America they willingly chose. Instead of regretting the loss of mail or familial contact and genetic bonds, we must be thankful so many Holstein citizens quickly lost contact and awareness of any relatives still in Germany. We must be thankful that within a mere few generations our Iowa community had been well absorbed and accepted within the vibrant expanding frontier and character that formed America in 1940. Because, given the genetic reality of the past, many young warriors from Holstein fought against a Nazi War Machine in which some of their relatives were participants. My 4th cousin, Claus Ruser, was born on May 7, 1921, in Barsbek of the Probstei, in the province of Schleswig-Holstein, Germany. He served on the Russian Front and died on January 15, 1943.

Man in the Sky

My interest in war as a new teen-ager was limited to play-acting and the implements of war. It would be another half dozen years before I would have to face the implications of potential real war as applied to myself and my peers. We came to be old enough that it was God that began to perplex my age group now, not politics. Religious training changed from Sunday School for children to Confirmation School for young adults. For us Lutheran boys the main payoff here was we would get to drink wine in the rite called Communion approximately four years before we could legally buy beer in South Dakota or seven years before we could buy our own wine in Iowa.

Sunday school was basically for children. Concerned parents wanting to provide some religious education for their youngsters would bring them in an hour before the church services and we would sit with an instructor in classes grouped approximately by age. Every teacher of the class was a volunteer and every one of them was earnest in what they were trying to teach. I can't remember a single incidence of participating in the process other than knowing I was in those classes. I do, however remember one assembly in the church basement, all of us lined up in rows sitting in metal folding chairs when, for some reason I cannot equate to Christian teachings, the instructor at the front of the room, asked of the students, "Who is your favorite movie star?" to which Brian Bruning, sitting in front of me boldly responded, "Victor Mature," with his spoken emphasis applied to "Mature". That brought a subdued chuckle from all us boys.

I can pinpoint in my fading memory now only two definite Sunday School teachers. One was Mrs. Striepe, wife of our Pastor. She was kind, but stern, we knew better than to mess around with Mrs. Striepe. Being the wife of the Reverend she was automatically accorded more respect. Paul, her son, was within our class and was always in attendance of course, and we didn't want to embarrass him. That relationship probably helped keep us in check. The other teacher I had was a tall slender, attractive lady, who was cordial and friendly and able to relate to us kids better than the older Mrs. Striepe. Little did either of us recognize the possibility at the time, but I later dated the Sunday School Teacher's daughter for a number of months before I left Holstein for good. It struck me then that I was glad I was a good little boy in her Sunday School class because I think it helped enable the permission the daughter had to seek during our short forays around town together. Perhaps that was the best lesson of all from my Sunday School classes: treat others as though it may not be the last time you will be dealing with them.

One's religion in a small close-knit town is not a closely held secret. All of us youngsters, even at our adolescent age knew of our peers exactly who was Lutheran, who was Methodist, who was Catholic, and who didn't go to church. Yes, if the community is small enough, which Holstein was then (and still is), there were only those four categories. The good thing is you generally were accorded no malice because of the category in which you lived.

Geri Bruning, mother of Brian, had four children, two of them within one year of me in age, and she very kindly would often arrange to pick me up and give me a ride to religious class, Geri being of the same faith as my parents. Initially it was Sunday School, later, when I hit seventh and eighth grades, it would be for Saturday morning confirmation classes taught by Reverend Striepe. Because I was able to ride with Geri and her family, my parents could stay home for an extra hour on Sunday or on the Saturdays during confirmation classes my father could keep working on his farm projects. Some days Geri would drive onto our farm yard to pick me up at the house. Other mornings, when the weather was pleasant I would walk up our lane and then up the gravel road to meet Geri's car at the stop sign on top of the hill. One morning Geri's gas tank already was registering a big "E" for empty when she picked me up. She very skillfully turned off the engine at each downslope hill and coasted as long as she could before restarting the engine and proceeding up the next hill. We made it to church on time. I was most impressed. When I finally complimented her several years ago on this adroit accomplishment, she had by then forgotten what she had done as a young mother that impressed me so much, but we each laughed and shared in the feeling of a solution at the time being well executed.

Reverend Striepe taught his puerile charges as best he could. But hormones were stating to creep into our blood stream, along with questions creeping into our brain. There was a small war going on inside many of our brains as to what was more important: understanding what sex was all about versus understanding what God was all about. With the implication of permanent and everlasting Hell lurking around the edges seemingly intertwined between the two vast subjects it was indeed a time of discussion and learning. For the God part of it the primary instructional material was a little blue book called "Senior Catechism – Luther's small catechism in question and answer form" by J.A. Dell, D.D. published by The Wartburg Press. For the sex part of it, we were basically on our own, no guidebook of questions and answers was to be had.

Reverend Striepe did with us as well as he could. He did not shy away from any of our probing inane questions and I regarded our Pastor as wise in the mysteries of the Lutheran Church, to be listened to in earnest. We asked all the normal questions which by this time I am sure he had heard a hundred times before, but which to us seemed original and unique at the time. Where exactly is it that the Big Man in the Sky is located? How can he know everything? What does omnipresent mean? Are you really sent to Hell just for cursing? How can you have three entities within one? And on, and on, and on. Some of the braver more reckless boys would occasionally try to conjure up the perfect question thinking this time they had the Reverend in a philosophical trap. Never happened. There was always an intricate answer which the Pastor gave which left him seemingly all wise, while it left us struggling students still scratching our heads.

Attending confirmation classes wasn't all so bad. It gave each of us one more opportunity to be amongst our friends, one more outing away from home, perhaps an opportunity to get out of some chores on the farm. The thing that scared us the most was a final oral quiz given by Reverend Striepe. He alone was in charge of deciding whether we "passed" and were accepted into the congregation as "adults" and allowed to participate in the sacraments of the church, such as communion. But the scariest part of all was the quiz or testing process was given in the large church sanctuary with any church members that wished to do so being allowed to sit in as witnesses to the process. Perhaps it was all part of a grand scheme to get us to start praying. If so, it worked. "Oh Lord, please let me pass the test tomorrow, and if it be thy will, please have the Pastor give me only the easiest of questions."

Mike

As my classmates and I entered seventh grade we sensed a change was being thrust upon us; more was expected of us as we advanced out of elementary school and entered junior high school and were only one step away from being in senior high school. It seemed noteworthy to us at the time anyhow. In junior high we had a home room and something called study hall and either we or our teachers sometimes roamed from one specific classroom to another, all very different from sitting in the same desk in the same room with the same teacher throughout the year. This fundamental change then elicited other changes around us, our scholastic performance began to matter a bit more, some friendships altered as we discovered more about our peers around us, and we subtly sorted into ability groups or modified social groups. The other thing we boys discovered was that girls were no longer just classmates and friends with longer hair, but instead some had bumps coming out of their chests and girls began to hold a new type of attraction for us, not as someone you could choose who would run fast on your team, or to be on your side for playground games, but as someone you might consider for the initial experiment in binding heterosexual relationships best characterized at the time as "puppy love", and the terms "Boyfriend" and "Girlfriend" acquired a new meaning different from merely describing the sex of your friend.

Mike Brosamle became my best pal during junior high. We shared common interests and abilities in sports, playing tackle, attitudes. He was physically built about the same as I, tall, slim, fleet of foot whether playing tackle or football, he had a charming and pleasant, easy-going personality. Mike was willing to take some risks in teasing and carried a pleasant grin while doing so. Unfortunately, he was also subject to taking some risks beyond teasing friends and simple tomfoolery. One day in sixth grade as we were all sitting quietly in our desks doing a recent assignment while the teacher was engaged in grading papers at her desk in front, Mike leaped from his desk and began slapping the side of his pants pocket in obvious frustration and some pain. All eyes in the room immediately fixed upon Mike gesticulating and waving his arms about in a veritable frenzy. Shortly thereafter we all learned some wooden kitchen friction matches he had in the pocket of his blue jean pants had rubbed against one another and ignited. He couldn't tease his way out of that one and instead became the recipient of much teasing during the next recess period.

I was turning into kind of an "A" and "B" type student whereas Mike was rather a "B" and "C" type student. I think Mike picked up on this difference before I did and began to take good advantage of it as opportunity allowed. He would ask for my assistance or an explanation of the new mathematical or scientific teachings we were being asked to absorb. Because we were also in the same religious confirmation class at church we had even more time to share together. One Saturday morning while we were supposed to be engaged in comprehension of one of the Ten Commandments, Mike, sitting next to me at a long table, instead was helping to design what became my signature set of initials, written with a bold flourish in cursive. As an engineer in a large corporation I continued to use that distinctive grouping of initials in signing off on many of the documents I was then preparing. Periodically I remember their origin from my pal, Mike. Who can predict the simple means by which one can impress and then be later honored by an old friend? My initials as cursively struck down upon paper have outlived the inventor by many years, but we cannot say Mike is gone as long as someone remembers him. Mike gave me memories. Holstein gave me memories. Those who live there and have lived there have memories. The memories of all form a complex ethereal fabric that envelopes the community. If one could see only the threads of Holstein memories the density would be greatest over the town with diminishing threadlike tentacles reaching around the earth.

Mike even gave me his girlfriend. Now that is a real pal. OK, it really wasn't like that but sometimes I think of it in that serendipitous manner. In the fifth and sixth grade time spectrum, Mike and Judy developed what youngsters sometimes do beginning at that age, they developed a special fondness. Their fondness was most exemplified by writing little notes to one another, notes carefully folded to hide the contents, and then passed to one another at recess or the start of a class or during lunch hour, the notes then tucked into a pocket or text book to be read during a selected private opportunity. Very cute. I remember seeing this activity and being a little jealous, not of Mike or Judy, but of the process of having a special friend one could share private expressions with. And Judy did begin to strike me as cute, attractive, and that pony tail she sometimes wore as her hair-do of the day fit her face perfectly. In temperament and appearance, she was perhaps a bit of a cross between Debbie Reynolds and Judy Garland.

As elementary school wore on into junior high I became more attracted to Judy and she to me. We exchanged comments, laughs, time together on the playground or at lunch time and somewhere in there she and I began to exchange little "secret" notes in the same pattern which I had observed between Mike and Judy. I worried about offending Mike and upsetting their dynamic and I didn't want to lose my friendship with Mike over a girl, but I wanted what I sensed Mike had with that girl. Fortunately for all of us at the time, emotions seemed to be in tune with one another simultaneously and as Mike and Judy's relationship at that "girlfriend-boyfriend" stage cooled, hers and mine warmed up. Mike stayed my pal, Judy became my girlfriend. Of course full credit must also be accorded to the web of friendships surrounding the three of us. Other friends such as Karen or Bryan played their fundamental roles as well in this experiential and experimental stage of our young lives. Bryan, who was a first cousin to Mike, would probe his network of friends, and others to ascertain if Judy really liked me better or Mike better, and then get back to me with the latest rumors. Karen would assess Judy's feelings and then get back to me with today's story line of how Judy felt or what Mike was thinking. Diplomatic maneuvering between various representatives of the world's nations must surely have had its beginnings in the tenuous negotiations of first love by the participants and their friends.

Apart from notes passed on a nearly daily basis, youthful affection in our Junior High did not really have much outlet for expression prior to one being able to have a driver's license and access to a car. There was, of course, increased time spent sitting next to one another as opportunity allowed, or time at school outside of class, not necessarily always on the playground, we still had our own set of friends to maintain after all. There were the five minutes spent after school prior to boarding our respective buses. The main events, I suppose, would have to be the few (two per school year perhaps, certainly less than four) school dances which were organized by some members of the faculty as well as several concerned parents, held in the school lunch room, apparently as practice and preparation for our social lives lying out there ahead of us in the world of high school. On a practical basis this meant that Judy and I and any of the other few "couples" that had been created had an accessible partner they could actually hold onto during the dance and enjoy the process, pretending they had a "Date", when in fact all us kids were merely attending an open event hosted by the school system with transport handled only by willing parents. Continuous dancing with a single chosen partner was not condoned nor allowed, but one could look forward to enjoying and holding onto that special someone when possible.

Tractors and Wind Tunnels

Not only were education, relationships, and obligations expanding in school, but also obligations and expectations were expanding for me as a maturing member of a farming family. Just as for centuries previously in Germany, children were expected to fulfill roles to assist the family in the survival and advancement of the whole family unit, in Holstein, Iowa the same expectations existed. As a younger child one of my first assignments was to ride in the oats-seeding wagon in the spring as Dad sowed the new crop, and to keep the hopper of the end-gate broadcast seeder filled. The wagon used was now towed by Dad driving our 1936 John Deere model "A" tractor but in fact it was the same wagon which had formerly been towed by Dad's horses in the years prior to my birth. Each spring we jacked up the wagon and mounted anew the old-fashioned, large-diameter rear wheels with their wooden spokes, wooden hubs, and steel rim, which had formerly been used when the wagon was pulled by horses. These old wooden wheels had two remaining advantages for a farmer besides that of avoiding the expensive purchase of a new grain drill. One, the wheels positioned the seeder higher in the air above the ground for a more effective seed broadcast width than the rubber tires normally on the wagon during other seasons of the year, and second, the left rear wheel was fitted with a chain-drive sprocket gear. Power was transferred from this gear by a chain to other gears on the end-gate seeder, which turned a spinning broadcast disk that scattered the seeds. Like most horse-pulled farm implements the mechanical action was ground-driven, no outside power source was needed other than pulling the wagon across the field, be it with horses or an engine-driven tractor. With the scoop shovel and a young boy in the oats-filled wagon box, Dad could keep driving the tractor and my main job was merely to keep the seeder topped off with oats. At the ends of each pass across the field, Dad would signal to me with an arm wave and I would either engage or disengage the lever which controlled the shut off port and the whirling broadcast disk. In most years we would also be simultaneously inter-seeding either alfalfa or clover seed in a separate hopper but this seed, being much smaller in size, did not need frequent replenishment.

Twenty years later when Jean and I began our own farming operation on the 140 acres we had purchased in Wisconsin, it was with a fair amount of embarrassment and chagrin I discovered I would not know how to analyze if I had applied the proper amount of oats seed to the soil. All those years of helping my father and watching him get off the tractor after the first hundred yards of seeding to walk behind the seeder, bend over, and look at our work, I failed to realize what he was doing and why. I had purchased a power take off powered broadcast seeder for my own farm from the local Tractor Supply Company and was preparing to seed our first crop of oats the following morning when I realized I did not know how to tell if I was applying the proper amount of seed to the ground. I also realized I wasn't the farmer's son I thought myself to be; I lacked some fundamental knowledge a good farmer needs to know. Too little seed applied per swath and our stand of oats and thus its future yield would be too sparse, unproductive, and let the weeds get ahead of the crop. Too much seed applied per swath, and I would have a crowded crop, stunted growth, but, worse yet, I would run out of the precious commodity before I had the field fully sown. That evening I frantically called Dad for advice and discovered what it was he was doing out there pacing across the swath he and I had seeded, periodically bending over and placing his hand on the soil, almost as in supplication. The answer was not terribly complicated but it came from 50 years of his working the soil and asking his own father the same question. You can't always learn adequately without asking the right questions now and then. "Gary, you put your flat palm down on the ground and count the seeds covered by your hand. If your hand covers an average of seven seeds, you've got the right amount." Fifteen million nine hundred seventy one thousand one hundred sixty seeds later and Jean and I had planted our first 10 acres of oats. Thanks, Dad.

Dad had purchased the used John Deere "A" some years before I was born as he gradually transitioned out of the work horses he had utilized since being a young farm boy himself. It was Dad's tractor, dare I say his favorite, because it remained on our farm until my parents moved off the farm to Holstein in 1980. The other reason I would give to declare the "A" as Dad's tractor was he was the only one in the family who could reliably start that tractor. The "A" had the old standard magneto ignition system and petcocks on each cylinder to relieve the compression for the hand starting of what I came to think of as a mischievous engine. I am proud to say I finally did learn to start that tractor, but never could I consistently count on the fact like Dad did. In one of the "A"s recalcitrant times when it had failed to start for me for some field assignment I was given I would march down to the hog house where Dad was moving sows and confess my inability to start the tractor this morning. He was never angry with my request, never said much, he would just accompany me back to where the tractor was parked. Then in my youthful vision and my mind's eye I see him reach out and stroke the front of the engine like one would stroke the muzzle of a horse, he adjusted the petcocks, reset the choke, reset the amount of gas feed, set his feet just so far apart, balancing upon the ground like an acrobat, grasp the heavy steel flywheel as a wrestler would grasp the arms of an opponent prior to the start buzzer, each hand spaced about 150 degrees apart, turn his head to the left slightly, and with relative ease he quickly flipped that wheel 90 degrees counterclockwise, and the 36A started. My Gawd! I had been twirling that flywheel until I was wheezing and turning blue in the face. He starts it with one flip. Dad closed the petcocks, closed the choke, reset the gas and headed back down to the hog house. I climbed on Dad's tractor and drove off on my assigned mission, silently stunned once again with the power and knowledge of a professional. And when I eventually met my father-in-law, another Holstein area farmer, I would watch him start his John Deere B tractor with the same proficiency.

Sometime after I watched the last two work horses take their lonely last ride out our farm lane, and before I started driving tractors, Dad purchased a used John Deere Model "MT" to do the more light-duty type of work around the farm. The old "A" was still the most powerful tractor we had. The "MT" was one of the first John Deere tractors to utilize a high-speed engine with vertical cylinders and an in-line crankshaft to the transmission, as opposed to what had been the now classic, low-speed horizontal cylinders with crankshaft perpendicular to the tractor's length. And, best of all, the "MT" had an electric-start engine, this young man's dream. It was a swell little tractor, and in fourth gear it could go like the wind.

My first work assignment with the "MT" was to cultivate corn, a new responsibility for me that would gain my Dad a lot of time to devote to other farm necessities. The tractor was purchased with a two-row corn cultivator, which was mounted onto the front of the tractor, and positioned up and down with hydraulic power at the touch of a lever. It must have been a dream come true for Dad who for years had cultivated behind a team of horses, applying his own arm strength to raise and lower the cultivating shovels, in addition to handling the horses' reins. My initial try-out and training took place in the corn field right behind the honeysuckle bushes north of the machine shed. Dad explained the process, gave me a short demonstration with him behind the steering wheel, then it was my turn. I am afraid that for a relatively calm and mild-mannered German farmer, he may have very nearly felt compelled to throw me off the tractor after I ripped out the first dozen yards of his carefully tended corn plants. Dad's explanation of what to do when and how to do it made good sense at the time, but when it came to me taking over complete control it all fell apart between my head and my hands in a maze of: keeping the tractor propelled straight ahead and not always counter correcting the direction of motion, looking at both sides of the tractor and cultivator simultaneously and balancing out the variable spacing of the corn rows, positioning the corn rows between the shields not on one side of the shield or the other where the plant would immediately be treated like a weed and ripped by its roots from the supporting soil structure, recognizing the rows to be protected are the little corn plants not the area between the rows, raising the cultivator at the end of the row and not letting it plow up the driveway beyond, lowering the cultivator upon immediately reentering the cornfield and not ten yards into the field leaving those weeds unscathed. Oh, it all happened so fast and all at the same time! Gradually I figured out the process and the timing under Dad's tutelage and eventually he took the risk of going back to his other tasks and leaving me to master the process. With practice and more time to develop my abilities I conquered my self-imposed problems and became a skilled cultivator. It quickly became one of my favorite farm jobs. Being trusted, knowing I could do the job well, being a contributor to the farm welfare and income, driving unimpeded through the clean air and breezes of my youth, toasting in the warm bright sunshine, being in charge of the power beneath my feet and at the ends of my arms, cultivating corn in an Iowa farm field is something I could easily volunteer to do again. It was that comfortable. But they don't cultivate corn in Iowa anymore. That too is gone along with my youth.

That MT tractor turned out to be my favorite work horse. As my skills developed I was assigned the task of keeping our small group of one-half dozen calves supplied with water while they were grazing the small patch of mixed grass, mulberry trees, pines, and several mighty elms northwest of the house as a supplementary pasture for them after they were separated from their mothers and left to rear themselves. They kept the weeds and sheep brush under control within the small 1-2 acre enclosure and helped preserve the main pasture for the rest of Dad's herd. There was no water supply within several hundred yards, and that one was merely our old hand-pump cistern. Dad had put an old corrugated steel cattle tank in one corner of the fence and my job was to keep that filled with water as needed by the calves. To do this I would hitch the small 2-wheeled 4' X 6' cart with rubber tires to the MT tractor, drive down to the barn hydrant, put our four 10-gallon stainless steel milk cans with friction fitted round lids into the cart, and fill the cans with water using a hose from the hydrant. These stoutly constructed and heavy containers were left over from Dad's days of cooling milk in the concrete milk cooler prior to its pick-up and purchase by the local milkman. When the new milk pasteurization and milk cleanliness laws came into effect, Dad and other small farmers like him elected not to make the expensive transition to processes ensuring a fixed sanitary standard, and the milk coolers and stainless steel milk cans became obsolete very near to the time when horse drawn equipment was becoming obsolete on area farms. This left the shiny silver milk cans available for other innovative uses – like keeping bullhead fish alive from the Lake Okoboji environs until one got home to the farm and cleaned them up for supper and an extra meal or two besides.

With the four milk cans brim full, lids tightly pushed down to avoid any spillage, I would drive the tractor and cart up to the fence corner of the calf lot and back up to the fence, lift each can up to the fence top, and dump the contents into the calves' water tank, about a 90-pound heft effort per can. The real accomplishment though, what really made me proud, was not the physical wrestling of 360 pounds of water and steel but the precise positioning of the back of the 2-wheel trailer cart up to the fence while backing up the tractor and trailer. It was a learned skill fraught with trial and error, mixed with luck and scientific observation, nurtured with cursing and rational aforethought. The main problem was dealing with three sets of axles, six wheels and the rear of the trailer moving in the opposite direction of the front of the tractor when in motion and turning, all while looking 180 degrees backward from the steering wheel. Like many other tasks, once you get it, it gets easier and easier, until you wonder why it gave you such fits and conniptions when you were learning. A dozen years later on our farm in Wisconsin, I was to garner the same pride in myself when I at last mastered the ability to back up a farm wagon with four tires, two axles and a pivoting tongue with the same skill I had developed on that John Deere MT while watering our calves. Even that modest farm skill though, which any good Iowa farmer of the time had to have, palls in insignificance to my utter amazement at watching a farmer from my friend Bryan's neighborhood south of Holstein. Bryan and I, working summer jobs between high school years, were hired to help stack hay bales in a semi-truck being loaded for delivery to a drought stricken area of Nebraska. The magical fellow drove in to our corner of the farm pulling two flat rack wagons hitched one behind the other, and proceeded to back the entire rig into the tractor-width alley way of the nearby barn to park it for the night. My mouth hung open as I gazed with quiet admiration at a skill level I would have declared impossible to attain. Furthermore he really did no correction as is sometimes necessary for such feats, such as pulling forward a bit, re-aligning the wheels and trying again. He just purred the whole string of wagons and tractor smack dab down that narrow slot and shut off his engine. He maneuvered six sets of axles and 12 wheels with five pivot points as easily as I had mastered the simple 2-wheel trailer, but it was several magnitudes more difficult. Just another Holstein farmer totally unaware he was leaving impressions behind for an added 60 years he hadn't planned on, and never knew he had done so.

Not all my "jobs" with the MT tractor met the qualifications of farm work. I remember one in particular that was more along the vein of pursuit of scientific knowledge. Or, maybe just messing around with what I thought should be possible. In the early 1950's America was in pursuit of greater and greater speeds with airplanes and from movie news reel clips or television I had learned of a device called a wind tunnel which helped engineers and scientists figure out the best streamlined shapes to hurtle through the air with the least resistance. Now, had I already been old enough to drive I could merely have stuck one of my streamlined shapes out the car window into the wind stream, and measured the resistance. As it was, I was not yet driving. As it was, I had not yet developed any shapes that needed testing within a wind tunnel. What I needed first was the wind tunnel.

In my youth window fans became a popular consumer item in advance of the invention and sale of air conditioning for homes. On those nights when the temperature crept higher and higher in the upstairs of our home and the wind had died down, and a soft soothing breeze was no longer moving through the quiet curtained corridors of our second floor bedrooms, the nifty new 24-inch, 3-speed window fan from Sears and Roebuck was put to use to help us sleep. The rest of the year that window fan was available for air propulsion in my experimental wind tunnel. The fan was normally stored upstairs on the north side of the stairwell and it was a spot where I could leave the tunnel set up for my experiments and modifications of the tunnel design. I could stand on one of the steps, about four or five steps down, and the fan and tunnel would be just at my mid-chest height, perfect for making adjustments with my hands, and for bending slightly to peer into the bowels of my creation and to mind-craft future modifications.

The tunnel itself was constructed out of stout corrugated cardboard sheets, the cardboard cut from packing boxes we had received in the mail and stored out in our Summer Kitchen available for uses on the farm as whoever saw fit. The cardboard's highest possible use for me, of course, was to be transformed into a wind tunnel, the pieces were carefully designed and then cut to size with my mother's paper scissors and with the 4-bladed jackknife I always had in the pocket of my at-home jeans. The bottom of the wind tunnel was flat and rested on the floor as did the window fan. Each side and the top of the tunnel consisted of cardboard triangles which converged down to a smaller opening, the outlet of my tunnel, with the whole entity affixed to the window fan with generous applications of masking tape and electrician's tape, the stickier the better.

The attained wind speed at the end of the tunnel was compared to the tunnel-less window fan's speed by using a common and cheap meteorological instrument in use on many farms of the time and generally molded in conjunction with a tubular rain gage. The rain gauge was held in plastic clips on one side of the device, while on the other side a plastic vane was hanging with miles per hour markings arrayed in an arc. Passing over this arc was the movable, pivoting vane mounted perpendicular to the miles-per-hour indicator. The pivoting vane had two heavy steel balls molded into place at the bottom end such that at rest, with no wind passing against the movable vane, the vane hung straight down and registered zero miles per hour. As wind increased in speed the entire device swung with the wind and kept the hanging pivoting vane in alignment with the direction of the wind. Then, as the wind increased in speed, the movable vane pivoted out farther and farther as the wind force increased enough to lift the gravitational resistance of the steel balls, and the wind speed could be noted on the speed marking array. It was a clever and cheap device, perfect for a boy's experiments.

I would hold the wind speed indicator in front of the tunnel-less window fan and note the wind speed at various points across the surface of the fan outlet as a base reference of the speed the fan produced without a tunnel mounted on the front. Next I mounted my cardboard tunnel to the fan using as much tape as necessary to contain and constrict the fan's output of breeze. I held the speed indicator up to the new and much smaller outlet which the tunnel created and noted the new speed. Hmmmm, this was not a very impressive increase, particularly when I compared the speed at my tunnel outlet to the speed of some air escaping back near the fan grille where I was having trouble sealing the total normal fan outlet. I discovered the wind speed there was actually greater than at my tunnel outlet. Disappointing indeed.

During my available free time over the next few weeks I added several more modifications and tunnel additions to my original fabrication, each addition further constricting the outlet until I got down to a 2-inch by 2-inch opening and attained a maximum speed of 28 miles per hour. After I concluded I could almost bicycle down the big hill toward Jensen's at that speed and that I had apparently reached the maximum potential of the Sears window fan and Gary's tunnel, my cardboard creation gradually accumulated dust and was eventually ignominiously retired to the bonfire when I decided I could no longer afford the space it took to store it. Forty years later, when I was serving a stint as a technical service engineer assigned to fan specialties for The Trane Company in La Crosse, Wisconsin I came to understand more fully why that window fan couldn't do what I wanted it to do so many years previously. As I look back upon this and other experiments of youth I see now it is not so important that I failed to attain my goal of high wind speed, but that the fan and other experiments I delved into on the farm carried with them tools of teaching that rose beyond my own perception of what was important at the time. Like life itself, it is not the immediate end goals that are important; it is the whole of the journey.

Within the process of the window fan and cardboard wind tunnel experiments still lay the quest for higher and higher speed of artificially created wind. It was at this point the John Deere MT became the power source for my next wind tunnel and the highest speed I was able to produce on my own prior to being able to hop into a car, roll down the window, and drive down the road myself. Roaming through the grove one day north of the chicken house, puzzling over my difficulties with the upstairs wind tunnel, I came to where my father had parked an obsolete, no longer used, single row corn picker. Examining it afresh I noted it had a fan mounted on top of the husking rollers with three wind outlets and three flexible tubes on each outlet which directed airstreams strategically into the bowels of the picker to blow out chaff, weed seeds, loose husks, and pieces of corn stalk, all in an effort to have only clean ears of corn being carried up the elevator to the waiting wagon pulled along behind the picker. But this fan was constructed dramatically differently than our window fan.

The corn picker fan had four blades mounted parallel to the axis of rotation. Air was pulled in along the rotating axle at the two ends of the fan. The three outlet ports were located perpendicular to the rotation axis. This was no quiet air mover. This was a blower. Now, noted my young budding engineer mind, we are talking wind speed. The fan was driven by a simple V-belt and attached drive wheel, and secured to the picker with few enough bolts and nuts that within one-half hour I had the whole fan assembly removed from the picker and was carting it to the garage where we housed our MT tractor.

Searching the farm and junk piles for the proper part for the next assembly I finally came upon an old V-belt drive wheel and with a clever combination of wood shims and more bolts rummaged out of the tool shed was able to secure the drive wheel to a power take off (PTO) connector that I could slide onto the PTO drive shaft of the tractor located in back of and under the driver's seat. Next task: find a suitable V-belt. Done. It was always very rewarding to have been able to find many components already available on the farm of my youth and on our current farm in Wisconsin. Oh, sure, they aren't always exactly perfect for the task at hand, but they will do. And found items in farm collections are always very affordable.

The next stage involved mounting the old picker fan to a stout old wooden plank (you guessed it, salvaged from another pile on the farm), pivoting one end of the plank off the upper storage floor of the garage, and suspending the other end from a block and tackle. By adjusting the block and tackle I could apply sufficient upward pressure on the V-belt running from the tractor drive wheel to the V-belt drive wheel on the fan to put the belt in tension for operation of the fan. After backing the tractor just a few more inches to get vertical alignment, I hopped off the seat, and engaged the PTO. Some shuddering of plank, some chaotic oscillation of V-belt, some wobbling of PTO drive wheel occurred, but everything hung together and kept working. Loose dust and leaves were flying about the garage, the flight ways of errant wasps going to and from their nests were thrown askew, but I smiled the grin of accomplishment, and immediately knew I had attained a new speed record. After blocking off two of the discharge ports and affixing a straight, but short, outlet tunnel, I ran to fetch the wind speed indicator and held it in front of my latest wind tunnel. Sixty miles per hour! Talk about a satisfying day on the farm!

I have no idea what my Dad really thought when he pulled into the garage that night after his long day at the farm service office in Ida Grove and saw his MT hooked up to a discarded corn picker blower there in the corner of the garage. Nor what he thought of the open tin can I sometimes had mounted on the muffler discharge opening (that can added such a pleasant tonal and resonant quality to the sound of power). I do not recall my parents denying any experimentation on my part as long as I didn't cause any lasting damage or harm to what secured our economic livelihood. They provided me the freedom to explore boundaries of action and imagination and I am very thankful for their putting up with me.

And Dad got what he needed out of me and I imagine that helped hold me in good stead. If one gives favors in exchange for favors received, each party gains. Perhaps it is as simple as that. Perhaps Dad merely shook his head upon seeing that latest weird arrangement of tractor hooked up to swinging plank with corn picker blower mounted on top and exclaimed, "Awh, heck, Gary's a little strange, but he doesn't cause much trouble. I'll just ignore this and hope for the best, whatever he's up to." Perhaps the MT and I gained a few points in his ledger book when we volunteered to hand-load some old accumulated manure in the cow yard left over from a winter's worth of feeding the steers and heifers, and we used the manure spreader to get it out to the fields. One summer, pitchfork in hand, I hand-loaded the spreader, and, driving the MT out to the field as my rest reward, spread load after load where Dad suggested until 50 loads later, the cow yard was clean again, ready for another winter's feeding. I remember my internal pride of accomplishment for a job well done. I do not recall the pain in getting to that point. There must have been some pain. I can rationally conclude there was, but the pain went away, the pride remained.

My mother's single biggest contribution to the economic livelihood of my family was the 80 acre farm she had inherited from her father. Through the kind grace and loving relationship she had with her dear brother, my Uncle Fritz Schroeder, Fritz participated in the legal transactions involving disposition of my grandfather's estate and Fritz left my mother in sole possession of the 80 acres where I was raised, where she and Fritz were born and raised, where my parents raised me and my three siblings. Mother, in turn, passed on this magnanimity in quiet terms to my father. She allowed him to run the farm, and to the rest of the world and even within the broad ranges of my extended family, it seemed in the traditional sense that it was Dad's farm and he was the decision maker for the major choices to be made each year in the economic needs of the farm. Dad and Mom knew better of course. They played the roles expected of farmers and farmwives within the community, but they knew and respected what each actually brought to the partnership that was their marriage, and I know of no arguments that ever occurred about these issues.

By the time the 1940s were closing, it was already apparent to my Dad that more income was needed to sustain his family. As a result of his natural interest in the appropriate means to farm in a sustainable fashion and from the farm magazines he consumed, Dad was an early adopter of contour farming, which is farming around the hills instead of up and down them. With the development and spread of farm programs to control farm production and hence crop pricing, Dad began to work part time for the local Agricultural Stabilization and Conservation Service (ASCS) which had been established in each county as a means of applying these farm programs to the local level of neighborhood farmers. His part-time assignment, which added a few dollars to the monthly family income, was to work as a crop field size measurer and as a measurer and calculator of the amount of stored grain on area farms participating in the government farm programs in affect at that time.

His part-time work impressed the right people and he was then asked to become the full-time Office Manager of the ASCS in Ida Grove, the county seat for Ida County. In this position he had responsibility for a half dozen clerks and secretaries who worked for the ASCS, as well as part-time workers such as he had been, all to the end goal of managing the federal crop support and conservation priorities of the government at the local county level and then reporting the results to the state office in Des Moines. In addition to managing and running Mom's farm, this was his main job task throughout the bulk of my school years in Holstein. The income was never enough to remodel the house for indoor plumbing while I was at home, nor enough to upgrade the old John

Deere 1936 A tractor, or indeed to buy any new farming equipment (any purchased equipment was always used). However, Dad's ASCS income was enough to prevent the bank from foreclosing on our mortgaged farm. And Dad's vocational efforts were enough to enable his family to live richly, if not to richly live.

For several years, while Duane was at home to help in the task, Dad also rented some additional farm land on the edge of Holstein. As these rented acres were six miles away from our farm, the transportation of equipment to and from the rental property and the manual labor involved basically ate up any additional profits. When the opportunity to renew the rental lease came about, Dad passed up the venture.

On Sunday afternoons in rainy weather or during the harsh winter, after we had attended church, purchased the Des Moines Register's large Sunday edition at Kerslake's Drug Store and returned home, Dad worked on another potential avenue toward trying to help his family's constrained economic situation. The Register routinely ran a difficult cross word puzzle competition each week. If you entered all the words in the puzzle exactly as the Register defined to be the correct answers, you could win a major cash prize of several thousand dollars. Now that would have been very handy in our household. Dad tried and tried, several times getting within a single letter choice, but was never able to land a cash prize. I think he enjoyed the puzzle competition though, at least I hope so. He would work diligently at the kitchen table, sometimes with a bowl of fresh popped popcorn nearby, dictionary at his side, paper puzzle cut out and laid beside his pencil and pen, pencil in lightly, then when he was sure of his choices, go back over in ink, seal it in an envelope, stamp the envelope in the corner with a three-cent stamp, and mail it off the next morning.

The Holstein I Knew Then

As I matured into the teenage years, my community of Holstein became intimately familiar to me. No longer tethered to my parents I could roam into my favorite stores either on my own, or depending on the errands of my parents, I might also accompany them. Holstein's population has always been in the magnitude of 1400 people. That was the size while I lived there. It remains about the same size now. Like many small rural communities, Holstein has seen a large amount of change in the past half century. Fortunately for the community, VT industries, originally Van Top, maintains a large manufacturing and shipping complex in Holstein and enables an employment base to sustain the population base. This means the community can support businesses supplying basic necessities like a few common groceries and gasoline. It also means the community and its residents can afford quiet small town living with neatly maintained and comfortable homes. However, Holstein is no longer the complex and interwoven set of interdependencies it once was when it was the center of a farming area that supplied all the basic needs of both the area farmer families, and the people living in the town.

The stores I entered in my youth had all the products one could need to sustain a satisfactory life. Other small towns of the area, towns like Alta, Kingsley, Odebolt, and Moville had a similar complex of interdependent stores enabling a productive and basic economic existence for the families of that community. No matter where one lived in northwestern Iowa, one did not need to travel more than perhaps a dozen miles to get everything required for a household. It was only if one wanted a much larger choice that one needed to travel to the bigger communities, communities like Storm lake or Cherokee or Sioux City. But whether it was furniture or groceries, a farm implement repair part or fuel, a haircut, clothing, or personal items, you could obtain and pay for that item in your local home town shopping web of stores.

Whether as a pre-teen or a teen-ager I entered the stores of Holstein now on my own, their familiarity embedded in my conscious actions through experiences shared initially with my parents. I didn't recognize it as unique at the time, because it was not unique in the world I was raised in, but store owners and operators often would address me by name, or, if not by name, they at least knew whose son I was. The web of the community went beyond the exchange of money for goods. It extended to the web of a social exchange of concern and friendship for people as individuals. Once a small infant of Henry and Sophie Ruhser I was now becoming a recognized community member in my own right. My parents bought furniture at Hansen's Furniture Store. I would walk into Kerslake's Drug Store to buy a ten-cent cone of butter brickle ice cream from Bill, or occasionally orange sherbet just for a change from my favorite flavor. Down at the street corner south of Kerslakes, the corner where I would meet my future wife before a dance when we were 19, I would step down the stairs to Lloyd Luft's barber shop and get my hair cut. You descended below street level to his shop and I had passed from having to sit on a little board across the arms of his barber chair to being able to sit in the chair itself. Very comfy. To guard the steps going down a large railing was mounted around the steps. On top of the railing were mounted small metal wrought iron teeth to prevent the local citizens from sitting on the top rail and risk falling into the stair well. Very thoughtful on some city father's part to have come up with this innovation to insure safety and prevent law suits. I always thought it was rather a pity one couldn't perch there in comfort and pass the time of day.

Across the street from Lloyd's Barber Shop was the Ten Cent Store. Obviously it must have had a more official name, but to me it was always the ten cent store. As a small child I would accompany my mother to this store, where she would probably buy some cloth or some buttons or a kettle or frying pan, but I would toddle over to the toy aisle to stare at the amazing collection. As an older boy, the ten cent store was where I bought a young boy's necessary fighting equipment, cap pistols and the rolls of percussive dots, known as "caps," which would bang when struck with the hammer of the cap pistol or other hard object. Most impressive was to take my Dad's heavy blacksmith hammer, position a whole roll of caps on the farm sidewalk and smash it down upon the whole roll. Now that was a BANG. Also luring were the plastic rocket shaped devices with fins, which were thrown into the air and the single internal cap would be exploded by the protruding firing pin upon its return descent and impact on the farm lane. The ten cent store toy aisle also held the ever-mesmerizing sparkle wheels. Held between forefingers and thumb the wheel would rotate and come into contact with flints throwing off sparks which appeared brightly colored when viewed through the tinted translucent lenses within the wheel. These were all really great toys which added immeasurably to the experience of my youth, and likely now cannot be purchased anywhere. Those safety people and lawyers sure do mess with people's lives. In my teenage years, the ten cent store no longer held what I once needed and craved.

Halfway between the main intersection and the Lutheran church where my father and brother once donated their labor time to the construction of the two story educational addition, stood Jim and Maria DeWitt's bakery, the ultimate home in Holstein of savory and olfactory temptation. Upon entering the bakery and seeing Maria DeWitt or Lurene Stamp, our neighbor lady and member of the LAG club, who could resist purchasing a fresh loaf of bread or some donuts, (multiple flavors and types were available), or perhaps a half dozen "Long Johns" which were next to the end of the display case, or some "Elephant Ears"? Next to the bakery was the Locker Plant on the corner. As a small boy I accompanied my father once to fetch home some frozen beef we had stored there in one of the lockers. I was aghast at how cold it was in there, how foreign the artificial light looked as the bulbs glared down through a haze of cold fog, and how thick and heavy was the entry door we passed through. However would I be able to push it open myself? How do you know the latch will work when you try and get out? I kept close to my dad's legs until the bright sun burst forth upon my constricted eye pupils once again and I was free on the sidewalk of the great outdoors.

About one half block south of the main intersection in Holstein was the movie theater, one of the best assets in our small town to my way of thinking, because we had what many small towns our size lacked, a great picture show. The movie theater was especially important in order to view and spend time with Roy Rogers and other cowboys when I was a little kid, and very important as a viable and acceptable destination for those first self-propelled dates as a 16 year old teenager. Across the street from the picture show was the old post office. How fascinating it was to see all those tiny postal boxes from the back side as my class of second graders toured the facility one afternoon.

Next door to the post office Robert, father of my good friend Roger, built a new clothing store. One particular product line was Key blue jeans, special to me because several promotional offerings included a two-bladed pocket knife. You can't be a very successful farm boy without a good pocket knife in your pants pocket. During Robert's time in the Air Force in World War II while he was flying 50 missions over North Africa and Europe he often thought about starting his own clothing business when he returned home to Holstein and his wife. Very recently I learned from Roger yet another example of the warm conviviality and caring concern emanating about Holstein like a warm embrace in those neighbor-helping-neighbor days of the mid 20th century. Robert and his family lived next door to Bill Zeman, owner of the only clothing store in Holstein at that time and Bill, speaking as neighbors do in their shared back yards, found out Robert was looking to engage in a new business venture, independently as his own boss. Bill mentored him concerning his idea for a clothing store and continued to provide hints and helpful advice of how to do so and what to watch out for. Robert followed Bill's suggestions, opened the store, and it proved to be a family success with the help of his charming wife, Muriel. How often can we imagine a story in which a monopoly business encourages the establishment of a competitive store? As time went on Bill and his wife, Lillian, continued to be very close friends of Robert and Muriel and acted as an auxiliary set of grandparent figures for their children. This relationship of Bill and Lillian to Robert and Muriel is a wonderful example of the compassion of the community I was raised in. I'm sure there are many other examples similar to this one. It was this type of cooperative behavior that made Holstein a good community in which to live, and a source of pride for its residents. Now, as Time insists, Robert, Muriel, Bill, and Lillian are no longer with us. They served their community well. The bold aluminum sign, with Robert's surname, once part of the marquee occupying the front of Robert and Muriel's clothing business, now hangs in the living room of a cabin overlooking a long beautiful lake in Northern Minnesota, a pleasing reminder of lives shared.

Walking down Main Street going north back to the main intersection in my mind, I next encounter Helen and Ethel's, a popular bar and eatery. Roger and I would occasionally grab our supper of burger and fries there, in spite of Coaches Gerber and Kraii advising against "greasy" food prior to the track meet or football game in which we were participating. We hoped they wouldn't be out on patrol and find us there. Next door to Helen and Ethel's was Ruhlow's Hardware, whose local competitor was Boothby's hardware. Both stores still had the marvelous rolling ladders with which to access items stored on the upper shelves, and both were able to supply the .22 cartridges I needed for my rifles. No need for an age check in those days. If you could fish a dollar bill out of your own pocket, you could walk away with a couple boxes of bullets.

In the next store north, Bill Zeman's clothing store was being transformed into Sorensen Clothing. Bill Sorensen was my dad's cousin and Bill had worked for Mr. Zeman. Sorensen's Clothing had a tall ceiling and on the north wall of the store were arrayed several mounted herbivore heads, including a moose and an elk; surely there must have been one or more deer as well. Having never seen live animals with the size of the racks on the moose and elk, as a young man I was very impressed with those animals. Mounts and sufficient space to hang them were both very rare and, having devoured the hunting stories in Outdoor Life and Field and Stream, I was somewhat jealous of anyone who had bagged and claimed these animals for display. But the heads just hung there, quietly keeping the secrets of their demise to themselves. I imagined a solitary hunter out in some remote wilderness in the midst of the great Rocky Mountains slowly stalking each of these animals and meticulously selecting an individual for the large rack of antlers which hung before me and then putting that animal in his gunsight. I have often wondered, "What became of those mounted big game heads?" Whatever it was, not enough honor was accorded to a young boy's vision of the past.

The exhibition most memorable in the store, though, was Bill's handiwork with common store string and plain brown wrapping paper. Whether it was a new pair of bib overalls for my father or a new pair of jeans for me, one left the store with the purchase personally hand wrapped in the twinkling of an eye by Bill's deft touch. He neatly folded your purchase on the expansive smooth wooden counter top which was his main work area for dealing with his customers. At one end of this counter sat his reliable old fashioned hand crank ringing cash register. At the other end, leaving room to fold and wrap in the middle, a large roll of plain brown wrapping paper was suspended at both ends horizontally by a slender wrought iron rack which also held a large spool of white string on top of it. Bill would grab the paper end, pull out and tear off just the right amount of paper to contain the purchase and wrap the paper around, flipping the contents and package as needed. Next he reached up to the string roll, pulled on it and quickly bound the string around and around the assembled package in two crossing directions. Lastly Bill applied a quick knot to the string, fingers knifing in accuracy like thrown darts, and then he broke the string by hand to separate it from the spool above. Accompanying this process all the while was Bill's calm, low voiced personalized chatter of, "How is the family doing?" and "What do the crops look like this year?" and other conversation which could not but be that emitted by a friend, not just a business owner.

At the main intersection of town, opposite the granite edifice of the Holstein State Bank, the financial hub of our small town where I signed up for my first checking account sometime in high school when I was starting to save money for college, were the steps leading up to Doc Wagner's dental office. That was where my mother received her complete set of false teeth and where I reluctantly committed myself after too many years of never having been to a dentist. Now children are introduced gradually to their dentist from infancy. Then, as a young teen-ager I toughed it out, trying to outlast the pain of deep tooth decay while attempting to fall to sleep — too many nights in a row. The pain was bad enough it brought out the Christian Lutheran in me and I tried nightly prayer, supplication, and Bible-reading. After a couple chapters of the Bible each night, split evenly between the Old Testament and the New — one never knew if the old God, Yahweh, or the Lord Jesus was going to be the best bet — I would always end my effort with The Lord's Prayer, under the assumption it represented one's best and deepest effort. After a few months of this I had to conclude God wasn't going to come to my rescue and decided instead that I had better try modern technology. I told my mother it was time for me to see a dentist. Doc Wagner yanked out several of the worst offenders, his wife acting as nurse, and patched up a couple more. Should have given in and seen him sooner. Knowing when to give in and when to carry on is a critical decision precipice that all of us have to learn and face repeatedly.

One block west of Doc Wagner and the bank lies Vollmer Motors, one of the few businesses still carrying on in much the same tradition as it did in my youth. Recently my school pal and good friend, Gary L, bought his new Buick there in spite of residing hundreds of miles away. Now that's small town customer service and buyer loyalty. As high schoolers we boys would make an annual trip down to Vollmer's as well as to Tharp and Baumann's Ford garage to view the new cars each September. Today at a small distance, I can't recognize most cars as to brand. I routinely walk over to look at the rear bumper and trunk area of current automobiles, where the brand and model emblems are most predominantly displayed, to answer my wife's inquiry as to what car we are observing. Then and yet now, my male peers and I can tell at a glance the '54 Ford, the '56 Chevy, the '55 Oldsmobile, the '60 Plymouth, and on and on.

In my mind's vision, after leaving Vollmer Motors I cross the street and head back east to the main intersection of town, where the bank sits on the northwest corner. Under the bank building, down one of the longest flights of stairs in town outside of those rising up to the American Legion Club, was Doc Martin's lair, always smelling richly of antiseptic and good stout cleansers. Blindfolded and transported in an air cushion, I would still have been able to tell my host where we were located merely from the stout medicinal odor of his premises in the high ceilinged basement of the building. Once each year, before the start of school, my peers and I would line up in Doc Martin's hallway for a group physical. He would listen to each of our chests through his stethoscope with his eyeglasses on and staring at an obscure point somewhere off our left shoulder. He was quite officious and we wanted his approval. Then he instructed us to do 25 jumping jacks, all of us waving about in an un-coordinated frenzy bouncing off the marble floor, and he would again listen to our hearts and breathing, sign our approval forms, and we would be fully authorized for another year's worth of battle on the gridiron, the basketball court, and the cinder track.

Down the street, headed north, passing the twin pillars of the bank, the next door north was Stolley's Drugstore, right across the street from Kerslake's Drugstore. Stolley's would become my post sports practice, post school hangout on many late afternoons after I started driving. It had that beautiful perfect mix of wire-formed chairs, white soapstone soda fountain counter, upright silver soda and water dispensers, an expansive mirror on the wall in back of the counter, and an air of ambience perfect for the high school crowd. In grade school I was a devotee of Kerslake's. In high school I was a devotee of Stolley's. I always felt somewhat guilty of my mixed loyalty and as a teenager would occasionally slip back into Kerslake's for an ice cream cone, or some warm cashews from his lighted case, or a magazine. In retrospect, I'm sure Bill, his wife, and his helpers, all being small town residents of our inclusive community, knew full well of the allure of the high school hangout and accepted it as being a factor in the community they could not compete against. In today's vernacular the two competing drugstores were engaged in market segmentation. In the 1950's and 1960's both drugstore owners and their staffs were merely living life as they best knew how, supporting the community, helping each other as neighbors when the need suggested, and providing a service for their customers.

At the far end of the block right before one got to the railroad tracks, which had been so fundamental to the establishment of the town, across from Moser's John Deere dealership, was the Blue Eagle. No other name was necessary. If you said you were at the Blue Eagle, everyone knew where you were and how to get to you. The Blue Eagle was a cross-cultural eating, drinking, and recreational establishment which catered to all age groups and varied interests. In the front portion was a tall, wooden lunch counter, sturdy and massive, in a U-shape with grill and coolers in the midst of the U and stools set all around the outside of the counter, where one could order burgers, fries, soft drinks and modest sandwiches. In back of the lunch counter area, separated by a wall with wide door and windows to view the action, was an eight lane bowling alley, one of the finest and biggest for miles around. My siblings remember when the pins were set by hand; I remember the community's amazement when the automated pin setters were installed. Adjoining the restaurant and bowling alley, accessible by two separate doors from either facility, was a long narrow room with a bar for serving beer to thirsty adults in front and a pool hall in the back. Multiple billiard tables were set about, their green velvet surfaces absorbing the lights positioned over each table; racks of pool cues adorned the wall on both sides of the room. My brother and his buddies would often engage in games of pool amidst their fraternizing. I was mesmerized by the art of the game, the care exercised by its patrons, the pacing back and forth to determine how to shoot the cue ball for maximum results, the effortless but cautious rotation of the chalk upon the cue tip, but I never got into the game. For me the Blue Eagle was a place to meet a family member for my ride, and because it was open longer hours than many business places, it was also a place I could go to use a public phone therein to arrange a ride home. One time when I went to the Blue Eagle after some sports practice or school meeting to use the phone, I dialed in what I thought was our home number, and was astounded to hear in response, "Murphy's Mule Barn, Murphy speaking." I was so aghast and flustered I immediately demurred and was attempting to break off conversation with a quick, "Sorry, Wrong number!" when my sister Gloria broke out laughing and asked if I was ready to be picked up. Sheesh! For a guy who already had some phone phobia problems, she sure didn't do me any good, but it's been a great laughable family story now for over five decades.

Businesses, cars, people, visions, conversations, steps, railings, memories – they all fuzz and fade and brighten and go dim and in and out of my mind like fog, like reality, like history, like a dream, like time passing through a funnel of being. Holstein as a town and community is still there. And I'm still here, but the Holstein I knew then is gone, gone to the past. That is the way the world works of course. Nothing stays the same. But I am struck by the fact that I did not realize the temporariness of the world about me at the time. Someone might have even taken the time, effort, and care to try and tell me then that what I saw around me would never be the same, that it would inevitably change. But I suspect I would not have listened or believed in such a pronouncement anyway. The young are not programmed to concern themselves that much with the far distant future. For that, we must all be thankful – it gives society a necessary immediacy of thrust through the present. But why then, the other end of this spectrum, why this me sitting here gazing backwards? Sociobiologists postulate our memories evolved in response to survival needs. Our forebears needed to have memory to know where to find the edible plants year to year, where the best hunting could be had seasonally, which herbs might help us through a fever, and to discriminate enemies from friends. So now I utilize what evolution developed to assist my physical survival, to instead aid me in my mental survival. Like a good song, like a good story, I replay the memories to know where I have been so that I can be most comfortable with where I am. And what about sharing memories? Sharing makes the song, the story, the memory last longer.

Sex Education

On my way to high school, scurrying through those middle transition years of junior high, as a young teen age boy I was still wrestling with the difficulty of my self-taught sex education. Progress was slow. And German families, for all their vaunted endorsement of education and schooling and the origination of kindergarten, were really not all that great in dealing with a biological imperative, turning it somewhat hypocritically on its head and making it into a taboo subject. Maybe they didn't feel it was necessary, after all, more than half of us classmates were reared on farms. Admittedly I might have been a little thick headed and slow to correlate physical commonalities of animals to humans, but the amygdala portion of my brain was beginning to beg for some explanation from my cerebral cortex as to the whole subject of sex and how specifically it functioned in humans.

To their credit, the Holstein community and the Holstein school system did have some rudimentary sex education for girls transitioning into the menstrual cycle. But nothing was provided for boys, not even a very good explanation of why the girls were all taken, no boys permitted, to a short (less than one hour?) secret, educational session focusing on their entry to the world of menstruation and womanhood. One moment the whole class is sitting together in the same room. The next moment all the girls are being led out to a different room. And we boys knew it wasn't the assigned hour for girl's gym workouts. We boys were left in a quandary with question marks on our faces. But we could tell something was up. And the rumor mill started.

I really don't know why the two sexes were treated so differently. Sex education wasn't part of my schooling provided by the Holstein school faculty. The rest of the boys and I were just forced to maintain some type of holding pattern in one of the classrooms during the girls' special education. One of my more aggressive and assertive, and apparently overtly inquisitive, male peers managed to somehow covertly obtain one of the pulp magazine brochures which had been provided strictly for the independent use and safe-keeping of the girls. Naturally, he was inordinately proud of this solitary investigative spy accomplishment, and shared it with some of the rest of us guys, safely gathered in some remote corner of the school grounds. To most us, specifically me, the contents didn't make a lick of sense. And the chief spy never allowed any of the rest of us private viewing of the document for further independent study.

So for sex education, I basically struggled along on my own, too embarrassed to ask for any assistance from any adult, too independent and fearful of peer teasing to ask any of my same age associates. I was, however, a good student and willing to devote myself to a rigorous self-study program. Accordingly, my hidden vocabulary increased considerably as I utilized the dictionary, and then looked up the meanings of words used in the definition. My sexual lexicon was enhanced immensely by the seven inch thick massive old dictionary kept above our stairs. I would pull the heavy tan book from its storage location, flop it on the floor on the south side of the stairs, stand on the 4th or 5th step down, and prowl the pages. On the north side of the steps, on a shelf under the sloping roof, was our trusty complete set of encyclopedias. When these were used in concert with words found in the big dictionary further enlightenment often followed. For pictorial representation, the undergarment sections of the old Sears Roebuck and Montgomery Ward catalogs found in the Summer Kitchen were a readily available resource. Even so, the most curious parts of sex education were still hidden from open access and full understanding, but at least I had gotten down to one thin layer of cloth over the female and the last thin layer still hiding the unknown. Occasionally, pictures in the National Geographic magazine carried in the school rooms or library eliminated even that last layer of clothing, but usually only partially and always in the context of foreign tribal habits, not quite offering the same allure and detail as I was seeking. Young pre-teens and early teenagers of today have it <u>SO</u> easy with information about sex available on a readily-accessible silver platter compared to the effort my peers and I had to put forth to comprehend, and, yes, appreciate sex and its attraction. I must fight to overcome my fundamental jealousy of their sex education opportunities, both via formal means and the informal means of today's entertainment media.

 My real breakthrough in my personal study of sex and all its intricacies, my real coup d'état against the system of education holding me back from things I needed to know, had its origin in an Omaha, Nebraska book store one summer. Each summer of my late childhood and early teen years I was allowed the opportunity to stay in the family home of my sister Delores. I always enjoyed those summer visits and the chance to spend more time with my siblings, all of whom were then living in Omaha. Delores and her husband Earl would put in a request for chocolate milk to be added to their weekly door side delivery, a treat unheard of on our own farm with its cows and bland daily white milk. Then too there was the daily run of the ice cream man tinkling his little warning bell on each block, to which children and mothers would scurry out and buy a treat. I didn't find any of those driving up and down our gravel roads in Ida County. About ten blocks north of Delores's home was a brand new shopping center, with a very complete book store unlike anything I had seen anywhere in northwest Iowa, let alone been allowed to visit unsupervised. By then I was allowed to walk there to spend some time while Delores was occupied in the chores of raising a family. Perusing the many sections of books, veering from my normal interest of astronomy and outdoor sports, I came upon an area devoted to marriage and family. After pulling down several books and reviewing their fascinating contents, I carried the book called, A Marriage Manual, A Practical Guidebook to Sex and Marriage, by Hannah and Abraham Stone (both M.D.'s, they must know what they're talking about!) and in its 39th printing (a good sign!) by Simon and Schuster, up to the checkout counter and the matronly lady behind it. "Aren't you a little young to be purchasing this book?" she asked, apparently taking it upon herself to define the morals by which I should exist. "Oh, it's not for me," I replied, "I'm buying this for my brother, he's getting married next month." Transaction completed. Book received in plain brown paper bag. Mission accomplished.

Talk about an answer book! Written in question and answer format, the book included a wealth of questions I hadn't even thought of yet. I transported it home to my room in the bottom of my suitcase after my parents came to pick me up at the end of the week and devoured the contents cover to cover. Thus the formal data content portion of my sex education was now complete; all that was lacking was implementation and practice. That too came over time.

The book's value did not end with a single reading by myself; it would prove to be a valuable reference source not only for me but for my future wife several years later. As word of its possession and value spread amongst my closest friends, they too checked it out of my closeted library as we wended our way through our high school and college years. A half dozen or so of my friends and their wives thus owe a small percent of their sexual prowess and knowledge to a young man who walked into an Omaha bookstore and bought a non-fiction book, which the checkout lady didn't especially want to sell to one so young.

Paradise Valley

Summertime was still preferable to school time. Because of my Dad's job in Ida Grove and the fact my mother never learned or had the incentive to drive, and because my siblings were all engaged in their own lives in Omaha, I spent a lot of time alone. Once in a while I wished I lived closer to town so I could bicycle in and spend an afternoon with Roger or Paul or Mike, but I never wished to actually live in town. Basically, I enjoyed my time alone and do not remember any periods of loneliness or boredom. I was comfortable with my life as a pre-teen or young teen, and enjoyed life as I chose to structure it. There were the assignments of farm work from my dad or mother including cultivating the corn with our MT Tractor, daily livestock chores such as gathering eggs at noon to reduce breakage, mowing the lawn, the worst part of the latter being starting the stubborn one-cylinder mower engine. But I had an abundance of time to spend as I chose in those days.

My dog, Tawny, a tan and grey coated Norwegian Elk Hound, was a constant companion outdoors. Dad brought him home after work one night and Dad and I made a comfortable little nest of hay for him in the barn during our other chores. I knew his name before I saw him. Not until many years later when we were clearing out our parents farm home did I realize where his name had originated in my subconscious. There, buried in a pile of books upstairs under the encyclopedia shelf, was a book about a special dog one of my siblings had read as a child, titled "Tawny". My Tawny and I were each the correct age to imprint upon one another and he became a long lived and beloved family member. Tawny and I would wrestle on the lawn or in the hay of the alleyway of the barn, or play tug with a piece of stout rope, or sit quietly on the lawn resting and gazing about, or go on hikes together over the whole farm, each of us with our own preference for what aroused our curiosity, mine determined largely by sight, Tawny's selected largely by his nose. We constantly checked each other's presence to assure we did not separate too far from one another. Tawny was a farm dog, not a house dog. In inclement weather he might be welcomed into a corner of the porch, there to curl up on a rug or watch us through the porch window, but each night he slept in the concrete cave-like tunnel formed because of the way the steps leading up to our porch were constructed. Each late autumn I would tidy this cozy enclosure up a bit and deliver a heaping deep pile of fresh clean oat straw for Tawny to prance into, make a circular depression, and lie down in.

 I enjoyed my bicycle and treated it as my mechanical horse. It enabled a faster means of getting over the hill to Jensen's pasture and exploring the roads and views around the section of land in which our small farm was located. And the speed attained as I coasted down the hill to our house yard or the hill down to Jensen's was exhilarating. On many a trip, whether it was to bike ride to Jensen's pasture or south to a terrific creek hole found by Duane and filled with scrappy little chubs, I would have my fishing pole mounted in the handlebar basket like the jousting weapon of a horse-mounted knight. In the basket would be the worms I had freshly dug from the soil behind the cattle shed, where rain falling from the roof kept the soil moist and worms were found in profusion churning soil around the roots of hemp, pigweed, dandelions, and other weeds growing there.

    I didn't always bike to the good fishing creek in Jesse's pasture. Other times I would walk and carry my fishing pole down through our pasture, past the Big Hole, past the cottonwoods and our dump, down to our small corner of pasture containing the same creek as Jesse's and which had run down through the neighbor's pasture from the east. I spent enough time there each summer to know where the best holes were for holding fish, where the deep runs were, where the shallow stretches were. My favorite technique was really quite simple but very successful on the hungry and abundant chubs inhabiting the water there. I would use only a small hook, no sinker, freshly baited with a wriggling worm, and flick it and six to eight feet of line to the water with my rod tip, and let it slowly settle to the bottom, sometimes in the best holes as much as six feet down. Generally before the worm hit bottom my rod would be dancing through the air with a chub. Sometimes, but with much less frequency, if the hook and worm made it to bottom, I might catch a Bullhead. To me at the time, this was a veritable big game fish, rare and chunky with volume. Florence Kastner's pasture had some good fishing in it, but generally I headed downstream and followed the creek through Jesse's pasture.

Over time, and through biking and walking to the upper and lower reaches of the big creek, I roamed and covered two miles upstream and two miles down. Many an afternoon was spent in idyllic wonder and curiosity as I followed the water's edge, looking for the deepest water, seeing tracks, observing the little volcano-like diggings of crayfish, jumping the occasional Jackrabbit, keeping an eye out for cattle approaching me, noting taller grasses where pheasants might lurk in the coming autumn, pondering the omniscient sound of nature, feeling the inner me content in the outdoors. The most exciting of these explorations took place immediately following the big rainfalls of six inches or more every few years, for then major flooding would inevitably take place and new fishing holes, bigger? deeper? broader?, might be formed and I would be the first to find them. It was after those floods that I would see our 50-pound sledgehammer come out of storage as Dad and I would gather up the fence repair tools, toss them in the little two-wheeled trailer hooked to our tractor and drive down to the Big Creek to repair the fence. Depending on the magnitude of the flood, our border fence keeping our cattle in and the neighbor's cattle out, could get washed out from the base of the creek bed and be strewn in stringy ligaments of barbed wire laid out downstream from whichever remaining post had not gotten ripped out by the force of the water, and accumulated debris. Then Dad and Duane would walk into the creek, reposition a post along the fence line and drive it into the liquid and mud with the big sledgehammer until the post, which had been given a pointed end with our axe, finally stood firm in the gravel below.

I didn't need to bike or fish to enjoy my time alone. I was equally content with hiking and roaming the neighborhood, pretending I was a new explorer, or just being myself and finding out what existed in the outdoors with me, where the jackrabbits were, how the Reed Canary Grass came to be so thick and lush, where the rocks came from, how close the neighbor was farming to the waterway, where the deepest erosion was, which crops were doing well, which tree limbs had broken off since my last visit. A favorite destination was a stack of hay bales, which the neighbor piled several years in the midst of Mabel Sherman's section near what I called Paradise Valley.

On my afternoon or early evening forays to Paradise Valley in late summer or early fall when the sun was slanting through our pine grove, I would wander past the old smoke house, past the mulberry trees now bereft of fruit, swing my legs over the top strand of the fence, trod the road up the second hill, and then enter Sherman's section through the wide, normally open field gate, and hike the slanting field edge trail down to my mystical valley. The valley had always been a calming retreat since I was introduced to it by my brother, probably while I was serving as his fetch dog during an afternoon pheasant hunt before chore time. Since that introduction I had returned frequently on my own or in the company of Tawny. These visits were not so frequent as those to my own farmstead special places chosen for their convenience, but often enough I came to know the valley and its rewards well, and to ration my visits there to preserve the important factor of rarity, like a gem taken out of its box for admiration in solace.

My reward was daydreaming, and it seemed the haystack was a tall altar edifice I could climb and then nestle into some comfortable crevice of bales, held not as an infant in a mother's arms but as a rational thinking being held in the pocket of what the outdoors, the earth, and in particular, this valley, this pile of bales, provided for me – an observational retreat to see what was in front of my eyes or to facilitate my vision inside to my inner being. Perhaps today the scientists might call it free-thinking, or the psychologists might call it an adolescent's exploration of self-motivation. I called it daydreaming and there was a vast range of subject material: what I would do after high school, is there a god, is there a hell, how to grasp infinity, how did life originate, are there pheasants resting near here, which creek hole should I fish first next week, how to straighten the front wheel on my bike, what modifications can I make on the wind tunnel, what did Mike mean when he made that comment about Judy, and on and on, until the sun sank low enough and I knew it was time to walk back home, back home to the world that existed as real and obligatory, and away from this valley and its comfortable nothingness which provided the everythingness I needed at that point of my being. Hovering around the core of daydreaming though, as an enveloping outer shell, was the outdoorness of free air, wild animal spirit, moving Iowa air, cloud patterns above, the voices which the grass and trees made, the blue of the blue sky, the red of the sunset, totally at the opposite end of the sensory spectrum as when you sink your head to a pillow in a dark room late at night. The paradisiacal setting of my valley gave this young man an enriched setting for his daydreams.

Leaving the Boy Behind

Leaving the ignorant innocence of junior high school and a somnolent last summer as a boy, beginning in mid-month, August, 1958, I was thrust into a chaotic, tortuous, enriching, fulfilling, frightening, embarrassing month of forced and rapid maturation to manhood which included a marriage, a death, a physical and mental hazing, self-acceptance, and the self-forged will to carry on. I came upon this compressed period of life experience only recently through a chronological assessment of my personal history. It was not that I have remembered this as any type of a particular burden all these years. I remember each event but it was not until preparing for this autobiography that I recognized so many of these significant (to me) events took place in such a short span of time. And it is only now that I can see the bang, bang, bang rapid pace of events in a young man's life probably contributed to a self- imposed memory wipe in order to cope with the grief caused by premature loss of a young friend.

On August 17, 1958 I served as best man to my brother Duane when he married Helen Riescheik in Falls City, Nebraska. I was the same age as Helen's sister, Marjorie, who served as bridesmaid. Duane and Helen enjoyed this congruency of our ages and engaged in some modest match-making efforts between Marjorie and myself, but our acquaintanceship was not capable of a self-sustained flame. Helen had several brothers each several years older than me. They took me under their wing after the wedding rehearsal, we were joined by several other young men, and I was introduced to the back country road carousing and beer-drinking of southern Nebraska down near the Kansas border. The process was very educational for me and their practices and avoidances of the law would be adopted by me and my compatriots in Iowa as we wended our way into the future trying to turn into responsible adults after we had engaged in the frivolity and experimentation of our late teenage years.

Duane's wedding is memorable to me for two reasons: 1) I was impressed with his level of joy and commitment to what my family all accepted as a lifelong promise. It seemed a big step which I had trouble grasping. He seemed to have no difficulty and was eager to proceed. I wondered how one could be so sure of such a major life event and that commitment to forever. 2) I fainted at their wedding while they were taking their vows. How embarrassing! There in front of all the attendees. But after a few minutes sitting down in the first pew I was able to rejoin them and their union was completed. No, I don't think it was the late-night carousing on gravel roads that did me in. It was the water. At our farm home in Iowa and where I now live in Wisconsin we were blessed with good-tasting, hard water. At the Falls City, Nebraska farm home, we endured strange tasting soft water with an odd flavor and so I did not drink enough during our visit to maintain good hydration. Hence, what with all the warm wedding clothes, a very hot afternoon in the church, some nervousness at being the best man holding the rings, I was doomed to keel over. It was an important lesson in proper hydration.

Eight days after my brother's wedding, my young friend and classmate, Bruce Ladewig, was shot and killed in an accidental unintended discharge of a .22 caliber rifle. News of such a tragic occurrence in a close-knit community like Holstein spread quickly. Inevitably, the better you know someone, the more shocking the news is when you hear of their death. The news surely was horrible for his closest relatives and family. But for his peers, his classmates, and his close friends, of which I was one, his death exploded like a weapon in our emotional hearts, and because we were all the same age as he, within a year of all being 14, we were all unprepared for the pain it caused and totally inexperienced with how to deal with it. Sure, some of us had lost family members, perhaps an elderly grandparent or older aunt or uncle, but Bruce was our age, was one of us, and yes, too young to die. But he was dead and we remained and our world was whirling on. How then to deal with this new reality?

Bruce died in the same week that High School football practice had commenced. For those of us who signed up for football, and Bruce had, it was a big, longed-for transition to the realm of high school and varsity sports. Our coaches were tough, fair, and successful and each of us wanted badly to succeed for them and to grow into our role as participants in the sporting history of Holstein High School. I am sure we had all looked forward to joining this near-ritual activity of high school football practice, would all have been excited and nervous at the same time, eager to be assigned our uniform, helmet, and number. Instead we had to cope with internal feelings of loss, of wondering how his death affected Bruce's soul, of questioning how we were to act, and what we would reveal only to ourselves about death.

Our classmate and friend died before grief counseling was provided to young people in situations like this, before a school system would choose to call in professional social workers or psychologists, before our parents had internet access to look up how to help their children through grief. Ours was a German community, not exactly the touchy-feely, group-hug type of community. By and large I think we were judged to have moved out of the world of children and were expected to deal with death as an adult would. But most of us didn't know the means to deal with death. So we all dealt with Bruce's death in our own way, pulled forward by the force of a caring community, if not necessarily a demonstrative community. Relatives, close friends, and all manner of Holstein community residents gathered round the bereaved to offer their condolences and support. All of us had learned some necessary steps of how to do this along the way of life in a community where nearly everyone knew everyone else, at least to some degree, and relatives and friendships lay about in the profusion of community time shared together along the road of growing up or old together.

My second greatest shock at Bruce's death happened 44 years later when a fellow classmate, Bette, was sorting through her house for a move after our class had held a 40th class reunion and found a copy of Bruce's funeral service bulletin and sent it to me. In this bulletin I discovered I was one of Bruce's pallbearers. I reread the contents and paused at the list of six pallbearers to slowly read my own name, confirm it was my name, and then to sit quietly at my desk to ponder why, after more than 40 years, I couldn't remember my role as a direct participant in his funeral service. It was patently obvious to me at that point that I hadn't handled Bruce's death as professionally as I had thought. I wasn't angry with myself or feeling guilty, I was just very surprised I could not recollect my role in the funeral, even with this potent proof in front of me.

    Forty-four years after Bruce's passing, I became strongly motivated for several weeks to relearn the details and to try to understand why I hadn't remembered them. I retrieved his obituary. I read the articles about his accident from the local newspapers, both the Holstein Advance and the Ida County Courier. I wrote my best friend, John, and asked what he remembered. But I really could not re-capture any personal memories of my participation in Bruce's funeral. I remember various play activities with Bruce from my youth, I remember his smile, I remember his house and visiting in it, I remember him coming to our farm. But I can't remember that funeral. The brain is a powerful, complicated organ, well known for its occasional malfunctioning, and admittedly capable of defending itself from ongoing harm. I can only assume in some strange complicated manner, my mind was operating to protect me and keep me going.

Sometimes we can only do what we have to do. I had to recognize my friend was gone forever and get through that funeral. I did that. Forty-four years later I found out how.

The next big event in that tremulous month of starting high school was the annual ritual of initiation, which, in our case, should really be spelled with a capital "I". Who amongst my class could forget our initiation into high school? Who amongst my class wants to remember it? Our initiation into high school is referred to as "freshman honor day" in the annual school publication known as "The Moo". In spite of that day's officious and reverential name, it was anything but an honor or honorable. Our initiation was one of many in a long line of a once-a-year hazing ritual at Holstein High School, officially sanctioned by the school board, the school staff, and much looked forward to by the seniors. As many events, rituals, celebrations are prone to do, this one gradually changed over time to culminate in our initiation. I say culminate because nearly all, perhaps all, of my classmates will agree it was one of the worst, most embarrassing, most harassing initiation events in Holstein High School history. I say culminate because to my knowledge, the magnitude of harassment and exhibitions of silliness were gradually reduced over time after our initiation, and eventually eliminated. I presume credit should be given to the parents, school staff, and school board members that observed our initiation, but I have no proof of that. All I can declare is ours was the worst. Classes before us, classes after us did not suffer their initiation into high school to the degree that the Class of 1962 did.

Not that I would say now I regret having had to endure our initiation event, or that it was a painful experience forever adversely marking my psyche. Indeed, like the successful participants in any hazing ritual I am in fact proud of my accomplishment, proud of having made it through the event, proud of not breaking down, proud of having some of the seniors tell me, "You did well. You took what we dished out and handled it without care and in good fun." But, in looking back at some of the old photos of the initiation, I do see pain, great embarrassment, fatigue on a few of those faces, and I'm sorry for them it had to be thus. For we the graduating class of 1962 there was no escaping from tradition. However, as I learned at my recent 50th high school class reunion, some of my classmates suffered physical bruising and still carry great resentment for the way they were treated during our initiation.

Our initiation occurred on Friday, September 5, 1958, only a few days after the school year had begun. The senior class of 30 members planned the day and the events that we, a class of 48 members, would be performing in. Each of us freshman had to craft a wooden paddle to particular dimensions and thickness, to be given to the senior to whom we had been assigned. The seniors could use said paddle on any of our behinds throughout the day. Awards were given for the best paddle construction and paddle decoration, the reward being a pie in the face. Each of the boys had to dress in a diaper, that was it, just a large cloth diaper. Each of the girls were mandated to come dressed as hoodlums. Many "fun" events were planned and prepared by the seniors. At each event we had to line up, gather round, and participate. Among these events: scrubbing clean the large concrete floor of the local bandstand in the city park with toothbrushes and water, dipping our faces into a galvanized bathtub filled with a vile grayish-white liquid to bob for some mysterious floating objects while on hands and knees, tossing fresh eggs to each other from a gradually increasing distance until the eggs burst as we attempted to catch them, crawling on hands and knees rolling moth balls through the grass with our noses. Throughout the events our hair and bodies were generously anointed with water and powdered cornstarch, and our skin marked with lipstick. Judging from the pictures, the seniors had a lot of fun. Judging from the pictures, for us freshmen it was an endurance contest. Most of us endured, and left any pain and humiliation suffered behind us. We completed our rite of passage and were granted the right to be treated as fellow high school students.

The next event to unfold in my emotional gauntlet of weeks from mid- August to mid-September, 1958, followed within several weeks of high school initiation, within three weeks of Bruce's death, within a month of Duane's wedding, not to mention within the stress of new high school classes, my budding romance, and the excitement and challenge of football practice. This event was my brother's shivaree, an Americanized variant from the

French word "charavari". I had never heard of a shivaree until one was being organized at my parents' farm for Duane and his wife, Helen. Duane and Helen were making a planned weekend visit to the farm from Omaha, where they were living now as newlyweds, to deal with wedding presents which had arrived at or been taken to our home. As such, they were perfect and unknowing candidates for a surprise party on Saturday night.

The charavari had its French historical origin in being a stigmatizing social event meant to keep a particular couple in line with customs and morality of the community. As the word and the custom migrated across the Atlantic to French Quebec the meaning and practice subtly changed until in the early to mid-20th century the shivaree came to be a "noisy mock-serenade for newlyweds" and was performed in locales along and west of the Mississippi River.

Friends, neighbors, and relatives who knew Duane well were all invited and sworn to secrecy and told to drive out and assemble in a line-up alongside the country road north of, and not visible from, our farm. At a duly appointed time early in the evening the lead car pulled out and every car there joined in a long caravan and came driving onto our farmyard honking their automobile horns, banging on empty pots and pans while hanging out the car window, yelling, screaming, generating as much joyous noise as possible until the newlyweds were forced by their loving family to step out the porch door and greet the numerous well-wishers. What a surprise it was! Duane and Helen had been led to believe they would have a quiet night at home with my parents and me.

It was a grand evening. The Summer Kitchen had been cleared out for the seating of guests and tables for card games. Card tables and portable chairs flew out of the closet and were set up around the living room. Cakes and cookies, soda pop and beer, were set out and made available in the house kitchen and in the Summer Kitchen. There was an abundance of laughter, mirth, joshing, jokes, conversation, good wishes, and camaraderie galore. As was typical of events in farm homes at that time, as the night wore on, the women folk mostly gathered together in the house, the men folk were relegated to the Summer Kitchen, and the entertainment of card games for those interested gradually commenced. Celebratory cigars were available and being doled out to anyone who wished in the Summer Kitchen. Although the box was quickly passed in front of me in jest, I was quicker yet and grabbed one and lit it up for a few puffs, to the unbelieving eyes of Duane and my father. They smiled in surprise, and I got away with it without any disciplinary measures being taken. Inch by inch, step by step, I was making my way into what I saw of as their adult world. Practicing, play acting, but nonetheless, making my way. It was a particularly fun evening for all involved, and typical of the shared joy which a small close-knit community could generate at that time, which I, as an aging man, in spite of its being a cliché, can call the good old days. It was my first and last shivaree.

My entry into high school meant the world was expanding for me, as it was for my peers. Now we had study halls, our own library, no recess periods, but a modified noon lunch time, classes we walked to instead of the teacher coming to us, a different disciplinary code, the pressure of conforming to upper classman's concept of how we should behave socially. My relationship with what was now commonly known as my girlfriend, Judy, was also expanding. I could sit with her for a time at lunch if we so chose, we could talk between classes or walk together to lunch, there were more school dances being held, some after sporting events like the home football games.

Judy and I were fortunate in that Judy had an older sister, Janet, one of the seniors, and Janet seemed to have adopted us as worthy of match-making. I'm sure I have Janet to thank for conning her then steady boyfriend, Dean, into providing transportation to the hayride. That early fall, my local Luther League, a church group for the teenage spectrum, organized a hayride as entertainment for one of their meetings. Several farmers were courteously coerced into pulling flat-rack wagons on a meandering tour over the sparsely traveled gravel country roads at night with their tractors. Each flat-rack wagon, an 8 foot by 16 foot flat bed of planks mounted on a four-tired running gear, had a single row of straw bales around the perimeter of the flat-rack, with loose straw spread on the floor of the wagon to help shelter participants from the bumps. Cooler outdoor temperatures in the evening could be expected so blankets were provided to add a layer of warmth if needed. Dean's mandated assignment from Janet was to drive to my farm, pick me up in his 1949 Ford, and come to the sisters' home for their pick up, It looked to me like a genuine double date, no parental driving needed, just one car with a couple in the back seat, and a couple in the front seat, me and Judy's first "real" date. I felt horribly shy, naïve, and a little embarrassed to be alone with Dean on the way over to our girlfriends' house, but I desperately wanted the end result.

The end result was a lot of experimental kissing under a blanket on top of the straw at the rear corner of the flat rack, as we explored this act of affection in a beginning girlfriend-boyfriend manner, unfettered by teachers standing in a corner, or adults intensely monitoring our actions. It made for a memorable evening. There wouldn't be that much kissing between us until more than a year later when I got my own car and became independently mobile. I always associate the song of Buddy Knox, "Somebody Touched Me" with that evening and with Judy, although I can no longer remember how that association came to be. Perhaps the song was playing on Dean's radio as we drove over to Janet and Judy's home, perhaps the song was merely quite popular at the same time as the hayride, or perhaps I adopted it post-event due to the lyrics, which, in addition to the title, include, "… in the dark last night."

High school studies and assignments took some getting used to. In junior high school we had been introduced to the concept of homework, but I never really worked at it. New learning, new facts, new concepts, came fairly easy for me and so I never really had to apply much effort. I suspect for me there was some play-acting at being a high school student while yet verging so closely to being, and occasionally relapsing, to the immature child from grade school. Mr. McKnight, our high school science, physics, biology, and chemistry teacher, had by now the experience to recognize scholastic potential in students, even though individual students might not have yet recognized their own potential. I was one of those students who did not yet have a clear view of what I could be.

One day, early in our first semester as freshman science students, Mr. McKnight held me after class, along with my pal Bryan, and several other boys, for a personal exhortation. Yes, we were all boys; no girls I know of got the special session. Girls didn't need the session. But as boys, we were too frivolous and full of ourselves—we needed shaking down. We all sat in our desk chairs lined up in a short row. Mr. McKnight stood directly in front of us, too close to us for this to be a casual visit, occasionally propping one foot up on the seat of another chair facing us, his back slightly arched, one elbow resting on the knee held up in the air by the chair seat, his index finger extended from the arm on his knee, and pointed accusingly at each of us as he addressed us both individually and as a group. He told us, in no uncertain terms, that we could do better than we were. He had looked at our junior high grades, he had assessed results of our Iowa Basic Skills testing, he had by then come to know us as individuals, and he said unless we straightened out, and straightened out right now, we were wasting our potential. He did not address us derogatorily, he addressed us as a caring partner. He did not address us as children, he addressed us as adults. He did not threaten us, he challenged us. He did not withdraw his support, he volunteered it. It was a good lecture. Mrs. Christie was a very good English teacher and made me a better writer, Mr. Gerber was a very good mathematics instructor and honed my abilities in that field, Mr. McKnight made me a better student, period, and he did so before any further laxity on my part would adversely affect my high school grade point.

Getting good grades and understanding the latest concepts our teachers were introducing us to were fairly easy for two of the Gary's in my class, not quite as easy for the third Gary in our class. Gary must have been a popular name when we were all born in 1944. It occasionally provided a little levity when new teachers would call upon one Gary and all three of us would answer. In order to foster his education and performance on homework assignments, the third Gary for a period of time would telephone me in the evening to check his answers to the homework or to seek a few hints about how to master the subject at hand. Those of us in the country were then all on party lines as were we three Gary's. Although party line residents had different phone numbers, each phone on the line would ring. You were expected to answer your phone only when your coded ring sequence came through the line, but anyone could, and some people on the line would, if they were curious or had time to kill, "listen in" on the conversation.

The phone in my home was, for many years of my youth, the classic, now antique, wooden box on the wall. There was a mounted transmitter microphone, a bell shaped devise, on the center front of the wooden box, adjustable only up and down. If you were too short or if you were a child, you had to stand on a box to speak into the phone. Below the mouthpiece was a small easel built onto the front of the phone for your convenience in taking a short note if that was necessary. The ear piece device, rather trumpet shaped, was held to ones ear, normally with the left hand as when it was unused it was mounted in a cradle on the left side of the wooden phone box. If you were short or tall you had more flexibility with the ear piece because its connection to the wooden box was via a cord several feet long. On the right side of the wooden box was a rotating handle that one would crank to secure the telephone operator at her switchboard in Holstein, and then verbally provide her with the number you were trying to reach. Our phone number was 33-F-032, which means we were on line 33 of the Holstein switchboard, and our ringing sequence to get our attention was three long rings and two short rings. If you heard 3 longs and 2 shorts, the call was for someone in your household. If you heard any other sequence the call was not intended for you and you were expected to be polite, but you could still listen in to overhear the conversation between two other parties. This, of course, was considered socially impolite, but that did not stop some people from such "rubber-necking."

Somewhere in my teen age years my home updated to a "modern" black plastic phone and rotary dial, but for a time there was still several years with the black phone when one could tell a phone call was going through to someone on your line and you could listen in. This "listening in" allowed Gary and I to meet a new Judy (Judy Cowan, not girlfriend Judy, turns out there were also 3 Judy's in our high school class, apparently that name was as popular as Gary) on the phone a year or two before she transferred to our school system and became a classmate. Judy and her parents had moved into our neighborhood and were living next to Mabel Sherman's house down the road a mile and thus were on the same party line as I was. When Gary would call me, she knew the ring sequence for my phone and would pick up the phone too and chime in on the conversation between Gary and me. We were having conference calls in the rural wilderness of Iowa long before the concept of conference calls was even introduced. It was quite a surprise for Gary and I to hear her voice for the first time and then, as our continuing conversations unfolded, to discover she was the same age as we were. As the homework continued, the calls continued, and our three-way conversations continued. It was fun for all three of us to explore the world of teen age conversation with someone we had yet to meet physically. The following year her parents transferred Judy into our school system and she became a classmate of Gary and me. The magical mystery of the female voice on the line was a mystery no more. Gary's scholarly pursuits began to veer off the college path I was on. The calls ended.

Although none of us classmates would have bet any money on it, the third Gary would become one of the most loyal participants of our class reunions. I enjoy seeing him at these rare events and we talk about those phone calls of our youth. Gary's and my roots, as for so many folks around the Holstein area, are entangled over the expanse of generations. His dad and my dad worked for the same organization of the government during the period my dad was office manager in Ida Grove. Gary and I played on the same school sports teams, went to the same classes, rode the same school bus, our families went to the same church, he and I lived four miles apart. That's commonality enough for a lifetime of memories, I suppose. But there's more. In the Holstein area, there's often more. Gary's great grandparents and my great grandparents, none of which either Gary or I ever knew personally, lie in the same small "Norwegian" cemetery only a few yards from one another. The cemetery is two miles from each of our homes. The farms Gary and I grew up on were once owned by our respective great grandparents. Gary and I aren't the closest of friends, but we still meet and reminisce at the class reunions. But in these old historical deaths, the shared grieving of a long past neighborhood which mourned our great grandparents passage to the graves, the same neighborhood in which Gary and I were born and raised in, and being related to those neighbors who lived near one another 50 years before Gary and I were born, he and I are bound commonly together in a unique way increasingly rare in 21st century America.

The Cottonwood Rocket Club

During junior high Roger, my classmate and son of one of the clothiers in town, was becoming one of my good friends. As we classmates aged and matured, as we began to exhibit our scholastic performance and personal interests as developing individuals, we began to subdivide our friendship groups. Without realizing it at the time, we were coalescing into new friendships based on who we were becoming. Roger became my good friend as we entered high school, then college, and he remains a good friend to this day. But in the beginning it was our common interests in rockets which propelled us together, pun intended.

When we were just entering eighth grade, on October 4, 1957, Sputnik was launched into earth orbit and ignited the international space race and the popular knowledge of and interest in rockets of all sorts. By then Roger and I, and then Bryan, who had been born one day earlier than I in the next room down the hall of the Cushing Hospital, were well acquainted with American, Russian, and German rocketry because of our scientific bent and interests in things that moved fast and dangerously. We knew of Wernher von Braun and his work with the German V-2 project from World War II. Von Braun had come to America after the war and was greatly involved in America's development of the Redstone and Jupiter rocket series, which launched America's own first satellite four months after Sputnik. America's Robert H. Goddard is generally acknowledged to be the father of modern rocketry and we had read of his contributions to the science of rocketry.

Roger, who graduated from college with a degree in aeronautical engineering and went on to work with things that moved fast and dangerously, and I started our experiments in rocketry with paper match heads. I had read an article about making tiny rockets out of paper matches torn from those small match books then commonly available. They were free everywhere, in bars, at motels, at cigarette sales counters, paper match books galore. The price was right for a couple of young teen agers. Who knows where I read the article. It could have been the Boy's Life magazine perhaps. It could have been passed on to me by one of the Meyer boys, my second cousins, who knew how to make a B-B shooter pistol out of a clothes pin, and which we used rather recklessly on the school bus. One thing I do know. I did not learn it from the Internet.

Once I shared the concept of match head rockets with Roger, we couldn't wait to get started. Per the instructions, one laid a common steel fabric pin along the length axis of a single paper match ripped from the book. Next you folded and wrapped a small square of aluminum foil from Mom's kitchen around the match head and pin and crimped the aluminum tightly around the pin and match, and then withdrew the pin leaving a tiny exit hole for the hot gases. After laying the foil-covered match in a suitable launch rail (we made ours folded from more tinfoil), you held a lighted match under the head of the wrapped match until the head inside the foil ignited. Presto! Self-sustained flight attained. We were on our way. Alright, only several feet of flight, but we were on our way.

After proving out the operation, naturally, being amateur engineers without realizing one day we would be real engineers in the industrial world, we began to study and postulate on potential weaknesses of the design and how to improve the length of flight. We crimped the head of our missiles to a point to improve the aerodynamics. We cut off the paper handle of the match and left only the head in the foil to reduce the weight of the match rocket. We added one or two heads of additional matches to increase the propulsive force and fuel content. We added tiny amounts of black powder that we had extracted from .22 bullets we had disassembled, but this added heat began to melt the skin of the tiny rockets.

Most of our match rocket experiments were carried out inside the porch of my farm house where we eventually attained the design limits of such a flying craft by launching them about 12 feet and hitting the lower side of the opposite wall, right underneath the bedroom window in said wall. I do not recall very many of our experimental flights occurring at his parent's house. It may be that with Roger being the first child, his parents might have frowned on this activity in their home as being potentially injurious. Whereas, I was the last child, my parents were tired of worrying about their children, and if I was occupied with my friend, then they could go on about their adult pursuits.

Given the success of our venture so far, we shared our results with Bryan and we joined with him to form the Cottonwoods Rocket Club, known as the CRC, named for the cottonwood trees in our pasture which we perceived would one day be an excellent launch site for future flights of bigger rockets. The cottonwoods area of our pasture and the nearby farm dump had some erosion channels cut into the soil which would provide a revetment to leap into prior to ignition of our designs. We pondered individually and together on how to make a bigger rocket, how to secure fuel, what was needed for sustained flight, where to get the materials, but, more fundamentally, how do we get to the next stage of our interest in rocketry. We would write up small reports of ideas and proposals and pass them in school to our fellow members of the club. A rather diverse series of experiments began to unfold as we read on our own, studied school courses, and discussed our ideas. Our efforts were not necessarily vigorously focused. After all, we also had girls to pursue, learning how to drive, and jobs at each of our own homes. Because we lived several miles apart from one another and did not yet drive on our own it was difficult to get together outside of school very often.

In retrospect it seems rather a small miracle none of us sustained any injuries due to our experiments, We should have had some kind of a safety officer looking over our shoulders but then, of course, it would not have been nearly as much fun and we would not have learned as much nor developed as many fond memories. In retrospect, I am sorry we didn't have enthused mentors like Homer H. Hickman, Jr. had and describes in his book, "Rocket Boys: A Memoir" about Homer's experiments, far more successful and numerous than our own, with amateur rocketry in Coalwood, West Virginia. Hickman was performing his rocket experiments during the same time period and at the same age as we were. At the start of Homer's interest in rocketry in 1957, he had basically the same interest, knowledge, and enthusiasm as we did, but through the vagaries of time, personal drive, access, and contacts, Homer and his friends carried rocketry to a far higher plane than Roger and Bryan and I could even conceive. Mr. McKnight could have been our mentor in a different world, but Mr. McKnight and we all had numerous other priorities and obligations.

In our world, in the late 1950's, we did what we could. Roger had a CO_2 powered pellet gun and conceived that empty CO_2 cartridges might form the body of a powerful engine if we could figure out what to put inside. The small end made for a terrific nozzle so Roger drilled out the small hole formed by its use in his rifle, inserted some type of flammable substance lost to memory, strapped down the "engine", and ignited it. Results: engine body too heavy, propulsive force too weak. Failure. I had a butane-powered camp stove and small butane-filled cylinders, about the size of a 12-ounce soda can. Roger and I discovered that if you insert the small air pin used to fill basketballs and footballs into the rubber closure at the end of the butane cylinder, the enclosed butane would spew forth into the atmosphere. We held the cylinder immobile mounted near the ground with the aid of a nearby brick pile, inserted the filler pin, and using a long stick with match tied to the end of it, we quickly ignited the escaping butane. Results: made for a terrific flame thrower but no propulsive force. Failure.

Some experiments were only indirectly related to rocketry. There was a documentary movie at that time which illustrated our scientists' explorations of what reactive forces could be expected on the human body in the event rocket flight became feasible in the near future. One method to understand G-forces on humans was to monitor their response when placed in a contained transit down fixed rails while propelled by a rocket powered sled. A different method was to put the volunteer in a capsule on a long rotating arm and submit the human to centrifugal force, which could be varied by speed of acceleration or deceleration or by the speed of revolution. I decided I could apply centrifugal force to a mouse and monitor its response.

Early that fall, in 1959, as the nights got cooler and winter was approaching, I had discovered that a few mice were living in the straw leftover as fresh bedding in a small portable hog house that was then unused and was located in the field on the other side of the south willows. I discovered the mice on a day when one of our farm cats, accompanying me on a short hike, came into the building with me and quickly went into stalk mode before plunging head first into the corner and capturing a mouse between the straw and the floor with her lightning fast paws. The cat, naturally acting quite proud and not wanting to share her supper with me immediately went outside and devoured the mouse. I discovered, with a little practice, some quick moves of my own, a little laughter at myself when I erred, and a tin can, I too could capture a mouse.

Having proven my ability to obtain subjects for a centrifuge, next I turned to design of my centrifuge. I took one of my Dad's small hand drills, the kind with a crank handle on the side and capable of holding a drill up to ¼ inch diameter, and inserted into the drill chuck a ¼ inch diameter rod which I had bent at 90 degrees to provided a rotational radius of 13 inches in length. At the end of the rod I attached a baking soda can into which I could insert a mouse and, with bolts and brackets, attached the entire rotating assembly to the mid-point of one of the pivoting doors in the portable hog house, such that the full diameter of rotation could be passed through without hitting anything and which still allowed me to grasp the drill handle and bring the centrifuge up to speed.

Between formulas from our high school text books and a little research in the encyclopedia, I calculated I could bring a mouse up to 35 ½ miles per hour if I could crank the drill handle 1 3/5 times per second. My calculations from that time further suggested a one ounce mouse would exert 13 pounds of centrifugal force at the end of the rotating arm. That may very well have been true because once I got the drill handle up to speed the door which the centrifuge was mounted on was rattling something fierce. Another calculation showed my mouse would be subjected to 208 Gs. I think my exuberance at working the newly discovered formulas was exceeded only by my ignorance at understanding what it was I was calculating. I know as I got into the world of high school mathematics and the formulas of physics, I was fascinated by the plugging and grinding involved in a good formula which yielded a single definitive answer at the end. It was a special kind of magic to me, and if done properly, a single correct answer always resulted. But you still had to know what you were doing and select the correct formula.

My notes from October 31, 1959 when I was fifteen years old:

"Today, I caught a small mouse, and put him in my Centrifuge 1, and put it into motion. I did not think, however, that the capsule was revolved 35 mph, but rather approximately 27-32 mph. Later when I removed the mouse from the centrifuge it had lost a lot of its former ability to function speedily (when running, etc.) and also its balance was completely ruined and it did not recover in the 5 min. observed although it did improve. After 5-10 min., I again put it in the centrifuge whereby all of its functioning ability was immediately reduced. An increased heart beating and breathing was also observed. A tiny drop of blood was also observed in the capsule, evidently from an external opening probably the mouth or nose. After the experiment the mouse was exterminated to save suffering and to 'aid the cause of the cats'."

Fortunately our pre-astronauts and human subjects had much better options for their post-flight care than what I was able to offer to my hog house mice.

On another day, I had caught a mouse and decided I wanted to get that mouse up to more than 35 miles per hour in a centrifugal rotation. I went down to our well by the creek in the pasture east of the barn and disconnected the motor from the pump jack of the well pump by taking off the V-belt. I attached a one foot long piece of wood I had brought from the workshop to the drive wheel on the motor and strapped my little furred subject to the end of the wooden stick by wrapping it round and round with white adhesive tape from our medicine cabinet, stood back, and plugged the power cord into the electricity outlet. Zingggg! I knew within a few seconds the mouse was no longer attached to the centrifuge. I quickly unplugged the motor and saw all that remained was remnants of mouse fur in the adhesive tape still attached to the stick. I looked and looked around in the path of rotation but never did find that little fellow. For all I know he was the first mouse launched into space. Certainly he was the first mouse launched into the space above our pasture.

In our mathematics classes at school Mr. Gerber was introducing us to the complexities of quadratic equations and the parabolic curve. For some months now my cohorts of the Cottonwoods Rocket Club and I had already been determining how best to bring our eventual rocket or front nose piece back to earth following the big launch of our rocket yet to be invented. An obvious easy solution would, of course, be to use a parachute either deployed or dropped out of the rocket upon its peak height being attained and then turning over to start back down. But within half of those beautiful parabolic curves displayed on the blackboard and illustrated in our math textbook, I instead saw the long flight path of a glider that plummets earthward, then levels out in its path to land horizontally on the ground instead of plunging into it vertically like an arrow.

Data was required. Further experiments were needed. Designs were drafted. Plans were made. I crafted several small 8-12 inch long gliders, their bodies cut from wood and shaped to form with a drawshave in Dad's toolshed, their wings cut from flat tin with a tinsnips. I affixed the wings to the body with thumb tacks and nails and bent the rear wing edges up. As the glider dropped straight down the passing air going over the rear wing edge would pull the entire glider body toward the same direction as the rear wings were bent, and, given a long enough flight path down, the glider would land horizontally, just like any other glider. Given the success of America's space shuttle craft, I can see there were minds a lot greater than my own, which had similar ideas, much better training, much more money. Such is the pace and diversity of scientific inquiry. I'm glad I joined in.

Dad was repainting the farm buildings at that time and had purchased a tall 32 foot extension ladder. Taking my gliders and a data sheet for recording the results I would mount the ladder to the east end of the machine shed when the cattle weren't below me but were instead out in the pasture. I climbed up the ladder, glider in hand, to both the 15 and 25 foot heights. Then I used a plumb bob, sometimes I just dropped ball bearings straight down, to determine where the glider would land if it had straight fins and wings with no pitch in the rear edge. Then I dropped the gliders from the exact same point and noted where the glider nose impacted the soil and rotting manure below. Back on the ground I measured the distance the glider had moved out compared to a straight line down. Noting these distances and the 15 and 25 foot drop heights I now had three points on a parabolic curve and the basis for comparing gliders and wing forms and for calculating what the vertical height should be to accomplish a horizontal landing. This was fun! Much better than a video game. But, again of course, unknown to me at the time, other youngsters were engaged in simple experiments that eventually created the computer revolution many of us now use, myself included as I type away on a laptop.

One day, when Roger was out on our farm and we were wending our way through the day and needing a diversion from our futile efforts of coming up with a satisfactory rocket, we decided we should make some whiskey. Why not? Companies made it. It is a manufacturing process, is it not? So, therefore we should be able to make our own. We knew our parents didn't want us in their own small supply. And this would be a way to drink some, to taste the forbidden fruit, so to speak, without needing to bother them, to upset their time schedule, with little things like parental rules.

Before implementation, knowledge was required. How very valuable libraries and encyclopedias are, Roger and I gathered what we could. Living on a farm I had ready access to clean small grains, oats were common, some barley was available, some wheat was still being mixed into oat seedings for some lost reason, and corn was abundant in any farmers corn crib, although our recipe did not include any of the latter. We mixed up our concoction with water and some yeast from mother's kitchen and while it fermented went about the construction of our still.

One-quarter inch copper tubing lay available in a coil in the old toolshed, left over from Dad's hooking up the living room oil heater to an outside 50 gallon tank. A metal funnel was placed over the top of a Folgers tin coffee can, with its small end crimped tightly to the copper tubing and served as the boiler. My little green Coleman butane camp stove was our heat source. The tubing was coiled through a 5 gallon bucket of cool well water and was the condenser. Our still site, rather than being hidden in the woods like some southern moonshine operation, besides that we didn't have any suitable woods, was in the upper story of the machine shed, in the same location where Dad stored the end gate broadcast seeder. It was a remote site which Dad only ascended once a year to get the seeder so was deemed safe enough for our illicit project. Besides that we could run our still no matter what the weather as we had a dry roof overhead.

With fermentation complete and my parents gone for a few hours Roger and I climbed up to our still and commenced the run. Being only very amateur tinsmiths and metal workers our biggest problem was the escaping steam from several poorly-made joints and seams once we had our mash mix up to boil. We were in danger of running out of hands as we struggled to hold our collection bottle under the dripping end of the copper line while frantically pulling handkerchiefs from our pockets to wrap around the loose joints in an attempt to seal them off and simultaneously risk scalding and burning ourselves from the heat and escaping steam while holding all in place, plus manually controlling the temperature setting of the stove. Grinning and bearing our way through the pain and complexity, we at last managed to fill our bottle with crystal clear unknown proof Iowa made moonshine. How proud we were.

Volumetrically, our southern competitors did not have to worry about us competing in their supply line. Roger and I collected about 2-4 ounces of whiskey which we put into one of my mother's empty food coloring bottles. We knew aging and oak were important to the total process so I inserted several slivers of clean oak into our bottle and tucked it away for aging and maturation. The hiding place, perfectly secure from any prying parent or my dog, Tawny, was behind the cupboard in the Summer Kitchen inside the wall space where I had managed to loosen one board. Even if one opened the cupboard door, a rare likelihood, and moved the storage boxes to look at the wall, one could still not readily perceive the wall board could be lifted out. It was essentially as good a hiding location as what my brother had when he crawled far under the concrete foundation of the corn crib and inserted a personally hand built wooden treasure box into the recesses between the supporting joists. I had found his secret some years after he had forgotten about it, but being a good brother, never revealed its location to anyone. Till now, that is. Secrets too can have an expiration date.

At last, months later, the oak slivers had changed the color of our whiskey to an aesthetically pleasing soft golden tan. We sniffed the mildly aromatic wonder, we admired the beauty of our work, we brought our lips and tongue to the bottle and tasted our product, and our conservative fear values took hold of our danger seeking restless side. We tucked the bottle back in its hiding place, and eventually poured it away on the ground. Apparently the challenge of making whiskey meant a lot more to us than the drinking of it. In the matter of the primary challenge, we had succeeded.

Roger and I continued our research on appropriate fuels and small rocket design. We zeroed in on zinc dust and powdered sulfur as the best fuel. Nozzle fabrication for the engine was hard packed clay. At the back of a science magazine I had found an advertisement for a chemical catalog and had sent for it, then ordered our selection of chemicals in the quantity and grain size configuration we had chosen. The absence of heavy regulations for shipping and who was ordering the product in the late 1950's made this quite simple and my parents did not closely follow what I was up to. My life till then as a good little boy was paying off.

Before the rocket fuels had arrived I discovered some lovely long slender wooden rods of about one-quarter inch square cross-section which Dad had sawn off the edges of the tongue-and-groove siding he was using in the remodeling of the chicken house. I commandeered the rods, sawed four of them to a uniform four foot length, and inserted them vertically into holes I had drilled in the center of a stout three foot square base constructed from two by fours and pieces of one inch lumber. The combined assembly then became the launch pad for our rocket. The four vertical rods would hold the initial upward flight of our rocket by containing the rocket body, one rod between each of the four fins we were using on the rocket. It was a beautiful launching platform, robust enough for the initial four feet of upward momentum, uniform fresh cut pine wood coloration, the delicate rods thrusting upward tentatively yielding slightly to our motions as Roger and I picked up the launcher and admired its construction and thought of its future utility.

At last the big day had arrived, launch day for our rocket. After months of experimentation starting with the little paper match rockets, months of learning and planning, weeks of acquiring the chemicals and rocket parts, days of rocket and launch pad construction, we were ready. Roger was able to come out to our farm one afternoon and we walked out to the pasture launch area carrying all our menagerie of pieces, wires, switch, launcher, rocket, fuse as the sun wended its slow summer way toward the western horizon of corn and oat fields, and the tree shadows on the pasture bluegrass slowly lengthened. It was a quiet and calm afternoon, perfect for launching our special creation.

We set the launch pad down in a flat area as far away as our 50 feet of old television antenna wire would allow us to still nestle into the safe confines of the old erosion ditch leading from our farm dump. From this point we could duck down below the edge of the dirt during our countdown. It was a rocket launch; you have to have a countdown. Fifty-four years later Roger was still using a countdown as we were launching water-filled pop bottles from a trebuchet I had built during my retirement on our Wisconsin farm. I was touched to note the tradition continuing. At the rocket launch pad we inserted a green cannon fuse through the rocket nozzle into the engine fuel cavity. Next we applied and taped an electrical resistance heating element to some exposed powder within the end of the fuse protruding from the engine. The heating element in turn was wired to our long length of antenna wire. This sequencing was necessary because the battery powered heating element was too weak to ignite our fuel mixture but the cannon fuse would become the high heat source needed for final ignition of the zinc sulfur mixture. Then we carefully lowered the rocket and ignition assembly into the hand crafted launcher. After a final check of connections and potential flight path we retreated to our revetment in the erosion ditch where we attached the wire ends to our switch and battery system.

"All systems ready, Roger? All systems go, Gary." We were anxious to see how high the rocket went and were ready with a visual protractor to spot the angle of the peak of the flight. With our recent new-found trigonometry expertise taught by Mr. Gerber, we could calculate the maximum height of the flight path. Roger counted down, "ten, nine, eight, seven, ...". Immediately after "one", he threw our switch and we waited for the ignition sequence. After a few long seconds we looked at one another, possibly uttered a "wha..?", were just about to raise our heads and look down range at our launcher, when "KABOOM!!", the loudest damned explosion we ever had the personal pleasure of attending, smashed into our ear drums, and resonated down the creek valley, the echo bouncing off our distant barn and reinforcing the torrent of sound careening in our skulls as we attempted to reason out what had just happened.

The lovely launcher was a total loss, a black charred cavity in its heavy wooden base, the four slender rods in hundreds of tiny shards. Rocket parts were even tinier; I don't recall collecting any pieces of the rocket. Our disappointment at not attaining flight status for our rocket was quickly exceeded by our thrill at witnessing what had just happened and being personally responsible for such a fine exhibition of power and noise. Gathering up what few pieces remained we eventually walked home and conjectured our nozzle opening was too small or had become clogged by fuse remnants. Time marched on, our interests diversified, the launcher was gone, we sought more time with girls, Roger and I each got our driver's license, and we never got back to the field of amateur rocketry. But it was great fun during the process. And we ended on a dramatic note. When I saw Roger again last year he told me how he can still replay and hear the resounding explosion of our rocket coursing through the valley. If two friends can make a fond memory that lasts more than five decades, you cannot say our rocket did not succeed.

On the Hunt

Incrementally, during those fast passing years of my youth, I became a more proficient hunter and each autumn I would look forward to the start of small game seasons and pheasant hunting. Perhaps more by tradition than from a deep underpinning of biology, pheasant season then in Iowa always opened on Veteran's Day. There were more pheasant-hunters in Iowa in the 1950's than there are now, and the opening was always a much anticipated event by those individuals who engaged in the sport. The legal bag limit per day was three male Ring-necked Pheasants by any single hunter. Deer were still a rarity in Iowa then and there was no local season for deer. Squirrels and rabbits were considered "easy" game to shoot compared to the explosive eruption of a pheasant powering out of tall grass or weeds or corn. Pheasants were an Iowan's "Big Game". Plus they were a tasty exotic treat to serve at the supper table.

The available armament for my hunting leaned against the chimney in one corner of our kitchen. I had worked my way up from: first the Red Ryder lever action B-B gun, then the ultra-safe single shot, bolt action Remington 512 in .22 caliber (the safety mechanism was automatically engaged with each cycling of the bolt), then my brother's Remington 121 slide action .22 repeating rifle, and finally my brother's pheasant shotgun, the big Remington 870 pump action 12 gauge. By the time I was in high school Duane was married and living in the city of Omaha. He knew I would have more utilitarian application for his rifle and shotgun than he would, and left both at the farm for me to use in my hunting pursuits.

And, pursue I did. If I was quick, on some days after school, I could still get in a short hunt for pheasants before the season closed daily near sundown. During the weekend, on both Saturday and Sunday, I could roam far and wide in my neighborhood, my home turf. I could not yet drive, so all my hunting took place via walking from my home to where the game was. Our farm was only 80 acres, but I hunted over nearly 3000 acres, the great bulk of the five sections of land I knew best and had hunted and had walked over and had camped upon. Four sections of land were adjacent to the section I grew up and lived on. Within the total of those five sections I came to know each weedy draw, each grassed waterway, each cornfield, each creek rather intimately from an outdoorsman's point of view. I knew the relative likelihood of a pheasant jumping from each patch or a rabbit from each brush pile.

In all those walks, hunts, and camps, I was never accosted by a landowner, nor did I ever ask any landowner for permission to hunt or enter their land. It was a different time, a different neighborhood, and a different relationship of people one to another than exists now. Each landowner likely recognized who I was from a half mile away as he drove past on the road or worked his field. Each landowner had a personal relationship with my parents. Each landowner granted me, the neighborhood kid, Henry and Sophie's youngest boy, the right to be upon their land without personally saying so. It just was. It came with the times and the relationships of neighbors with whom I was growing up to possibly become one of them. Of the sons of the ten near neighbors I knew best, at least six eventually farmed the lands they grew up on. Profits of each farm went to the individual landowner, but, as long as no harm was done, the environmental richness and warmth of neighborliness was available to all who belonged. I feel very fortunate to have been one of them and to have been treated as such before I knew what my place in the neighborhood could be.

    I missed my fair share of shots at pheasants. The long full choke barrel my brother had specially selected for his pheasant gun, which I was now using, was not amenable to flushes of the birds close at hand, but, boy, could it reach out and nail the distant gliding pheasant as he winged away. I got better. I got quicker. I got more accurate. One weekend Duane and his new wife came home to the farm for a weekend visit. Duane wanted to go on a pheasant hunt with me and had borrowed a shotgun for his use while he allowed me to use his trusty pump Remington. We walked up the small south valley near the small creek heading to its origin on the other side of the road. Walking effortlessly with guns over our shoulders we knew we would not see a pheasant until after we crossed over the road to the neighbor's land climbing first what we called the high grade. Stepping across the road to gaze upon the draw in which both Duane and I had once trapped pocket gophers when it was a pasture, we saw the change in farming and tilling practices as we looked down upon a mass of tall hemp and ragweed and corn stubble on both sides of the waterway, and prepared ourselves.

Guns were dismounted from their casual carry position. We crossed through the nearby open field gate and gripped stock and forearm of our weapons in ready-to-aim position as we got closer to what we sensed was active pheasant cover and separated ourselves from one another slightly. All of a sudden, typical of pheasants sensing danger, "cuck, cuck, whirr!" burst forth out of the cover in front of us and several hens along with several cock pheasants first rose nearly straight up, then began to quickly wing away. Immediately discerning the legal males from the hens both our guns flew up to take sight on our quarry. Hesitating just a moment, I allowed Duane first shot on this hunt because I regarded him as my guest, the person who accompanied me, and tagged along, instead of what historically had been our roles where I was the little brother accompanying him. Duane shot. And missed. In as much time as it took me to know he had missed, I fine-tuned my aim, and fired, "Bam!". That pheasant went down in a tumble of floating feathers. While seeing that bird fall I saw another cock still within range of the full choke barrel, while I was automatically cycling the pump, bringing a fresh shot shell into the chamber. Sighting on that bird while locking in the front motion of the slide mechanism, I reaffirmed my grip on the gun, and fired again, "Bam!" and my second shot took down the second cock pheasant. Calm gradually returned as the sound of gunshots echoing in the valley ceased and we saw the remaining pheasants far out of range now, winging silently up the south hill and descending into some standing corn awaiting harvest.

Duane looked at me, smiled with pride at his little brother, and said, "That's good shooting, Gary!". Bagging two pheasants after Duane had missed felt good, but better yet, was being the subject of his complimentary praise while he conveyed a somewhat subdued amazement at how far I had come in my hunter prowess since he was last able to witness my capabilities. I felt as though the mantle of family hunter had been passed from him to me. It felt good. And I felt older. I always kept my big brother on a pedestal above me, but he made me feel at that moment that we could be equals.

In the late 1950's deer hunting was not something Iowa hunters did in Iowa. At that time there just were not enough deer in Iowa to justify liberal seasons nor was there much chance of the Iowa sportsman being successful in his home state. To hunt deer, an Iowa hunter would choose instead to travel to Minnesota or Wyoming or Colorado. Our cousin, Delane, being as much a sportsman as my brother, wanted to hunt deer and had procured a Winchester Model 70 bolt action rifle in .270 caliber for this purpose. One day my family was visiting him at their farm south of Holstein and Delane and Duane wandered out to their pasture to sight in Delane's new weapon and to get used to how it operated. I had just passed somewhat beyond my youthful B-B gun stage and wandered with them as the little kid tagging along anxious to watch and see a high-powered rifle in action. I was too young to shoot Delane's gun that day but the activity very much impressed me with the noise, the reach, the recoil, the power, and I wanted somehow someday to be like Delane and have my own high-powered rifle. Seeing those mounted ungulate heads in Bill Sorensen's clothing store downtown and knowing they were taken with rifles very much like the one Delane showed us, made me want a high-powered rifle of my own.

For the next half dozen years after seeing Delane try out his .270, I *con*tinued to read Jack O'Conner's hunting stories in Outdoor Life Magazine, collect gun literature, study ballistics charts, dream of shooting my own big game, and look at the gun pages in the various catalogs of those days. And then, there in the pages of the latest Montgomery Ward catalog was my opportunity: a military war surplus British Enfield No. 4, Mark 1, in .303 British caliber, available for $11.95. This amount was nicely within the realm of my cash savings tucked into one of the drawers in my bedroom. Some of the readily available surplus military firearms of the day had very peculiar and rare calibers but I already knew both Remington and Winchester carried the .303 British ammunition. I didn't ask my parents. Deeming myself old enough for the decision, I filled out a catalog order blank, took my cash to the post office and mailed off the envelope with enclosed money order.

About a week later, two long toots of the car horn of our local postal delivery man let me know he had just left a package at our mailbox located at the end of our farm lane, the package being too big to insert into the mailbox. I walked out, collected the mail and the long cardboard shipping box from Montgomery Ward, and knew I was now the proud owner of a high-powered rifle, actually my very first personal gun, all the other weapons I used being the possessions of other members of my family. All very easy and very convenient at that time. Due to current social issues, due to the terrible deeds which have been done by terrible souls, due to revised codified laws of both the nation and most states, what I had done so casually is now totally impossible. Mom asked what was in the package. I told her I bought a rifle. End of discussion. I had a blessed rural childhood in a simpler age.

I took my package to the lightly used and weather-tight Summer Kitchen, placed it on the old table there, and eagerly removed the contents. I could barely discern I had received a rifle as the entire gun was thoroughly wrapped in a bulky translucent film of tough plastic sheet. After taking off this outer layer and a waxy brown paper beneath that I discovered the rifle was entirely covered, wood stock as well as metal parts, in a slime of sticky cosmoline, placed there over a decade ago to protect it from degradation and corrosion. You never can tell what the future will bring. The previous owners, the British government, having already cycled through two world wars, had been very cautious and had held this weapon and others like it, in long term storage in case of yet another war. My "new" rifle had been a left-over from World War II. Instead of war, given the vagaries of life, society, technology, and government and profit considerations, this rifle had made its way to an Iowa farm boy.

Over the next year or so I put in a lot of time and attention to that British military weapon. I cleaned off the cosmoline with lots of dry rags and gasoline and gun oils. The rifling of the barrel was in prime condition. The wood stock was in very good condition. Having been originally manufactured in 1944, the rifle had likely seen little if any battlefield use. I removed the military sights, filed down the bayonet attachment protrusions to blend in the contour, vigorously used steel wool to polish the receiver and barrel, re-blued the areas where I had removed metal, and installed a new Lyman front ramp and sight, and a rear peep sight. I retained the front fore end stock but cut it down to sportier length, sanded, contoured, and hand oil-finished the walnut to match the coloration of the original. I ordered two white diamond shaped plastic inlays, popular for hand finished and sporterized rifles at the time, and inlaid them myself on either side of the wood housing the magazine. I replaced the rear straight handle military stock with a walnut butt-stock ordered from Fajen's in Missouri which came rough-finished and included the raised cheek pad and pistol grip hand hold. I sanded the wood butt-stock, smoothed it, sanded again, and when finally satisfied with the grace, form, rounded edges, and yes, physical beauty of my work, I hand-rubbed the stock down with natural linseed oil and color-matched the newly mounted rear stock with the original front forearm stock. Very nice. I now had a good-looking high-powered rifle capable of taking down most North American big game. It looked in overall appearance very much like Delane's or Jack O'Conner's rifles, but was much more affordable, and had the added pride advantage of being very much my own hand-made product.

I shot at targets with my Enfield now and again, showed it to some of my friends and let them shoot it. Some months I took it with me to my college dorm room, just to have it around. There weren't a lot of guns at college then, but some of us had them and sometimes went target shooting for entertainment on a weekend. Forty years after I retrieved my first rifle from the mailbox at the end of our Iowa farm lane I used it to kill the single biggest buck deer I have ever seen while holding a rifle and having a deer license in hand. The deer had 17 points and was trailing several does through the brush and hardwoods of the bluff above me on our farm in Wisconsin. Now when I see the mounted head on our stairwell wall, I can see not only the details of that hunt in November of 2000, but I can see a teen-aged boy on an Iowa farm re-crafting a surplus military weapon to take with him into an unknown future, and I sit here marveling at seeing the whole picture backward in time, while simultaneously knowing the boy couldn't see what memories the rifle could still be providing 40 years hence.

Self-Propelled

Shortly before my 16th birthday, the legal age in Iowa for being able to drive un-restricted of destination, my father presented me with a used 1954 Ford car for my use. I was stunned. He hadn't discussed his plans with me nor did I have any input into his decision. But I was certainly pleased and had no objections. The car had been repainted to a two-tone red and white by the original owner, and was slightly modified with the addition of small fins, so popular in car design at that time, on each rear fender. The fins and color pattern certainly made it a unique and individualized car, but at the same time slightly embarrassed me by being too non-traditional. I didn't let those mixed feelings stop me from very much liking having that car and adopting it as my own, washing and waxing it in the summers on the lawn west of the house under the Elm shade. It had a six-cylinder engine with straight stick overdrive transmission. V-8's were popular at the time and coveted by any teenage boy but maybe Dad wanted the 6-cylinder to keep me from any late night racing he might have heard other older teenage boys of the area were engaged in. Pulling out from the stop sign on Highway 59 and then going as fast as possible, a popular competition was to see what speed the car could attain by the time you got to the first cemetery gate on cemetery hill north of Holstein. Outclassed by the V-8's, it was a competition I didn't have to enter. I was getting very involved in more after-school sports practicing and I think Dad saw having my own car as freeing up his time and responsibilities to me. Now I would be able to make my own schedules and get home for chores after the football, track, or basketball practicing was done. What I saw was a lot more freedom to pursue my own selection of off-farm activities and fewer time restrictions on when I could engage in those activities.

Having access to one's own car was a bit of a status symbol and allowed me to join a minority of high schoolers who drove their own cars after they were old enough to do so. I quickly got very used to being self-propelled and from then on drove myself to school each day, parking on the south side of the school gymnasium near where Bryan parked each day in his '55 Ford and Dennis parked his '57 Ford. After school, after whatever practicing for the day was complete, before driving home, I would stop at Stolley's drug store, the official teen hang-out. Wyleen would be behind the counter serving up cherry cokes or whatever one's favorite might be. The white soapstone counter had traditional silver soda and water fountains with manual control on top of them. Wire chairs surrounded round wire-legged tables in the front center of the store, wire-wrapped stools were lined up for perching at the counter. I don't remember much sitting though, too restrictive, many of us stood so we could move about our friends, greet and josh whoever might come in next. Bryan would stop in, Mike would be there, maybe Danny, maybe Roger, Paul, Mary, other members of the gang. It was a convivial setting allowing pleasant winding down after our physical exertion. There was some flirting, the normal teen age teasing, done with good humor. After 15 to 20 minutes of catching up on the latest news and rumors of school and our friends, one by one we would depart and get on home to our responsibilities.

One night a number of us had gathered at Stolley's for our normal drop in and adieu of the day. The main subject of discussion was the upcoming speech each of us would have to make within a few days as part of our English studies and beginning attempts at public speaking. Some of us had not yet selected a subject for our speech, others were nearly done with their preparation. I was standing near the candy rack, picked up a wrapped chocolate covered marshmallow Easter bunny, and in jest, carelessly said, "Maybe I should just give a speech on this candy bar". Mary jumped at the opportunity to perhaps corner me and forthrightly challenged me by betting me I couldn't do it, and that furthermore I wouldn't do it. Well! Not having any better ideas for subject material, I rose to her challenge, and before giving it any further rational thought concluded her bet was on. I have to admit it was probably not the best speech of the semester but it was received in good humor by the rest of the class students, and most importantly, by Mrs. Christie, our teacher. She smiled gently at my presentation with a bit of a question mark lurking there on her forehead as I reviewed the calorie count, ingredients, nutritional value, selection and color choice of the wrapping, its ephemeral appearance once a year, and its texture and taste. Who said you can't make a speech out of a marshmallow bunny?

Having a car, of course, greatly facilitated my big romance with Judy which we had been developing since 7th grade. Now instead of only attending the after-game dances we could also take in an occasional movie, drive around town together cruising up and down Main Street, making a U-turn at each end, and cruising up and down Main Street again. Judy's mother and I got along OK, Judy's father scared me, so I made sure to honor whatever curfew he had specified for Judy. With Judy being a farm kid too, it was nice I didn't have to park on some gravel road with her like some of my high school pals who didn't date country gals had to do with their girlfriends, and the consequent risk of getting rousted by teasing comrades cruising the same road or the local sheriff patrol. Judy and I always had the privacy of her farm yard when I pulled up and parked near their kitchen door and in front of their garage for our good night activity of hugs and kisses then known as "necking", the term fundamentally describing the expected limitations of that era. Their shaggy dog generally honored our wish for privacy once he came to the car door to remind himself whose car this was.

The relationship between Judy and I had by now been cultured through a handful of years and we were both comfortable with it and our relationship to the other. It was based partly on, obviously, the hormone-driven attraction to the opposite sex, but because of the amount of time we had spent together and how well we had come to know one another, included the more fundamental aspects of having a close friend, one you could trust, a person to share thoughts and conversations with, and then, perhaps even consider living our lives together out there in the now near future of post-high school. But ours was a relationship also based on two features which did not necessarily promote maturation to a self-actualized adulthood.

One is that ours was a relationship based partially on convenience. It had become convenient for us not to have to wonder who might ask us out on a date or to the next dance. We already knew the answer, so we encountered none of the risk-taking development of some of our peers who did not have a steady friend of the opposite sex. In the manner of learning how to be comfortable with more of a cadre of the opposite sex, we had become lazy and complacent. It was easy and non-challenging to just lean on the other. This added to our comfort level of being teenagers, but did not expand our capabilities of understanding other teenagers because a lot of our available time was spent with each other, and we were spending less time with others who might have furthered our personality differentiation.

The second feature which mislead us but felt comfortable, rather like a pleasant drug limiting our ability to stretch socially, was the addictive cachet of being one of the "steady couples" in school. The fact we were a steady couple meant we were in a minority which was accorded a certain fixed status level within our teenage world by others. This in turn meant we could feel perhaps better or unique from others who did not have a steady boyfriend or girlfriend for our having an established relationship as a couple when in fact we were no better or different from all of our peers. Any level of arrogance is unbecoming and potentially dangerous. Of course, both of these features are only recognized many years later as I ponder the past from an analytical perspective. At the time we were unaware of either and were quite content in our relationship being who and what we were.

    After all we classmates had gone through the annual tradition of ordering and receiving our class rings, I wore mine long enough to call it my own, several weeks or months, before electing to give it to Judy. My giving, and her accepting, my ring was the physical mark that we were now "Going Steady". This terminology was a potential prelude to an engagement ring and future marriage although by no means was this planned nor did this necessarily occur in all those high school incidences of couples who had done the same. Some persevered to marriage, most split apart as life carried them down paths unrecognized at the beginning. The receiver of the ring would wrap the band with adhesive tape to shrink its size and enable the ring to be held on her finger. Another option was to wear it on a chain around her neck as a necklace. Going steady with the giving of a class ring meant each was committed to the other and automatically meant, within the teen-age social context of the time, you would not date other individuals. Going steady bonded and cemented the relationship between the two parties involved while simultaneously declaring to others that an enhanced couple relationship had been established for all to know. I think each of us was proud and pleased to have taken this step, but, as with many other couples, we had no idea where it might lead us.

One Sunday, when Duane was home from Omaha for the weekend, my family drove up to Meriden to visit my grandmother Ruhser and my Uncle Clarence. We took the back road through Quimby and while headed there the subject of what I would do when I grew up and graduated somehow came up. I remember quite clearly that Duane turned to me and said, "You should be an engineer." I think it was the only time anyone had ever advised me what vocation I should be engaged in as an adult. I did not have the faintest idea of what an engineer could be at that time. To me, the only engineer I had heard of up till then was the fellow driving the train. Looking back I can see Duane had assessed my school grades, knew what I was good at, and based on his Korean War experiences as a member of the 841st Engineer Aviation Battalion, had a much better comprehension of engineering as a vocation than I did. Duane's casual comment had little meaning for me until several years later when I was engaged in engineering studies at Iowa State University. It was one of those instances where a person outside yourself recognizes who you could be before you yourself do. Now his comment makes sense. When Duane made it I think I only made note of it for its peculiarity.

Law enforcement, keeping kids on the straight and narrow, maintaining a peaceful and quiet community can be a challenge. Holstein seemed to do it with aplomb and astute application of jurisprudence, with just the right force, not too little, in which case wrong keeps being done, not too much, in which case rebellion makes the problem worse. In my case, it was just right, just as it was for so many others in a small community where caring adults exert thoughtful pressure fully cognizant of the implications for the social outcome.

Some of the older kids who attended the same high school as I did had dual exhausts behind their V-8 engines in the cars they drove and the vehicle could emit either a gentle rumble or a loud charge of power made manifest through noise. Given the modest six cylinders in front of my single muffler, I was jealous and sometimes yearned to be amongst the rebellious group who could proclaim their independence and quasi-adulthood through the singular act of being behind the steering wheel with foot on the accelerator as they rode atop dual, straight through mufflers and a powerful V-8 engine. Wasn't that what being a grown-up was all about? Oh, what peculiar visions the youth can have as they work through the transitory life of a teen ager.

My exhaust pipe had developed a large rust hole in front of the muffler. With some of the exhaust gases bypassing my muffler, the noise emitted from my little six was rapidly approaching the excessive level and I grew fond of it, in spite of it still not sounding like a smoothly cycling symmetric V-8. I and my father couldn't afford to replace the front exhaust pipe at that time but while under the car examining the problem, I noted I could cut an an empty tin can with both ends removed and wrap it around the pipe, bind it in place with two stout metal hose clamps, and the leakage problem would be corrected, and the engine exhaust would again pass through the muffler and the sound be appropriately reduced. I also noted I could cleverly turn on and turn off the loud noise by sliding the tin can fore and aft, covering or uncovering the rust holes in the exhaust pipe, and while reaching under the car with my trusty screwdriver, I could do that whenever and wherever I wanted. So, I would drive to town on a date with Judy or driving around with my pals and stop and uncover the exhaust pipe to "make noise" while I was in town cruising the streets. Then, before I took Judy home to her parent's house or before I entered my own farm yard, I would stop and slide the can over the rust hole and reduce the noise level.

After several weeks of making noise with my car, accelerating up and down city streets, easing off on the accelerator and getting that backfire staccato burst, the local gendarme, our town policeman, was stopped by my car awaiting me after school one day. He explained the mayor of Holstein, Mr. Ernie Carlberg, would like to see me at a specific appointment time several days hence, at his home. Did I know where that was? "Yes, I do, sir." In the last several years of high school I had fortunately learned the blessed simplicity of saying "sir" to those in authority and discovered it was quite helpful at times like these.

Not having been told exactly what this meeting was about, but with trepidation in hand, I presented myself at the Mayor's front door. Upon my knocking the Mayor came and let me in and kindly guided me toward the back of his home to what I presumed was his den or home office. I'm sure he must also have had a desk or office at City Hall. I am also sure he must have chosen his home as our meeting place quite volitionally with a sense this was the appropriate locale for what he was about to say. Mr. Carlberg bantered in friendly tones for a few sentences. I responded curtly but politely, before he got to his main point. It seems he and the police had received several complaints about an excessively loud red and white car with short tail fins, and the police had surreptitiously confirmed the complaints as justifiable. The Mayor asked if I would confirm these findings. I did. Then he outlined for me, rather briefly, not what I had done as being wrong, but why he and other responsible adults like him such as my parents, my teachers, my coaches, my neighbors, believed I would mend my ways. In other words, he caused me to think about living up to the expectations the community had for me, and that I was a better person than I was exhibiting through my actions. The Mayor did not notify my parents of the meeting between him and me. There was no need to do so.

Every few years, an exceptionally heavy rain would drench our area of Ida County and cause Ashton Creek, which my family referred to as the Big Creek, to go out of its banks and flood the adjacent pastures, including our own and our nearest neighbors. The farm immediately adjacent to our east border was owned by Florence Kastner. A new renter was occupying the farm and the neighbor came down to our line fence to join my Dad and myself as we worked on repairing the flood's damage to the fence where it crossed the creek. Dad, of course, being a life-long resident of the Holstein area, knew Lester Ellerbusch and I recognized him as being a member of our church, but I had never really spoken in conversation to Lester. By the occasion of our meeting in the pasture I had grown several more inches, put on a few more pounds of muscle and had recently gotten my driver's license and the red and white Ford. Lester was easy-going, courteous, and often wore a gentle grin that exemplified his spirit.

Apparently my stature as a strong and able teen ager, a near neighbor, and Hank's son had been on Lester's mind as he contemplated the work to be done on the land he now occupied. Several weeks after our pasture fence work he stopped in at our house to speak with Dad and me, and offered me the job of being his hired hand for the coming summer, if that was alright with both my father and me. Once I got the gentle nod of approval from my father, I immediately accepted, knowing as I now did that I would likely go on to college after high school and savings were important to that goal. I had been following in my brother's footsteps helping neighbors with day jobs of stacking hay bales or shelling corn, but being Lester's hired farmhand would mean a steady income every work day instead of just occasionally. This would be my first "full-time job", well, for three months anyway, eight to ten hours per day, five to six days per week, at one dollar per hour. I was very pleased. It was a fair wage and it would mean a tidy sum in the bank when I returned to high school in September.

I was a little nervous as I drove the one mile to Les's farm the first morning of my summer break from school. I parked my Ford close to their house yard fence under the spreading limbs of an old Elm which would shade my car during the hottest periods of each day, and stepped out not knowing exactly what I was getting into. Les came out of the house with his characteristic smile and greeted me in his "Aw, shucks" manner, described what needed to be done that day, what he would do, what I would do, "if that was OK" by me, and I immediately felt more at ease. I wanted to please this good man, my first "Boss", and, as it turned out, the best "Boss" I ever had in my long vocational career, which included dozens of bosses.

I no longer remember what we did that first day, but I remember many of my assignments from Les. They were often the typical ones of running a farm operation in the days of the early 1960's. Farms were still very diverse in function and operation. Lester and his wife ViLois, a wonderful woman, had a few chickens but those were generally the responsibility of ViLois and their children. There were cattle and hog fences to build and maintain, hay to cut and bale, hay bales to put away in the barn and stack neatly for feeding out the following winter, cattle to sort for sale or weaning, hogs to feed, corn to cultivate, oats to combine, weeds to chop or spray with herbicide.

Lester's biggest tractor, far more powerful and modern than any I had driven up until then was a diesel Case model 830. It had an engine accelerator one could control with your foot, like driving a car, instead of the manual fixed speed hand-set throttle I was used to. The Case had power steering which meant you didn't have to fight the steering wheel to set the course direction. It had multiple hydraulic cylinder actuators and three-point hitch capability. I was used to having three forward gears to choose from in the tractors I drove for Dad at home. This Case had more gears than I had fingers on my hands. It had four big cylinders, 50 percent more power than any tractor I had ever driven. It was definitely a young man's dream tractor. I worried enough about doing the wrong thing with Lester's big investment that I was very cautious about driving that large tractor, but I cultured my familiarity with it and came to look forward to manning it the next time.

The Case exemplified Lester's modern farming practices. But Les also had a very old-fashioned side to his farming. He had several work horses he occasionally used for the fun of it. After he retired from active full-time farming he continued to dabble in work horses and was a skilled multi-horse hitch driver. While I worked for him he had one of the oldest still-functioning tractors in the area, an old Massey with a front-mounted, hand crank starting mechanism. He had this old Massey permanently wedded to an ungainly frame of metal beams and reinforcing welds and rod which, with long pointed beams of wood sticking out in front, like a giant multi-tined fork, made up his hay buck, used for stacking loose hay. I've looked back and reviewed my time as the hired man of the Ellerbusch's multiple times over the years and I always come back to two fond memories: one is how well and rightly they treated me, two is giving me the old fashioned experience of bucking loose hay up into stacks.

Lester and I went up to the gentle hill north of their place, a hill sloped gradually enough you can drive an old tractor anywhere you wish, but high enough you can look down upon the broad expanse of the Ashton Creek valley, and feel basically like you are on top of the local farming world. On top of that hill Lester had a large field of coarse Sweet Clover cut down at the peak of its golden yellow bloom. He instructed me how to operate his old hay buck, gave me several demonstrations of the actions I would be taking, where to put the stacks, what to watch out for, and he walked home leaving me there the rest of the afternoon to buck loose hay into haystacks that would shed the coming rains of autumn. If I could choose one farm job from a time machine to go back and do again, it would be bucking hay with Les's old tractor that afternoon. I thank Lester for the trust he had in me and the gift of performing that job for him.

On some days ViLois might bring a sandwich lunch to Les and me depending on where we were working and we would sit in the shade of the car or under a nearby tree and chow down. On most days I would join the family at their dining table in the house for the noon meal. The noon meals were always delicious and filling, ranging from fried chicken to meat loaf to pork chops to cold cuts on bread, and the conversation was cordial. On one of my earliest meals in the house Les asked me to "pass the bug juice", gesturing his finger as he did so with glass in the other hand. In spite of the visual signals I was totally mystified and thought perhaps I had not understood him. Bug juice? "Excuse me?" said I. "Pass me that bug juice, please." ViLois was smiling widely by now and rescued me by declaring her husband was referring to the colored juice drink, Kool-Aid, which was perched near my end of the table. I passed the Kool-Aid, now recognizing it by its new moniker established by Les. About four decades later I was driving through South Dakota and had refilled my truck with gasoline when I stepped into the service station for refreshments and discovered real "Bug Juice" for sale in that station's cold drink refrigerator. Some clever company was marketing a fruit flavored drink using "Bug Juice" as their brand name. I couldn't resist buying a package and then sending the empty wrapping medium, a coated cardboard box, to Les and ViLois via the mail and to tell them of old memories, and that Les had been right all along. There really is "Bug Juice".

My parents were born in 1904 and 1905. Lester and ViLois were born two decades later, actually in ViLois's case, two and a half decades later. Their more recent course through life gave them an entirely different perspective of living as a couple than the example which my parents had presented to me. The time I spent watching Les and ViLois that summer was my first exposure in spending more time than a casual visit with a younger set of adults than my parents. It was enlightening and illuminating to my vision of what a good marriage could be. My parents were but one generation removed from the mores and culture of the Old Country, the Germany of our ancestors. My parents had a good marriage, a long marriage, based on mutual respect and affection, but they were not demonstrably affectionate. The marriage I had the honor of witnessing between Lester and ViLois was young and vibrant, they could tease and have fun with one another, they were more than merely affectionate - they were mutual friends and shared alike in their common world of a single union. I respected what I had learned about marriage in my own home but Les and ViLois provided a new and good example of a married relationship for me to attempt to emulate in my own unknown future.

    At the funeral of my best friend's father in Holstein, I had the pleasure of seeing Les and ViLois again. The years had marked each of us with Time's passage but we spoke with mutual fondness of the days when I was a farm kid, their hired man, in the days of Yore. ViLois remembers seeing me drive by their home each day as I journeyed to school in my red and white Ford, distinctive in her vision from a quarter mile away. What she remembered most was my morning punctuality, "Gary, I could set my kitchen clock by when you drove by each morning." Knowing now that a strong time sense is a potential marker of an engineer's mind frame, I suspect even she knew what I would someday become before I did.

    Another summer before college, I spent a number of weeks working for Eldon Blenner on his farm two miles north of ours. Eldon had been a good friend of my brother and both he and his wife were very affable. Eldon was the son of Bill and Lill Blenner and was then working the farm which Bill had farmed prior to moving to town. Lillian was my Dad's first cousin, once removed. Hence Eldon was my second cousin, once removed. I did not recognize Eldon as a relative at the time. All I knew was he was a good fellow, Lil was a member of my Mother's Let's All Go Club and served me lunch in the school cafeteria while Bill was a custodian of the school. It was fun for me to greet them at school as a neighbor kid who knew them outside of their school roles. The farm where I grew up is now owned and operated by Eldon's son and family. The circles of life and interconnectedness of the members of the Holstein community never cease to amaze me.

During that summer long ago Eldon had had a serious intestinal operation and was going to be physically incapacitated for a while. Fortunately, both for him and for me, he knew what he was getting into and arranged my employment with him before his operation. It was cultivating time, time to rip the weeds out of the new corn rows, and Eldon had a big Farmall tractor with a large cultivator mounted on it, where I spent a fair amount of my time while working for the Blenners. Our cultivator on our farm only handled two rows of corn whereas Eldon's was a 4-row cultivator, twice the mass, twice the coverage of what I was used to. But, once I got used to looking and covering four rows instead of two, it was still a very pleasant way to spend the day. The sun baked my shirtless bare upper body and the rows flowed smoothly through the corn shields as I guided the cultivator on path after path through the field. Some nights of those days when I had cultivated a lot I would dream visions of the corn plants gliding endlessly between the shields, because I had seen so much of them while I was awake. On those long days the engine purred beneath my control and idle thoughts pattered through my head as I steered through the waving green corn plants thrusting higher to maturity and gained the satisfaction of completing one field and then moving on to the next.

And then, suddenly, with summer passing quickly in the farming world, it was time to cut and bale the hay. There are few smells better than a field of hay, freshly cut, drying in the sun, the odor wafting to the nose, bringing with it memories of summers past, other hay fields, and the pleasant task of engaging in sustaining your cattle through another year with bounteous harvest. Eldon was able to walk now but still could not mount a tractor nor lift a bale, so he had called in his good neighbors and with them I engaged in the yearly task of cutting, raking, baling, loading the bales on hay wagons, just like the flat rack Judy and I had first kissed on, and then unloading the bales at the barn, putting the bales into an elevator for passage to the mow, and stacking them in the haymow for Eldon's disbursement to his cattle in the winter coming.

At the end of the day, bales safely in the barn, protected from any coming rains, the machinery parked for storage, it was time for the hay crew to celebrate their accomplishment, a good job well done. With Eldon on the way to recovery, he was able to join us out on his lawn and offered his earnest thanks to each of us for all the help rendered in this community effort. We neighbors, friends and relatives, sprawled about, sitting, reclining, on the shaded grass near the house while Eldon and Barb, his wife, brought out some end-of-the-day refreshments, meaning beer, a pleasant selection and abundance of beer.

I was then at that tender in-between age of being a hard working farm hand, driving myself from job to job, darn near an adult, but not quite, and not legally allowed to drink beer in Iowa at that time. Defining my sufficient maturity for themselves, the neighbors and Eldon concluded I had by then earned the right to engage in an adult's post-work refreshment. At this point, I had some practice on the back roads late at night in drinking a little beer, thanks to a kind, but older friend, and so accepted their exhortations to join in this customary winding-down exercise. It was my first "public" drinking and I couldn't have picked a better bunch of fellows to do it with. Under their gentle tutelage and teasing I joined the ranks of the neighborhood farm crew and tossed down a few brews, narrowly recognizing my alcoholic capability in time to still be able to drive safely home. I believe I was the last neighborhood kid to have the pleasure and rewards of working a farm job within the context of the old crews that had once gathered across all these farms in helping one another survive and thrive to the coming year in a spirit of mutual engagement. I am proud to have been among them.

Naturally, the decision of whether to smoke, confronted many young men, older boys, kids, whatever we were. I was among the group who answered, "Well, sure, of course I will." The only things being in the way were our parent's strong disapproval, and the fact that it was illegal to buy tobacco at our age. But that didn't stop those of us enterprising enough to find a way to engage in obtaining the product and practicing a bit. Even though, even then, in the 1950's we knew there was a strong link between smoking and bad health, a fact the rest of the country could not unilaterally admit for another 3-4 decades. A neighbor, several miles away had died dreadfully of lung cancer. He also had smoked several packs of cigarettes a day. I remember my parents' sad-faced condemnation of what he had done to himself. Even that didn't dissuade me from the goal to engage in smoking.

In the late 1950's Phillip Morris's Marlboro Man was riding the range, and I wanted to ride with him, cigarette dangling from lips as we each would sit astride our horse. Pall Malls, Camels, Winstons, Salems – there was a whole world of tobacco waiting to be sampled. My father used to smoke but had quit by the time I came along, several of my uncles smoked, half the neighboring farmers smoked. It was a popular thing to do at the time. And, because it was officially restricted to adults, naturally a number of us wanted to test the practice to see what all the fuss was about. It might even make us into men, seemed that way anyhow.

A popular story told of smoking corn silk behind the barn. To me, that sounded decidedly crude and unworthy, so I cannot speak of its attributes. I can, however, recommend alfalfa stems. My pal, Brian Bruning and I were still several years shy of getting our driver's licenses and were still roaming the neighborhood by foot and bicycle, camping near the local creeks, catching chubs with fishing rod and worms. There were several abandoned barns and buildings in the neighborhood that we sometimes frequented for a short visit in a bad case of curiosity or to escape that quickly developed rain shower we hadn't counted on. On one of those visits we had climbed on some hay bales in a haymow to look out the open barn window at the secret vista before us and were gnawing on some stems of the alfalfa from the bale, much as anyone does who pulls a foxtail stem or stiff blade of grass to put between lips and teeth, mostly for the jauntiness of it.

One of us noticed the stems, properly broken off between leaf joints, were hollow and we could draw a small breath through the stem. Furthermore, held and drawn upon thusly, they rather looked like miniature cigarettes, mildly fragrant like tobacco, but a rich dried green coloration on the outside, instead of white paper. One of us had matches along in their pocket. Like they say, great discoveries come by chance and experimentation so we lit one, or several, up, and the alfalfa cigarette was born. Properly dried in the bale, hand selected for uniformity and texture, the best of the bunch burned like incense, the lighted glow just visible, and self-extinguishing if you didn't take a draw frequently enough. Very satisfying for both of us. And, oh, so foolish! In a barn?!

As an older child, on one of those very rare trips to a souvenir community and associated shops galore, I had purchased a miniature realistic looking briar pipe, right down to the distinctive wooden bowl and black pipe stem, except sized so that the briar bowl would only hold about one-half inch of a cigarette. The pipe had laid around in my souvenir collection in my bedroom for a few years, until Roger and I figured it was time to give it a try. In that time the tobacco companies still gave out samples of their brand of cigarette in attractively packaged units of four which an enterprising and observant young teenager could discover or come across, along a roadside ditch or discarded in a downtown community trash receptacle while yet fully wrapped and thus "safe to use". Also, in the absence of finding our own, Roger could occasionally lift one cigarette from his mother's unattended pack lying unguarded in their home, as she was a moderate smoker just when we needed her to be.

    Carefully preplanning our activity on one afternoon, Roger and I slipped out of the house and hiked up to the empty granary and sometimes livestock building up on the hilltop south of our farm. There never were any intruders, but being careful lawbreakers, an always opened window allowed us to monitor for approaching strangers. Much like a military hilltop revetment we could scan the surrounding countryside for approaching adults. We took the concealed pipe and the one cigarette we had brought and inserted a one-half inch section of the cigarette into the tiny bowl and lit up, taking turns passing the pipe back and forth until the tobacco was quickly used up. Ahh, so this is what smoking is all about! Very distinctive. And so we passed from being casual admirers to being secluded occasional users. Being careful to chew copious amounts of the chewing gum we had brought along and washing ourselves in the nearby creek afterwards, we headed home with the cocky attitude of having sampled at last the forbidden fruit. And got away with it.

Over the months that followed, a couple more training sessions were held between Roger and I as we advanced up to the cigarette held jauntily betwixt our fingers, tapping off the ash like professionals. The next goal was to kick back in the comfort of our family living room and puff away like normal adults, unfettered by the need to sneak off to abandoned buildings or hidden recessed corners in the deep eroded sections of the bed of the creek. Roger had come out for the day, perhaps we had been working on the rocket project or torturing a few mice, when my parents announced they were going to be away a number of hours visiting a relative. The weather was mild and my knowing the location of this relative assured Roger and I the luxury of several hours for experimentation followed by bodily cleansing, obfuscation of any potential clues, and decontamination of the area. We knew by then the superior sensing mechanisms parents possessed to ascertain transgressions by their children.

I fetched the powerful window fan, the fan of my wind tunnel experiments, from the upstairs storage, opened the north window of the living room, and mounted it in the opening, discharging outward. Next I opened the south kitchen windows, the kitchen door, and the west window of the living room. No sense in taking unnecessary risks by not having enough air movement. And Roger and I sat down in the living room in the normal comfort of a cozy easy chair and a relaxing sofa, kicked back our heels upon the linoleum floor with scattered rugs lying about, and lit up. Yes, sure, the screaming whine of the window fan on high speed setting was mildly distracting and meant we couldn't hear each other speak without shouting a bit, but, man, that was living. One cigarette done each, we snubbed them out, proceeded to the cleanup phase, and returned to what had been occupying us before my folks had left. Reviewing this situation over the gap of a half century strongly suggests Roger and I must have put in about 1.2 man-hours of labor each for preparation, dismantling, and cleaning in exchange for the ten minutes of "relaxed" smoking. It's difficult to understand the logic of a teen-ager, especially when that teen-ager was you.

Over the next several years as we approached high school graduation, I and some of my peers dabbled a bit in the art of smoking without picking it up as a habit until we journeyed on to college. The experimentation and trial runs of having a cigarette in most of our experiences was actually likely numbered in the single digits as opposed to a weekly event. We were assisted considerably in not adopting smoking as a daily pursuit by the powerful personality and admonitions of our football and track coach, Coach Russ Kraii, known to all of us boys at least, as not Mr. Kraii, not Russ, just "Coach". Coach wasn't a great teacher of the social studies courses he taught in the classroom but he was a hell of a coach, with numerous conference championships to his credit in football, track, and girls' basketball, frequently taking our girls to the state meet. Coach was tough, he was sincere, he was honest, and he exuded the personal demands that made you want to please him, and to work for the good of the team.

I was being exceptionally stupid one day. I had discovered I could hide a cigarette inside of a fountain pen with its writing guts removed and had foolishly shown my device to my buddy, Mike Brosamle, while we were in the school gymnasium locker facilities having finished showering and cleaning up after a vigorous practice session of football. Without thinking, rather the trademark characteristic of all teen-age boys it seems, Mike blurted out in jest, in a teasing but too-loud tone, "Ruhser, what are you doing with a cigarette!?" Truth be known, there wasn't a good answer to that question. I wasn't even using or smoking on any regular basis at all at that point. I just thought it was cool that the cigarette fit so nicely and silently in the concealed disguise of a pen. An emphatic, "Shhhhhush!!" was quickly blurted out between the lips of all the guys standing around Mike and I, and Mike quickly realized he might have been too loud. He was. Within a few seconds Coach had tumbled out of his office down the hall, followed by his cohort, Art Gerber, to ask all of us assembled, staring gape-faced in his direction, as to "What the hell is going on down here?"

Well, there was no good answer to that question either. None of us were quick enough or foolish enough to come up with a good lie. We all knew Coach would get to the bottom of things. For those of us still in the locker room our planned departures for home were put on hold by Coach as, like a good detective, he called us back into his office one at a time for a one on one inquisition. Coach was not one to let things lie and fester as he grabbed the bull by the horns and quickly got the facts from each of us as to whether we were smokers, if we had tried, how often we smoked, why we smoked. After the questions came a lecture for each of us, individually crafted for specificity to the boy/man sitting in front of him, and then ending somewhat rather like the admonition from the Mayor, Ernie Carlberg. Coach told each of us what he expected of us, and how, if we didn't live up to his expectations, we would be letting down the team, the school, the community. We could ruin ourselves, our own health if we wanted, but not, by god, on his watch, not while we were playing for him. It was fair, it was reasonable. I mended my evil ways while I worked and performed in sports activities for this well-intentioned man, our "Coach." Experimentation and sampling of smoking finished for the school year, I put future smoking intentions on hold until I graduated. Some communities, some school systems, some coaches at the time would have sent letters home to the parents for this major infraction of, unpublished, but implicit, rules. That did not happen where I grew up. Each boy/man and Coach had made a verbal commitment, a contract, during the inquisition. Coach deemed that was as far as it needed to go.

    I understand some people literally hate their experiences in high school. That was not the case for me. I enjoyed it immensely and have a lot of fond memories. My best classes, the ones I looked forward to, were any of the English classes taught by Mrs. Christie, the math classes taught by Art Gerber, and the science classes taught by Mr. McKnight. Each of those classes supported me well in my efforts as I made my way through engineering in college. I owe some of my writing skills to Mrs. Christie, wife of the superintendent of our school system, and to the journal project she had each of her students write. She even went out of her way to review and help me on an essay I had written one summer and entered into a writing contest. Mr. McKnight's mandatory insect and butterfly collection during our sophomore year was not much of a hit with any of us boys, but it provides good laughter 50 years later as those same boys gather for reminiscing and bragging rights as to which of us performed the worst during that exercise.

I enjoyed and went out for all three of the major sports, football, basketball, and track, each of the four years I was in high school. Although I was one of the tallest boys on the basketball team, I never quite figured out that sport and never mastered the jump shot so I was one of the worst players and spent a lot of bench time during the games. And that was OK by me. I didn't want to embarrass my team by flubbing up, and always felt my role in basketball was to support the good players by being there at the games with them. The best part about basketball for me was when the whole team was out there on the gym floor shooting baskets and loosening up before the game while we were wearing those cool looking warm-up suits.

Track and football were my favorite sports. It is hard to choose the best between them because track is an individual pursuit of excellence in tightly defined events, whereas football is a team contest relying very much on every individual performing his role in having the whole team excel as a unit. I loved the high hurdles. It was my premier event and I set several meet records which had not been broken for a number of years until I came along to add my name to the record books. As happens, by now, my name has been erased by other skilled athletes with their own training, attributes, and inimitable goal of setting new records to supplant those I once set. Along with some longer distance medley running, Coach also talked me into running the low hurdles and it was great fun to run them with Gary L. The low hurdles were his premier event and it was exciting for him and me to get first for him, and second for me, as we placed one-two in several track meets in the conference.

The teams before us, and the seniors when we were mere freshman, had set an impressive record in football in our Maple Valley football conference, winning the conference championship a number of times. A few rumors slung about northwest Iowa suggested those big-boned, tough, and hearty Germans from Holstein were unfairly bigger than average and the result of our being formidable opponents had its origins in the northern European stock of which we were made. Whatever. Coach made sure we knew our job on football game nights against the opposing team was to beat them and presented resounding reasons for doing so during each half-time speech. My team never lost a home game while we were in high school and won every football conference championship for all four years.

I played "right end" every year and during my senior year wore the number 13, which I then adopted as my lucky number, and woe to the short half backs from other teams who tried to get out around me on their way down field. Coach's admonition to me during defense was to "never let them get around you, always turn the play in to the rest of the line."

Passing the ball was not used very much at all in High School football in those years, particularly by us. Because we were, indeed, a big team, usually our players' weight out-ranked the opposition and we had the heaviest front line in the conference, our prime modus operando was to run the ball and fight and slog our way consistently down field. But, once in a while, Coach or our quarterback, would call for a pass in order to distract the opposing team from assuming they has us figured out, or, because things were in a rare state of getting desperate. One night on the home field each team was scoreless, neither team able to get across the goal line, when the opposing team finally got a touchdown. Holstein, my team, was behind. Not something we were used to. Time was running down when the word arrived in huddle, go for a long pass. This meant I would have to run downfield, give a fake turn, then hang a 90 degree bend, and be available as a possible recipient of the pass. The ball was hiked. I ran, faked, hooked, and waved my arms so Bryan could see me. He threw a lofty, long, somewhat wobbling pass, and I went for it. Bobbling the catch ever so slightly, I was able to catch the pass, see the goal line in sight, and head toward it. Too late, some defenders from the opposite team nailed me and I was hauled down. But we were as near to our goal as we had been all night. On the next play our fullback, Joe, got the ball from Bryan and quickly powered his way to the touchdown. Then we succeeded on our conversion for the extra point and thereby won the game as we held the other team off from any more touchdowns. I didn't make the winning touchdown, but successfully catching Bryan's pass meant I had set up what then later proved to be the winning touchdown. Being good supporters of one another, the team was excited and pleased and back-slappingly tickled with what Bryan, Joe, and I had done that evening.

    The next morning, Saturday, as I was doing a few errands around the town of Holstein, I finally and gratefully found out a bit of what our halfbacks and fullbacks experienced in terms of the adulation of the greater community, not just each other's team mates, for doing a great job in helping the team pull off another win. Although it is a team sport, the scoring in football remains largely limited to a few members of the team, and thus, rightly or wrongly, it is nonetheless the touchdown makers that get more of the credit from the town. Pete Stein, who helped run the gas station where I fueled my Ford at 25 cents a gallon and which was owned by my classmate's father, personally commended my catch and effort. Later I ran into Bill Jackes, the friendly and courteous deliverer of my parent's fuel oil and farm gas supplies, and he too passed on his compliments and shook my hand on the "great catch". Wow. Verbally expressed compliments coming from folks other than our coaches and team mates meant a lot to my young ego.

About 45 years later my wife, Jean, and I were back in our "home" county doing a little genealogical research in the court house at Ida Grove, where the County Clerk, in charge of all county record documents, was Jim Clausen. In the small world of Holstein, which seemingly revolves as its own and exclusive solar system, I knew Jim fairly well, not because he and I had talked so much over the years, but because of his relationships to my parents. Jim had rented my parent's farm land for a few years after my father quit actively farming. Later, when my parents moved off the farm to the town of Holstein, their first dwelling there was a house they rented that was owned by Jim.

As we solicited the large brown journals of old vital records to review from Jim in the court house that day, his and my conversation turned to the "old days", and he recollected a football game one Friday evening some 45 years earlier. "Gary," Jim said, "you caught the long pass that set up the winning touchdown. Then my brother, Joe, went on to run the extra point conversion just as the third quarter was changing to the last quarter. No more touchdowns were made other than one for each team in the whole game and you guys went on to defeat Odebolt-Arthur, 7 to 6." Why, you could have pushed me over with a feather. I vaguely

305

remembered the game, and could recall the thrill of making the catch, and my pride at receiving praise from various community members. But I didn't know the score, or when the points were made and by whom, or who it was we were playing against, and I certainly didn't expect to have anyone standing in front of me who had a four and one-half decade old memory that he could rattle off in such detail. That's what I call community. That's another tiny sample of what Holstein means to me. It's not the football catch. It's the shared memories and the lives interwoven and the years passed as in slow motion on permanent replay.

The End, The Beginning

I had dated Judy throughout high school. With the advent of my own car in our lives, our relationship became closer because there was more personal private time spent together on dates. We were very comfortable with one another and had a shared continuity of friendship and conversation with our mutual friends, several of whom were dating each other. These friends knew our status, we knew theirs, and it helped bond all of us together within the high school dating scene. As we were within our last year of high school, Judy and I would sometimes visit each other's home during special holiday seasons such as Christmas, and thus began to meet each other's extended family members. We made special memories, staying out till sunrise on Prom night, caroling in the snow with the Galva Luther League, dancing at the post-football game dances arranged by the high school cheer leaders, going to movies in Holstein and Cherokee, driving up to Arnold's Park for the day on a double date with John and Vicki, Judy came to the home track meets and football games to help cheer me on.

One exceptionally snowy evening when I had no business doing so, except for teenage affection and Judy on my mind, my right rear wheel slid off the edge of the gravel road then covered in six inches of new snow while I was half way between Roy Beyer's place, brother of my wife's father, and Orville Johannsen's place, father of my life long-time best friend, John. Still over a mile from Judy's house, my Ford was immobilized. The wheel would spin but I couldn't crawl out of the hole I was in. Not without some further effort and thought. Nobody else was foolish enough to be out in this weather so any extraction from my situation would have to be of my own doing. Naturally, being a farm boy, I had one of my Dad's scoop shovels in the trunk and was able to remove much of the impeding snow from the wheel areas but that didn't help get me over the icy ridge edge of the roadbed intersection with the upper contour of the ditch. Traction is what I needed. Being an overtly prepared and cautious farm boy, I also had a set of what were called strap-on tire chains. They were chain segments with a web belt and buckle attached, which one could thread through the rim segments of the wheel and thereby affix chains to the wheel without having to jack up the car. So, I strapped them on to both rear wheels, hopped in, engaged clutch, and away I went. I think Judy was pleased to see me. Not so sure about her Dad.

By then, "going steady" as we were, my class ring in her possession, both of us seniors looking toward graduation, both of our post high school lives laid out before us there on the dawning horizon, things had progressed very slowly but deliberately and incrementally to the "serious" stage as each of us danced around the question of where our relationship would be three years, five years into the future. No plans were firmly drafted but the word "marriage" had slipped into some of our conversations as we each discovered the "future" was no longer so far away. By then we knew each other's families and accepted the expected life- long commitments of the spouses involved, our parents, brothers, and sisters, all of whom were older than we were, all of whom were married. Like me, Judy was the last child of the family. The good examples set by the marriages we knew best provided strong and powerful illustrations of what we would need to live up to.

At that time, being within several months of graduating in my final year of high school, I knew I would be going on to college at Iowa State, and I knew Judy would not pursue advanced education but would soon be entering the work force. More importantly, I also knew Judy was the only girl I had ever dated or known as a girlfriend. I knew each of our families respected and revered the state of marriage. And I knew I could not marry anyone without knowing absolutely there was no one more suited to be my life partner. I concluded I was not about to marry Judy, then risk later questioning if another woman would be a better life-mate, dump Judy, then get divorced. I did not want that to be a possible future. Given the sibling and parental examples in her and my world, we each needed a life-long commitment. I wanted the surety of positively knowing. And so, ... I knew I had to break up with her and date others in order to determine if we cared enough about each other to commit to forever. Mine was a cold, hard, rational decision arrived at over weeks of agonizing. Then there were more weeks of agonizing as I implemented my decision. Judy bore no responsibility nor fault for what was my sole action. She did not see nor agree with the situation as I defined it. It was a painful process for her and for me. Friends came to each of us with questions, concerns, comments, and, as needed, consolation. But I had thought long enough and hard enough to know there was no reversing of my decision or actions. I had turned the page and implemented a new future to see what would now develop. We were each into uncharted waters of testing new relationships, looking for unplumbed depths of understanding for what we had in the past, plotting where we should steer to, and how high to set the sails.

With track season over, the state meet in Des Moines completed, final course tests taken, graduation night was quickly upon me and my fellow classmates. Nearly 70 per cent of our class had been together since kindergarten. It would be another 13 years before we would spend as much time with a new individual as we had spent with each other during our school years. As was the established custom in Holstein, the community, our relatives, friends, neighbors poured forth from their homes to support and celebrate the new graduates. There is a picture showing the graduates leaving the ceremony and the gymnasium, biggest indoor facility available, seems packed to overflowing with area citizens. This was our big night and we tried to grasp the importance of the event, realizing full well it might be a long time before we saw some of our fellow students again, knowing things would never be the same, but yet, not knowing what would develop.

After the ceremony we organized ourselves into a receiving line to accept the well wishes of an abundance of attendees. Judy and her good friend, Karen, stood on one side of me. Amongst the attendees who shook my hand, made some gentle comment, was a tall and statuesque brunette, Jean Beyer from Galva, the little girl to whom I had thrown my heart way back in third grade, but we had left each other behind in the history of separate schools in neighboring towns. I had seen her picture recently in the local paper as the Salutatorian of Galva High School and recipient of a scholarship from Morningside College, but I would have recognized her anywhere. Thirteen months later we would meet again for our first date. Two years after that date we would be married.

We and the community had complied with local tradition. One town minister had given the invocation for our graduation event. Another town minister had given the benediction. Class pictures had been taken. Personal photographs had been exchanged between graduating friends. Each of us had written clever comments or significant thoughts personalized to the receiver on the back of our own photograph. The pictures of my graduated friends lingered from folder to pile to drawer until one day in my adulthood I organized them into a picture binder of old memories, stored in the base cupboard unit in the northwest corner of our living room, opened periodically as I drafted this memoir, pictures which help provide a key to unlocking the past-ness of a time of bygone history.

In the summer that followed I continued with local area farm jobs, baling hay and performing other farm jobs for the neighbors. Once, I calculated the sum total of hay handled by myself had amounted to several tens of thousands of bales. In the evenings that summer, nearly every night I went to town to cruise the streets in my Ford, get together with my buddies, check out the girls, went out on dates with some of them, and once in a while went to sample alcoholic beverages late at night with my pals out in the middle of some seldom-traveled country road. None of the friends I hung out with ever allowed a drunken pal to drive. These were not only good friends; they were caring and thoughtful friends.

In August, 1962 I had reached the end of a journey, which, as a child or grade-schooler I had thought lay endlessly before me. Now it was here. My time as a permanent resident in the enveloping arms of a small caring community of German ancestry and with a plentitude of inter-relationships was over. I packed the Ford and drove off to Iowa State University in Ames to enroll in engineering and to room in the massive Friley Hall dormitory with Bryan, the infant who was born just down the hall from me one day earlier than I, both of us starting our little lives in the same small hospital in Cushing, Iowa eighteen years earlier.

Epilogue

When we married on June 11, 1965 neither Jean nor I had any reservations about committing to one another forever. On this day as I write this sentence we are 48 years into the journey. We plan to continue to the end.

My big brother, Duane, died in a farm accident in Nebraska when he was 33 and I was 21. His death was the hardest thing I have ever had to deal with to date and it took me 10 years to accept his loss. Sometimes I would conjure up other reasons for the accident to have occurred because he was a skilled farm lad and knew the dangers to watch out for, but I now know some mysteries will never be resolved.

My young friend, Paul Striepe, son of the Lutheran preacher, was killed in Vietnam in 1968 by peoples who no longer are, but who we then called the enemy. Why can't we learn to just skip over the war part? Over the years I have had to come to grips with the haunting memories of him and me playing War as young children. His was one of the biggest funerals, if not the biggest, ever held in the community of Holstein as hundreds poured out to rally around his family and his memory. Support in times like that is never enough but Holstein does it very well.

My father died early in the morning of Christmas Day, 1984, when he was 80 years old. As I pass through the decades of aging that he experienced I periodically have the impossible wish of sitting down in easy chairs on my lawn and having a conversation between he and me, with him being the same age as whatever I am at that moment of wishing. What a conversation that would be. After writing this memoir I now think I might be able to guess his answers to my questions a little more accurately than I might have before I embarked on this effort.

My mother died in December of 1986 when she was 81 years old while she was the roommate of Catharina in the Good Samaritan nursing home of Holstein. Catharina was the mother of my junior high and high school girlfriend of five years. I am told that Catharina and my mother were good friends and enjoyed each other's company while at Good Samaritan. Catharina spent more time with my mother in the last two years of my mother's life than I had spent with my mother in the last 24 years of her life.

The home in which many of these memories were made was razed around the turn of this century by a cousin, the son of Eldon Blenner, Eldon being the man I worked for in 1961. A new home was built by my cousin in the exact same spot as the original home, the one I grew up in. I hold no ill will for this action. My home had fulfilled as many dreams, provided as much physical shelter, and mental comfort, as it was capable of giving. It was time for new dreams to take root and grow. I give the new occupants of this home and the farm on which I was raised my best wishes.

Although I have known and gone to school with John since he and I were five years old, he did not become my best, my lifelong, friend until we were both in college at Iowa State University. By then he and I had matured into different people than the ones we were as children and teen-agers and we came to recognize the many commonalities and philosophies we shared, their roots traceable back to Holstein. We now have each shared a strong friendship for over one-half century, and were Best Men at each other's weddings.

After four years at Iowa State University at Ames, Iowa, I became an engineer and worked for two of the larger corporations in America. Later I secured my Professional Engineer's License in Wisconsin and did some consulting work as well as teaching a few night courses at the local technical college. It was a profession which made ideal use of my youthful interests.

###

The End

Sources

These memories are my own, recollected as best as the vagaries of time and circumstance can render them. They may or may not match the memories of peers and friends who engaged in the same events portrayed. I attribute any differences to personal perspective and the passage of decades of time. But that does not change the meaning or relevance or reality to me of these events as told in this memoir.

Any mistakes or errors in my story are my own. I have tried to be accurate with respect to the historical facts included in the text by utilizing the following sources and can recommend each of them for a broader comprehension of the history of Holstein, Iowa. Listed initially are three excellent books which reveal a wealth of information about the origins of Holstein, Iowa and the individuals who participated in its development, followed by websites and other sources as applied to particular subjects in my memoir.

The Holstein Centennial Book 1882-1982, Corrine Yates, editor, Printed by Miller Printing and Publishing, Odebolt, IA.

Holstein Quasquicentennial Book 1882-2007, printed by Bell Books, Rich Hill, MO 64779.

Our Heritage A History of Ida County, Bruce L. Godbersen, Editor in Chief, Midwest Industries, Inc. Ida Grove, IA, Publisher, Printed by The Ida County Courier, Ida Grove, IA, copyright 1977.

Ocean sailing ship, Harriet, classified as a bark, and the ship passenger list:
http://www.immigrantships.net/v7/1800v7/harriet18470608.html

Immigrants' transit upriver to Davenport, Iowa on a riverboat:
http://www.celticcousins.net/scott/henrietta1847trip.htm

First railroad bridge across the Mississippi, the conflict with steamboats, and the role of Abraham Lincoln:
http://en.wikipedia.org/wiki/Davenport,_Iowa

German American Heritage Center and the Standard Hotel in Davenport, Iowa:
http://www.gahc.org

Colonization of the Volga River area in Russia under Catherine the Great:
The Volga Germans in Russia and The Americas, from 1763 to the Present by Fred C. Koch, the Pennsylvania State University Press, University Park and London, copyright 1977.

Colonization of the moorlands in Germany from 1760-1765:

Http://www.plaggenhacke.de/, a German website, the portion titled "Arbeitkreis PLAGGENHACKE, Kolonisten-und Familienforshung

Claus Ruser and his role in the Civil War:
Military files of the United States Archives

Definition of Shivaree and its historical context within North America:
The American Heritage® Dictionary of the English Language, Fourth Edition copyright ©2000 by Houghton Mifflin Company. Updated in 2009. Published by Houghton Mifflin Company

www.ingramcontent.com/pod-product-compliance
Lightning Source LLC
Chambersburg PA
CBHW071301110426
42743CB00042B/1137